AFTERMATH

AFTERMATH

GENOCIDE, MEMORY AND HISTORY

EDITED BY KAREN AUERBACH

MONASH University
Publishing

Monash University Publishing
Matheson Library and Information Services Building
40 Exhibition Walk
Monash University
Clayton, Victoria, 3800, Australia

www.publishing.monash.edu

Monash University Publishing brings to the world publications which advance the best traditions of humane and enlightened thought.

Monash University Publishing titles pass through a rigorous process of independent peer review.

www.publishing.monash.edu/books/agmh-9781922235633.html

Design: Les Thomas

National Library of Australia Cataloguing-in-Publication entry:
Title: Aftermath : genocide, memory and history / editor Karen Auerbach
ISBN   9781922235633 (paperback)
Series: History
Subjects: Genocide.
                Genocide--Political aspects.
                Collective memory--Political aspects.
                Memorialization--Political aspects.
Other Creators/Contributors: Auerbach, Karen, editor.
Dewey Number: 304.663

Printed in Australia by Griffin Press an Accredited ISO AS/NZS 14001:2004 Environmental Management System printer.

CONTENTS

This volume and the Aftermath conference were made possible
through the generosity of the Sunraysia Foundation
in memory of Dr Jan Randa

INTRODUCTION

Karen Auerbach

Violent conflicts that tear communities apart do not cease with the end of bloodshed; in the aftermath of violence, representations of the past often become a battleground themselves. In this collision between history and memory, addressing the wounds of the past becomes integral to reconstructing communities in the present. In the words of James Young, 'History is what happened. Memory is the recollection that binds what happened to ourselves in the present.'[1]

The relationship between memory and history is all the more fraught in the case of genocide. If there is always a chasm between the events of the past and our ability to comprehend them – if the past is a foreign country, as a British novelist once wrote – then that gap is even more challenging for scholars of genocide. The problem is not only that we struggle to accept that human beings can commit such acts of mass violence. The scale of killing also means that most victims do not have time to leave behind accounts and perpetrators often do not document their crimes, so that historians are faced with the challenge of how to reconstruct this past.

Yet the study of genocide assumes that how genocide occurred is explicable, even if 'why' it happened cannot be fully understood. In the case of Holocaust studies, this approach seeks to dispel the mystifications that see the Holocaust as an event somehow outside of human history; the latter approach seems to take the causes of the genocide outside of the hands of humans, which is perhaps a reaction to our hesitancy to acknowledge that human evil is present in history and therefore present in human beings. The comparison of the Holocaust with other cases of genocide is rooted in this assumption that the Holocaust, like any historical event, is explicable. And if the Holocaust can be explained, then we can apply study of the Holocaust to our understanding of other genocides, investigate similarities and differences, and use this knowledge to help us to respond to and perhaps prevent other genocides.

---

1   James Young, *The Texture of Memory: Holocaust Memorials and Meaning* (New Haven, Conn.: Yale University Press, 1994), 116.

Yet some scholars of the Holocaust have argued that the Holocaust is unique, limiting the possibility of comparative research with other genocides. Scholars of other 20th-century genocides, on the other hand, have often challenged this notion of uniqueness and more recently many Holocaust scholars have taken the approach that the genocide of European Jewry was unprecedented as the most extreme form of genocide known to us to date, but not unique. In fact many historians of the Holocaust now agree that the Holocaust can and should be compared with other genocides. Yehuda Bauer, for example, the prominent Israeli historian of the Holocaust who initially was an outspoken proponent of the idea of uniqueness, argues that 'the basis of intelligible historical writing is this comparability of human experience. If there are recognizable patterns in the unrolling of human history, then there is a point in examining them ...[2] The very claim that a historical event is unprecedented can be made only when that event is compared with other events of a presumably similar nature with which it shares at least some qualities.'[3]

While historians of the Holocaust have increasingly accepted the need to study the genocide of European Jews and other genocides in relation to one another, moving away from the debate over uniqueness, the field of comparative genocide has developed and scholars are increasingly applying methodologies from Holocaust studies to the study of other genocides. Yet the integration of the two fields of the Holocaust and comparative genocide is still tentative. Forums for new research in Holocaust studies, from conferences to journals, are still largely separate from the broader study of genocide. This volume, which grew out of a conference at Monash University in 2011, helps to facilitate that conversation. Its focus is how genocide is remembered and represented in both popular and scholarly memory, exploring in a comparative framework how memory of genocide develops and evolves.

The role of the Holocaust in shaping how other genocides are remembered, and the application of methodologies in Holocaust studies to the study of other genocides, are the starting points for the three chapters in the volume's first section. The relationship between the construction of national identities and memory of past conflict is a theme that runs throughout the volume, and it is the foundation for studies in the first section by Tom Lawson on 19th-century British representations of the destruction of the Aboriginal

---

2   Yehuda Bauer, *Rethinking the Holocaust* (New Haven, Conn.: Yale University Press, 2001), 17.

3   ibid., 39.

population in Tasmania and by Rebekah Moore on memory of the famine in Ukraine in 1932–1933. Lawson notes that while memory of the genocide in Tasmania – unlike memory of the Holocaust – is largely absent from contemporary British culture, the impact of colonialism on Tasmania's Aboriginal population was a frequent theme in 19th-century British culture. Yet as Lawson found in his examination of textbooks, newspapers, literature and other sources, these 19th-century representations at times depicted the anticipated disappearance of Tasmania's native population as an ultimately positive development. His research is part of an increasing body of scholarship that approaches colonial massacres of native populations through the lens of genocide studies, and although not all scholars agree on applying the term to these cases, their debates about what does or does not constitute genocide are themselves integral to how these events are remembered and represented. The Stalinist-era famine in Ukraine is a case in point, as Rebekah Moore shows in her chapter on the role of Holocaust memory as a foundation for commemoration and study of the famine. Moore argues that the Holocaust has shaped both popular commemoration and scholarly representations of the famine in Ukraine regardless of what term is used to define the mass starvations. While the study of Holocaust memory informs both Lawson's and Moore's studies, Kimberly Partee Allar's chapter about representations of female perpetrators of the Holocaust and of the genocide in Rwanda takes a more explicitly comparative approach. Focusing on guards in Ravensbrück and a range of cases in Rwanda, Allar argues that both popular and scholarly representations of female perpetrators have focused on a handful of sensational, high-profile cases, ignoring the broader population of female perpetrators. Like Wendy Lower's recent book on female perpetrators in Nazi Germany,[4] Allar's comparison of the two genocides seeks to incorporate gender issues more integrally into research on 'ordinary' perpetrators.

Central to the second section, 'Perceptions and Representations: Past', is a re-evaluation of how 'bystander' populations experienced the Holocaust as it was unfolding and struggled to reconcile the genocide with their own wartime experiences. Fay Anderson's analysis of Australian press coverage of the Second World War finds that, as in the United States and elsewhere, newspapers reported on the Holocaust during the war but failed to comprehend the scale of what was occurring. While Anderson

---

4   Wendy Lower, *Hitler's Furies: German Women in the Nazi Killing Fields*, 4th ed. (Boston: Houghton Mifflin Harcourt, 2013).

ends with the liberation of the Nazi camps, Salvador Orti Camallonga's study of Spanish memory of the Holocaust focuses on the first decades after the war, examining both political and journalistic narratives about the genocide. He argues that, aside from attention to rescue efforts that saved Jews (and this despite recent findings that collaboration also played a role in neutral Spain's relationship to the genocide), Holocaust memory in contemporary Spain was marginalised, and that this resulted not from the absence of Jews, but from variegations in postwar Spanish politics. The politics of memory and the formation of national identity are central to Camallonga's study, which takes a similar approach to Spanish memory of the Holocaust as Lawson does about 19th-century British memory of genocide in Tasmania.

The three chapters in the next section focus on interactions between contemporary visitors to sites of Holocaust memory and the narratives that those sites construct about this past. Generational differences in those interactions are at the heart of Laura Levitt's essay on visitors' encounters with the exhibition at the US Holocaust Memorial Museum, especially concerning the impact of photography and art, and of Esther Jilovsky's literary analysis of memoirs about visits to Auschwitz among survivors and their descendants. A generational perspective also shapes Suzanne Rutland's article about the development of 'March of the Living' trips to Poland among descendants of Holocaust survivors in Australia. She explores the politics of memory not only among victims and their families, but also, like Camallonga, among a European bystander population, focusing on the confrontation between conflicting Jewish and Polish narratives at Holocaust sites in Poland.

Complementing the third section's emphasis on visual representations in the transmission of memory, whether in photography or in museum exhibits, the final section examines Holocaust narratives in film, which have been central to the formation of popular memory. Drawing, like Allar, on increasing attention to gender issues in Holocaust studies, Adam Brown and Deb Waterhouse-Watson examine films that depict rape, situating them in the context of a growing body of scholarship about sexual violence during the Holocaust. They underscore the voyeuristic aspects of these films' representations of rape while also considering other films that counteract this tendency. Danielle Christmas's chapter, on the other hand, combines the perspective of film studies with the field of legal history, analysing films about Holocaust trials to examine both evolution and continuity in conceptions of justice before and after the trial of Adolf Eichmann in 1961.

INTRODUCTION

All four sections have at their root a re-evaluation of narratives of past conflict and a desire to understand how memory of genocide is mobilised in the aftermath. Tensions between history and memory continue to shape competing narratives, reflecting the fact the Holocaust and other modern genocides have not yet passed into 'mere history.'

Part I

The Holocaust
and other genocides

Chapter 1

'WE HAVE EXTERMINATED THE RACE IN VAN DIEMEN'S LAND'

Remembering colonial genocide in 19th century British culture[1]

Tom Lawson

Genocide, without doubt, is acknowledged in the memory culture of modern Britain. But a specific incidence of genocide dominates. Holocaust Memorial Day is observed annually on the 27th January. The Imperial War Museum, official archive of the nation's memory,[2] has a permanent exhibition on the Holocaust.[3] The Holocaust is a mandated part of the national curriculum, meaning that *all* of Britain's schoolchildren learn 'the lessons of the Holocaust'. The government also sponsors a scheme to send schoolchildren to Auschwitz each year, and in 2014 the Prime Minister launched a commission to report on the best way to memorialize the *Shoah* in the twenty-first century. Of course there is a much wider cultural presence for the Holocaust in everything from cinema to children's fiction. The meaning of these memories is complex, indeed contested, and might even be changing. However there is one fundamental and constant root – the assumption that the Holocaust, as an example of genocide, represents a transgression. It is the opposite of all that 'we' are, the very antithesis of the identity of modern, diverse, tolerant, liberal

---

1   The ideas in this article are explored at length in Tom Lawson, *The Last Man: A British Genocide in Tasmania* (London: IB Tauris, 2014).

2   Gaynor Kavanagh, 'Museum as memorial: the origins of the Imperial War Museum', *Journal of Contemporary History* (Vol. 23, No. 1, 1988), 95

3   For an analysis of that exhibition see Tom Lawson, 'Ideology in a museum of memory', *Totalitarian Movements and Political Religions* (Vol. 4, No. 2, 2003), 173–83.

Britain.[4] Indeed, that children learn about the Holocaust in the context of an education for citizenship says something important about the role that the memory of genocide plays in building identity in modern Britain.

It is notable, then, that there is no cultural presence for the genocides perpetrated within the British Empire, even if there is an increasing academic willingness to discuss the violence unleashed in the British world.[5] Yet this memory gap has not always existed. Intriguingly, during the 19th century, genocide at the hands of the British was present in all manner of different cultural forms – and what is more, the memory of destruction wreaked underpinned a variety of British identities. In particular, the destruction of Indigenous Australian groups was used in the 'mother country' to construct sometimes opposing senses of the British imperial mission. Specifically, the destruction of the Indigenous population of Tasmania was written and rewritten within a number of imperial discourses, which had at their root the idea of British identity, and indeed the very nature of the human race. Yet here genocide was not always, indeed not usually, represented as a transgression but in a much more positive fashion, often as indicative of Britain's role at the apex of human progress. It is this example of the politics of memory that is the subject of the following discussion, demonstrating that perpetrators remember genocides too.

The narrative of genocide in Tasmania is well established, but bears repeating here. Between 1803 and 1876 by various means British settlers murdered, displaced, deported and ultimately largely destroyed the Indigenous population of Tasmania.[6] This destruction was the result of both organised, government-sponsored action and the wrath of a settler community at arm's length from control (of either Hobart or London). After the move toward a more systematic settlement of the island at the beginning of the 1820s, violence between settlers and the Indigenous population became endemic as the latter sought to defend their lands from settler incursion in an 'intense frontier conflict'.[7] By the end of the 1820s, and under pressure from settlers literally demanding extermination,[8] the Tasmanian local government

---

4   For an extended discussion see Andy Pearce, *Holocaust Consciousness in Contemporary Britain* (London: Routledge, 2014).

5   Richard Gott, *Britain's Empire: Resistance, Repression and Revolt* (London: Verso, 2011).

6   There are number of comprehensive accounts, the most recent of which is contained in Lyndall Ryan, *Tasmanian Aborigines: A History Since 1803* (Sydney: Allen & Unwin, 2012). This is an updated version of Ryan's *The Aboriginal Tasmanians* (Crows Nest, NSW: Allen & Unwin, 1996).

7   Henry Reynolds, *An Indelible Stain? The Question of Genocide in Australia's History* (Ringwood VIC: Viking, 2001), 52.

8   ibid., 71.

– with the approval of the Colonial Office in London – sought, effectively by the militarisation of the entire community, to capture and confine the Indigenous population. Although this scheme was an embarrassing failure, at the same time the government in Hobart sponsored the far more successful enterprise of 'conciliating' the remaining Indigenous nations in Tasmania through the curious person of George Augustus Robinson. This conciliation would end with their removal – again approved in London – to an outlying island.[9] Robinson toured Tasmania between 1829 and 1835, convincing various groups to accompany him.[10] Most significant was the agreement brokered at the end of 1831 with the Big River and Oyster Bay peoples to accompany Robinson to Hobart and effectively desist from the guerrilla resistance to the extension of settlement in Tasmania.[11] While Robinson's conciliation was celebrated at the time as a peaceful means of control, designed in part to protect the 'Aborigines',[12] there is little doubt that he convinced Indigenous Tasmanians to accompany him by demonstrating that the alternative was extermination for their people.[13] Even if Robinson did not use violence, his success was therefore dependent upon the violence of the past. The surviving Tasmanians were confined in a government-controlled establishment on Flinders Island. This settlement, known to its inhabitants as Wybalenna, was a permanent settlement in which the Indigenous population was to be civilised – taught how to farm the land, engage in commerce and worship a Christian god. While Robert Hughes's description of this site as a 'benign concentration camp' is hyperbolic, it does follow the view at the time that it represented an 'island prison'.[14] And the Wybalenna settlement was indeed defined by the death and decline

---

9   Secretary of State for the Colonies Lord Goderich approved the removal in correspondence. Goderich to Arthur, 5 May 1832. NA PRO CO 280.

10   The most comprehensive account of Robinson's activities is his own. See NJB Plomley, *Friendly Mission: The Tasmanian Journals and Papers of George Augustus Robinson 1829–1934* 2nd Edition (Queen Victoria Museum and Art Gallery and Quintus Publishing, 2008).

11   James Bonwick, *Van Diemen's Land* (Melbourne: Black Inc., 2010), 293.

12   See for example the correspondence with which Lt. Governor announced a peaceful end to conflict in Van Diemen's Land to the Colonial Office. Arthur to Lord Goderich, 14th April 1832, NA PRO CO 280 / 34.

13   For example on 10 November 1830 Robinson recorded that he had told a group of Indigenous Tasmanians that the government would 'clear them off the land' if they did not follow him. Plomley, *Friendly Mission*, 305.

14   Robert Hughes, *The Fatal Shore: A History of Transportation of Convicts to Australia 1787–1868* (London: Vintage Books, 2003), 423; James Bonwick, James Bonwick, *The Last of the Tasmanians or the Black War of Van Diemen's Land* (London: Sampson, Low Son and Marston, 1871), 253.

of its population. The original population was around 220,[15] but by 1847 there were just 47 survivors.[16] These survivors were then transported back to Hobart to see out their lives as a kind of colonial curiosity at a settlement at nearby Oyster Cove. After the death of Truganini in 1876, Indigenous Tasmanians were widely, and of course wrongly, declared 'extinct'.

There is, of course, extensive debate as to whether the events described above constitute, by any definition, a genocide. There is not space to rehearse such a discourse here, nor a discussion as to whether the British settlers intended to destroy the Indigenous population 'in whole or in part'. But perhaps it suffices to say that contemporaries throughout the century, both those that believed that settlers should 'exterminate' the Indigenous population of either Tasmania or all continental Australia and those that (almost) despaired at their passing, believed that what was occurring was what we would now call genocide. From George Murray's famous warning to George Arthur, the then Lieutenant Governor in Hobart, that the destruction of the Tasmanian population would represent an indelible stain on the British government, to Anthony Trollope's brutal suggestion that the 'Australian black man ... has to go', the British recognised that what was happening amounted to a wholesale destruction. As *The Times* declared in 1864: 'We have exterminated the race in Van Diemen's Land'.[17] Indeed, it will be my contention here that it was in fact crucial to the role that memories of ethnic violence in Tasmania played in British culture that there had been extermination. It was the idea of extermination, in effect of genocide, that ultimately was used to bolster the idea of Britain's march to progress.

From the outset the accounts of that extermination that reached Britain were, in effect, memories. The geographical distance that separated Britain from remote Tasmania meant that it was only the traces of destruction that reached there from Hobart – through government dispatches, the accounts of colonists, and indeed colonial newspapers. Events written in the Hobart press, for example, might be repeated in London as news more than six months later in the 1820s. Thomas Richards has described empire as essentially a fiction, the idea of control over such vast territory little more than a fantasy.[18] This model can certainly be applied to news from colonies as

---

15   Reynolds, *An Indelible Stain*, 78.
16   NJB Plomley, *Weep in Silence: A History of the Flinders Island Aboriginal Settlement* (Hobart: Blubber Head Press, 1987), 172.
17   *The Times*, 30 December 1864, 6.
18   Thomas Richards, *The Imperial Archive: Knowledge and the Fantasy of Empire* (London: Verso, 1993), 1.

far away as what was then called Van Diemen's Land. For the vast majority of Britons who engaged with such a territory, it was a place in the imagination, a fantasy. That Van Diemen's Land was primarily, at least before the 1820s, a destination for transported convicts just serves to increase the sense that it was part of the imaginary – as did the fact that it was inhabited by 'aboriginals the lowest in the scale of human kind', themselves an almost fantasy people.[19]

Bernard Porter has argued, in answer to the Saidian claims as to its universal presence, that the empire was incidental to British culture.[20] But Indigenous Tasmanians and specifically their destruction were a recurrent cultural presence in Britain from the 1820s onwards. They featured in popular opera, children's literature and comic-book fiction, newspaper reports, art exhibitions and history books.[21] They were represented in museum displays, including from the 1890s the display of human remains, itself indicative of the role that the 'extinct' Indigenous Tasmanians played in a developing scientific discourse about the nature of existence and human origins. Not all representations of Tasmanians and their decline moved in the same direction, however; discourse ranged from an evangelical philanthropy which mourned Tasmanians' tragic passing to an overt racism which denied their common humanity. By the end of the century, readings of genocide in Tasmania had more or less coalesced into a narrative of the inevitable decline of the Indigenous population in the face of human progress to civilisation.

While the penal colony of Van Diemen's Land registered in the British imagination from the arrival of settlers in 1803, it was at first indelibly associated in the public mind with the brutality of transportation.[22] After the transition to more systematic efforts to colonise the island in the 1820s, there was greater engagement with the 'enchanting Elysium' off the southern coast of New Holland, not least through the publication of guides intended to lure emigrants.[23] But, because increased colonisation also led to greater

---

19   Characterisation comes from *Leicester Chronicle*, 2 May 1835.

20   Bernard Porter, *The Absent Minded Imperialists: What the British really thought about empire* (Oxford: Oxford University Press, 2004), 3.

21   Only some of these genres of representation are investigated here.

22   Coral Lansbury, *Arcady in Australia: The Evocation of Australia in 19th Century English Literature* (Melbourne: Melbourne University Press, 1970), 24.

23   CH Jeffreys, *Van Diemen's Land* (London: JM Richardson, 1820). See also George William Evans, *History and Description of the Present State of Van Diemen's Land, Containing Important Hints to Emigrants* (London: John Souter, 1824); Edward Curr, *An Account of the Colony of Van Diemen's Land Principally Designed for the Use of Emigrants* (London: George Cowie and Co., 1824).

conflict between settlers and an Indigenous population attempting to defend their land, this discourse was also defined by the attention that it paid to violence between the communities. A picture was developed in Britain of a colonial population at times under siege from the violence of 'pitiless savages'.[24] This narrative of conflict, in which the colonists were besieged by vengeful savages, was the same as that employed by government, both in Hobart and London, to explain the spiralling violence of the 1820s.[25]

In identifying revenge as the motivation for attacks on the colonists, the established narrative for escalating violence played into wider imaginings of Australia in the 1820s. Both in London and Hobart it was repeatedly stated that the spark for violence was the depredations of the original settler population. Because it was a penal colony, much contemporary literature constructed Van Diemen's Land as a hive of scum and villainy – into which Britain was exiling its most depraved citizens.[26] Within such a framework the idea that these fallen men had oppressed and tortured the innocent 'savages' sat particularly easily as it met with that other core assumption of English literary constructions of Australia – the idea of the 'noble savage'.[27] William Moncrieff's popular opera drew on both notions when it set the Indigenous population in conflict with the wild convicts of Van Diemen's Land, but crucially in alliance with the more respectable settlers. Moncrieff's narrative was therefore in line with the original colonial rhetoric of harmonious cooperation.[28]

By the time Moncrieff's drama was published in 1831, however, the idea of harmonious coexistence really was a fantasy of an apparently more innocent age, and reports that the Tasmanian population was already on the road to being exterminated abounded. Despite these dark fears, the idea that the Indigenous population could still be 'saved' or civilised was also a crucial part of public discourse concerning Van Diemen's Land. After the campaign against slavery bore final fruit in 1833, evangelical opinion had

---

24   See for example *Jackson's Oxford Journal*, 8 January 1825; 28 May 1825. It is notable that these reports are based on press reports from New South Wales and Van Diemen's Land. As such they are the accounts of the settler communities themselves.

25   See the correspondence between the two, some of which was published contemporaneously. AGL Shaw, ed., *Van Diemen's Land: Copies of All Correspondence Between Lieutenant Governor Arthur and His Majesty's Secretary of State for the Colonies* (Hobart, 1971).

26   Richard White, *Inventing Australia: Images and Identity 1688–1980* (St Leonards, NSW: Allen & Unwin, 1981), 16.

27   ibid., 10–14.

28   WT Moncrieff, *Van Diemen's Land: An Operatic Drama in Three Acts* (London: Thomas Richards, 1831).

turned its attention and energy to the sufferings of Indigenous peoples in the empire. Thomas Buxton and his associates campaigned successfully for the establishment of a select committee to investigate the problem of intercourse between Europeans and 'Aboriginal Populations'.[29] This committee, which took soundings from evangelical and missionary opinion across the empire, was haunted by the spectre of the decline of the Tasmanian population.[30] While they rejected the idea that the disappearance of native populations was the inevitable consequence of colonialism, the committee proposed an urgent reorientation of the relationship between settlers and 'Aboriginal Tribes'. Settlers were to bring civilisation to the savages, rather than destruction. In Australia the committee recommended, somewhat perversely, that this be done based on the model being adopted in Van Diemen's Land, pioneered by George Augustus Robinson. Robinson was himself fired by an evangelical passion to transform the 'wandering savages' that he found in Van Diemen's Land[31] into a productive, settled and Christian community.[32] After learning of Robinson's work, the committee recommended the appointment of several 'Protectors of Aborigines', answerable directly to London, in order to educate and elevate the Indigenous population – chiefly, as Robinson was attempting at Flinders Island – in the ways of Christianity and commerce.[33] Buxton went on to form the 'Aborigines' Protection Society' which would campaign on these issues for the rest of the century.[34]

At first glance, of course, Buxton's select committee appears to have been offering a critique of colonialism that, in its mourning for the nearly exterminated Tasmanians, was seeking to avoid a repetition of that calamity. Indeed to a limited extent that interpretation is correct: the Aborigines' Protection Society did act as a humanitarian and colonial conscience. However, it is worth pausing to consider the underpinning assumptions of the philanthropic reading of genocidal population decline in Tasmania in order to fully understand the role in which its memory was being cast. The committee

---

29   James Heartfield, *The Aborigines' Protection Society: Humanitarian Imperialism in Australia, New Zealand, Fiji, Canada, South Africa and the Congo, 1836–1909* (New York: Columbia University Press, 2011), 3.

30   Alan Lester, 'Humanitarians and white settlers in the nineteenth century', in Norman Etherington, *Missions and Empire* (Oxford, 2005), 73.

31   Plomley, *Friendly Mission*, 229.

32   ibid., 59.

33   *Report of the Parliamentary Committee on Aboriginal Tribes (British Settlements)* (London, William Ball, 1837), 83.

34   As James Heartfield argues, the select committee was the first act of the Aborigines' Protection Society. Heartfield, *Aborigines Protection Society*, 15.

accepted almost entirely the account, constructed in part by colonialists like George Arthur, that violence had emerged because of Indigenous Tasmanians' wild spirit of revenge. The original offence here was not the invasion of the land and the disruption of Indigenous communities' relationship with that land, but the unnecessary violence that accompanied it.[35] Thus even though the committee identified that it was 'we' that had caused 'desolation and ruin', the colonial project itself was not found to be at fault.[36] Indeed, philanthropists were in a sense arguing for a more robust and coordinated form of colonialism where the power of the metropole was much extended, as demonstrated by the Protectors and the idea that 'Aborigines' should be the responsibility of the home government rather than colonial administrations. Witnesses told the committee that colonialism had caused 'aboriginal' populations to 'vanish from the face of the earth',[37] and supported by some of the press, the committee translated that knowledge into a desire to deepen and strengthen the power of the metropole over the colonial periphery, in other words to extend the colonial project.[38]

Therefore in the minds of the survivors from the Abolition movement, whom, we should remember, regarded themselves as having just set free the former slaves of empire, the British Empire was both the problem *and* the solution. It was not the British invasion of Van Diemen's Land *per se* that had created a hellish convict society which, after systematic settlement and pastoral expansion, was responsible for genocide in Tasmania. Indeed the solution to problems revealed by genocide was the further extension of British power, in terms of both the state and its missionary outriders.[39] It was they who could enact the 'gradual extinction of savage barbarism' both, one must assume, in the settler and 'Aboriginal' populations.[40] In the words of Saxe Bannister, the former attorney-general of New South Wales, 'it is thus seen that our intercourse with coloured peoples has for the most part, injured them; but, at the same time, so far from those tribes being irreclaimably

---

35   *Report of the Parliamentary Select Committee on Aboriginal Tribes (British Settlements)*, 13.
36   ibid., vii.
37   *Report of the Parliamentary Select Committee on Aboriginal Tribes (British Settlements)*, 10.
38   See for example *Sheffield Independent* 14 January 1837.
39   At the end of the century one of the central figures of the Aborigines' Protection Society reiterated that the project had never been aimed at ending colonisation. Henry Fox-Bourne, *The Aborigines Protection Society: Chapters in its History* (London: PS King, 1899), 60.
40   See the following report from member of the Aborigines' Protection Society, Standish Motte, *Outline of a System of Legislation for Securing Protection to the Aboriginal Inhabitants of all Countries Colonised by Great Britain …* (London: John Murray, 1840), 11.

adverse to civilisation, it is clear that where justice has been done, where protection has been granted, and instruction provided for, their improvement
has been proportionately extensive'.[41] Genocide, in other words, did not
extinguish hope nor did it challenge the notion of the British civilising
mission. If it were Britons who were responsible for genocide, it was only
that scurrilous population that had been expelled, not those representatives
of the colonial class that sought control.

The hopeful desire to transform colonialism – to use the genocide in
Tasmania as a spur to a better and more liberal British future – was widespread in the later 1830s and into the 1840s.[42] Yet if the select committee was
the high-water mark of British humanitarianism, it was short lived. Even as
early as 1839, members of the Aborigines' Protection Society began to lose
confidence in the transformative possibilities of their vision of Protection
in Australia.[43] Again this turn to pessimism was informed by events in
Van Diemen's Land. George Augustus Robinson's hopeful reporting of the
possibilities of the Flinders Island settlement was continually undermined
by the prevalence of death and decline there,[44] and reports from the Protectors and other missionaries elsewhere in Australia offered no grounds for
optimism. Lancelot Threkeld shut his mission down in 1841 because the
'Aborigines' had disappeared.[45] There was no savage to civilise. Faced with
the clear indication that the darkest fears of the committee would come
to pass, that all the 'full blood Aborigines' on Van Diemen's Land would
indeed perish despite efforts to civilise them, even the most hopeful of
enlightenment liberal was moved to believe that in fact the extinction of the
'native tribes' of the empire might be inevitable.[46]

---

41   Saxe Bannister, *British Colonization and the Coloured Tribes* (London: William Ball,
      1838), 268.
42   See for example the published memories of a journey to Van Diemen's Land from
      two missionaries, James Backhouse and George Washington Walker, in James
      Backhouse, *A Narrative of a Visit to the Australian Colonies* (London: Hamilton
      Adams, 1843).
43   Patrick Brantlinger, *Dark Vanishings: Discourse on the Extinction of Primitive Races
      1800–1930* (Ithaca: Cornell, University Press, 2003), 37.
44   Vivienne Rae Ellis regards Robinson's reporting as deliberately fraudulent. See
      Vivienne Rae Ellis, *Black Robinson: Protector of Aborigines* (Melbourne: Melbourne
      University Press, 1996), 122–33. See also *Seventh Annual Report of the Aborigines'
      Protection Society* (London: Smith, Elder & Co., 1844) and Francis Nixon, *The
      Cruise of the Beacon* (London: Bell and Daldy, 1857), 24.
45   Rae-Ellis, *Black Robinson*, 155.
46   Herman Merrivale, *Lectures on Colonization and Colonies* (London: Longman, Green,
      Longman and Roberts, 1861), 487.

Across the 1840s and into the 1850s a more aggressive reading of the colonies was becoming common in literary culture and beyond. English writers such as Samuel Sidney and Charles Dickens were sympathetic to the settler communities, and becoming dismissive and contemptuous of the Indigenous populations of empire and particularly Australia.[47] Australia was no longer constructed only as the last refuge of the scoundrel, but increasingly presented as a land of opportunity. This was particularly the case within the context of the 'Gold Rush' of the 1850s, before which the 'savage man [was] cowed and overawed by the influence of a civilisation he can neither comprehend nor resist … awaiting … that speedy extinction to which some untraceable cause has doomed him'.[48] And for some, famously in the case of Dickens, there was an increasing sense that this was not a fate for which civilisation should apologise. Dickens's magazine *Household Words* contained an attack on the very notion of the 'Noble Savage' in 1853, in which it was stated very clearly that it was 'highly desirable' that the 'savage' be 'civilised off the face of the earth' in the course of the world's development.[49] Within the context of the 'heyday of [Britain's] imperial might' the genocide of Tasmanians increasingly became represented,[50] and indeed remembered, within a vision of the triumph of civilised man whose destiny it was, in the words of *The Times*, to cover the planet.[51]

This sense that the Indigenous population represented the past, and the colonial population the future, became embedded in a variety of representations of Tasmania and with it the idea of the Tasmanians' inevitable and wholesale 'extinction' became fixed. At the 1851 Great Exhibition at Crystal Palace, of the 349 groups of items from Van Diemen's Land 'only four represented the handiwork of its aboriginal population'.[52] Travelogues and natural histories invariably recorded the 'drama of destruction' in Van Diemen's Land,[53] while memoirists who recalled their time in Tasmania in publication seemed moved to account for the 'extermination' of the 'aboriginal inhabitants' of the island.[54] When Henry Jeanneret protested publicly at his

---

47   Lansbury, *Arcady in Australia*, 63–76.
48   *The Times*, 19 November 1851, 4.
49   Charles Dickens, 'The Noble Savage', *Household Wards*, 11 June 1853.
50   Russell McGregor, *Imagined Destinies: Aboriginal Australians and the Doomed Race Theory* (Melbourne: Melbourne University Press, 1998), 20.
51   *The Times*, 29 July 1869.
52   George W Stocking, *Victorian Anthropology* (New York: The Free Press, 1987), 275.
53   See for example PE Strzelecki, *Physical Description of New South Wales and Van Diemen's Land* (London, 1845), and reviewed in *The Times*, 8th October 1845.
54   Mrs Charles Meredith, *My Home in Tasmania: During a Residence of Nine Years* (London, 1852).

being removed from the job of Commandant at the Wybalenna settlement on Flinders Island across the beginning of the 1850s, he made clear to the British reading public within this framework what the purpose of that settlement was – to supervise the journey of the 'Aborigines' to oblivion. No effort, he assured readers, was 'spared by His Majesty's Government to render them comfortable here and happy thereafter' and they would be succeeded on Van Diemen's Land by an 'intelligent and loyal race' of colonial subjects.[55]

Throughout the mid-Victorian period the progressive 'decay' of the Tasmanian 'race' was reported to readers of the British press.[56] This culminated at the end of the 1860s and into the 1870s with accounts of the death of the 'last' Tasmanians, in 1869 the 'last man' – known variously as William Lanne, Lanny or King Billy, and then in 1876 the 'last Tasmanian' of all, Truganini.[57] Of course in reality Truganini was not the 'last' Tasmanian at all; a mixed-heritage community lived in Tasmania and its outlying islands.[58] This community did not go unnoticed or ignored, even in Britain – their existence was for example noted several times in newspapers, including those commenting on 'extinction'.[59] Why, then, were claims as to the extinction of Tasmanians after the death of Truganini so often repeated? In part it was of course because of the contemporary belief in the utter immutability of the characteristics of race, but it was also because the idea of extinction was itself, self-fulfillingly, important. The extinction of Indigenous Tasmanians demonstrated the inevitability of the decline of 'savage' races everywhere, and as such the destined triumph of civilised man. To deny that this people was disappearing from the face of the earth would thus have disrupted a sense of the British Empire's place in history and progress.[60]

The discourse that I have described above was rehearsed in the press coverage of 'King Billy's' death, as the history of settler/Indigenous relations

55 Henry Jeanneret, *The Vindication of a Colonial Magistrate* (London: Hope and Co., 1854), 63.

56 See for example *The Times*, 5 February 1861.

57 A large article on the last Tasmanians, looking towards their demise, was published in the *Illustrated London News*, 7 January 1865.

58 Ryan, *The Aboriginal Tasmanians*, xix – the argument of the whole book is essentially that the 'Aborigines did not die out in 1876 or in any other period of Tasmania's history'.

59 The population of the Furneaux islands is described as 'descended from Tasmanian Aboriginals' in *The Times* 23 September 1890. And the anthropologist Henry Ling Roth discusses an article on Fanny Cochrane Smith, a Tasmanian of 'mixed blood', in his *The Aborigines of Tasmania* (Halifax: F King and Sons, 1899).

60 Mcgregor, *Imagined Destinies*, 59.

on Tasmania was recounted. The vestiges of the liberal lament that the sufferings of the 'extinguished ... native population' could have been averted by a stronger and more centralised imperial control could be heard,[61] alongside mocking of the 'civilising' desires of the philanthropic approach which 'improved ... the aborigines of Tasmania ... off the face of the earth'.[62] Prior to her death Truganini was celebrated in the press. *The Gentleman's Magazine* published an interview with her, describing 'the last Tasmanian' as the 'merry as a cricket' survivor of a race whose 'lot' it has been 'to disappear at the approach of civilisation, like dew before the morning sun'.[63] But again it was not just the assertive rhetoric which saw that Tasmanians had disappeared in the face of progress that was constructing a sense of the rectitude of that empire. Even the critical discourse that looked back to the liberal philanthropy of the 1830s and 1840s repeated the idea that the British could have saved the 'savages'. Indeed later in the century, and in the context of a new mood of imperialism in Britain, the Aborigines' Protection Society again became active in calling for the kind of extended imperial control that had defined them in the 1840s. While based on outrage at the sufferings of Indigenous peoples at the hands of British settlers, it was also an articulation that the British state (if not its people) could protect the 'barbarous races'.[64]

Those newspapers that mocked such philanthropic urges came close to revelling in genocide in the same way that Anthony Trollope did in his guides for emigrants to Australia and New Zealand in the early 1870s. Following Dickens, Trollope did not seek to apologise for extermination, because he refused to apologise for colonisation itself. Colonisation of Australia and the entire globe had been of benefit to the human race and therefore could not be recanted, whatever the consequences for the 'Australian Black Man'.[65] Trollope mocked the philanthropic 'sect' which he felt,[66] perhaps not unreasonably, disingenuously sought to protect both Indigenous populations and the colonisation project which, as he saw it, was the root cause of their suffering:

---

61   *Daily News*, 19 November 1869.

62   *Penny Illustrated Paper*, 5 June 1869. See also *The Morning Post* 24 December 1869.

63   Account of the interview in *The Gentleman's Magazine* can be found in *Leeds Mercury*, 7 October 1876 and *The Ipswich Journal*, 10 October 1876.

64   Heartfield, *The Aborigines' Protection Society*, 54.

65   Anthony Trollope, *Australia and New Zealand Volume I* (London: Chapman and Hall, 1873), 72–76.

66   Trollope, *Australia and New Zealand*, 68

Here at home all of us believe that we were doing a good deed in opening up these lands to the industry and civilisation of white men. I at any rate so believe, But if so, we can surely afford to tell the truth about the matter. These black savages were savage warriors ... and we too, after a fashion were warriors.[67]

Perhaps the text that was most important in cementing an understanding of the significance of genocide in Tasmania was James Bonwick's *The Last of the Tasmanians*, which was first published following the death of William Lanne in 1869.[68] Indeed much of the newspaper reporting of Lanne's death was actually prompted by Bonwick's publication. Bonwick spent much of his working life in Australia, but his book was specifically aimed at a British and American audience, to highlight the iniquities of the occupation of Australia. Bonwick's message was, however, a contradictory one. He acknowledged the violence done to Tasmanians, lamented their extermination and pointed to the original offence being the occupation of the land. Yet he repeated the notion that the root of the violence was the displaced and immoral population. He was certainly patronising in his exoticisation of Indigenous peoples. At the same time, Bonwick was respectful of their culture and acknowledged that the transformation that George Augustus Robinson desired amounted to a destruction of that culture, which we would now call 'cultural genocide'.[69] But ultimately, in an act Trollope would have identified as intellectually dishonest, Bonwick suggested that the entire tragedy had resulted from a lack of care, repeating the sentiments of abolitionists when he stated: 'the concern awakened for his condition comes too late ... We cover our faces while the deep solemn voice of our common Father echoes through the soul, "Where is thy brother"'.[70]

By pointing to the common humanity of Britons and Indigenous Tasmanians, and echoing the famous abolitionist mantra, Bonwick placed his narrative firmly within philanthropic discourse. But he also pointed to a further role for Indigenous Tasmanians, or their memory, in British culture – the biological, ethnological and anthropological debate over human origins

---

67   Trollope, *Australia and New Zealand Volume II* (London: Chapman and Hall, 1873), 83.

68   James Bonwick, *The Last of the Tasmanians or the Black War of Van Diemen's Land* (London: Sampson, Low Son and Marston, 1871).

69   Brantlinger, *Dark Vanishings*, 126. For a discussion of the idea of 'cultural genocide' see Robert van Krieken, 'Cultural genocide in Australia', from Stone, *The Historiography of Genocide* (London, Palgrave, 2010), 128–155.

70   Bonwick, *The Last of the Tasmanians*, 400.

and the racial make-up of mankind. Indeed, one of the details of Bonwick's book that was most repeated after publication was its lurid allegations regarding the struggle over the remains of William Lanne, whose head was stolen in an effort to secure it for the Royal College of Surgeons.[71] Not only was this very public dismembering of Lanne's remains reported by Bonwick and subsequently in newspapers, but it also was the subject of a mocking poem by James Brunton Stephens. 'King Billy's Skull' pointed to the value that the skull would command in Britain precisely because of the importance of Indigenous Tasmanians in a debate that had seized the scientific community since the middle of the century.[72] That debate in turn points to the cultural centrality of the idea of extermination, because this was quite literally an existential debate regarding, to use a common misquotation, the 'origin of the species'.

Indigenous Australians in general, and Tasmanians in particular, were central to the debate on human origins because it was believed that these were the places to hunt 'cultural dinosaurs'.[73] Coming from the abolitionist discourse that insisted on the common roots of all mankind, evolutionary biology and anthropology contributed to a vision of man progressing to civilisation. It was claimed that the 'lower' races, like Indigenous Tasmanians, were peoples without culture who had been lost to development. They were, especially for the developing discourse of anthropology, examples of cultural hangovers from a previous age. And as had been stated since the beginning of the 19th century, Australian 'Aborigines' and particularly Tasmanians were amongst the 'lowest' or 'rudest' forms of man known to science. Within that context, anthropologists regretted the 'unhappy fate' of the Tasmanians while collecting specimens of their remains as survivors from 'pre-history'.[74] Tasmanians were themselves memories from a former time, and to study them was, according to John Lubbock, an associate of Charles Darwin, to have access to a primitive society and therefore to 'penetrate some of the mist which separates the past from the future'.[75]

While men like Lubbock believed that in Indigenous society they were seeing a glimpse of themselves in the past, a glimpse of the 'drift and cave

---

71   ibid., 393.

72   James Brunton Stephens, 'King Billy's Skull', *Convict Once and Other Poems* (Melbourne, 1888).

73   Adam Kuper, *The Invention of Primitive Society: Transformations of an Illusion* (London: Routledge, 1988), 92

74   Roth, *The Aborigines of Tasmania*, v–vii.

75   John Lubbock, *The Origin of Civilisation and the Primitive Condition of Man: Mental and Social Condition of Savages* (London and New York: Longmans, Green, 1912).

men' of Europe,[76] there was an alternative discourse that denied the common root of mankind. Thinkers such as Robert Knox instead argued that race was a much harder characterisation and delineated different species of men. Knox as a consequence foresaw a dark future, defined by racial conflict because it was impossible for different races to 'mingle' and therefore, as the 'Saxon' spread across the globe, the 'sure extinction' of 'dark races' would follow. Central to Knox's vision, however, was an understanding of the Tasmanian past: 'Already in a few years we have cleared Van Diemen's Land of every human aboriginal. Australia, of course, follows'. Knox's embrace of genocide as the natural law of interracial contact was also predicated on a sneering rejection of 'philanthropic' attempts to civilise the 'darker brethren' as a 'war ... against nature'.[77]

At first glance it might appear that it is only the overt racism of Knox, and indeed Charles Dickens and Anthony Trollope, that accommodated genocide into their world view. Yet the liberal discourse which in the 1830s and 40s had advocated that 'lower races' could be transformed and civilised had fewer and fewer advocates as the century progressed. Indeed by the later 1800s those who advocated the kinds of protection and 'civilisation' projects that George Augustus Robinson had pioneered in the 1830s were chiefly concerned with supervising the destruction of 'Aboriginal races', of making their disappearance from the earth and journey into history and oblivion as painless as possible. The idea that Tasmanians and other Indigenous Australians represented a kind of pre-historic hangover certainly allowed liberals to come to terms with the destruction in Tasmania more readily, because it could then be represented as a natural and inevitable process. As JG Wood reflected on the demise of Indigenous Tasmanians in his *Natural History of Man*, a popular publication that had originally appeared as a weekly serial: 'For the real cause we must look at the strange but unvariable laws of progression. Whenever a higher race occupies the same grounds as a lower, the latter perishes, and whether animate or inanimate in nature, the new world is always built on the ruins of the world'.[78]

As such, genocide in Tasmania became an important element in the progress mantra of the age. Nowhere is this more evident, especially looking back from the 21st century, than in the work of Charles Darwin. Darwin

---

76 James Backhouse Walker, *The Tasmanian Aborigines* (Hobart: John Vail, 1900), 1.

77 Robert Knox, *The Races of Men: A Philosophical Enquiry into the Influence of Races over the Destinies of Nations* (London: Henry Renshaw, 1862), 229.

78 JG Wood, *The Natural History of Man: Being an Account of the Manners and Customs of the Uncivilised Races of Men* (London: George Routledge and Sons, 1870), 68.

had first observed the decline of the Tasmanian population in his Beagle voyages. Coming from the same abolitionist tradition as the philanthropists of the Aborigines' Protection Society, he too had been unwilling to declare the 'extinction' of 'Aboriginal' races inevitable in earlier publications. By the beginning of the 1870s Darwin's position had hardened, and he used the example of Tasmanians in *The Descent of Man* in his account of the evolutionary progress of culture and the inevitable destruction of 'Aborigines' in the face of ascendant, triumphant, liberal man.[79] Like other monogenists, Darwin's account of man's progress from a common root both relied on and explained the destruction of Tasmanians; in a liberal age it was also a means by which philanthropists could come to terms with their violent national past.

Of course this debate about the nature of man and human origins went far beyond a narrow professional discourse between scientists. It was represented in school textbooks and in the end displayed to the public in a variety of museums. By 1900 visitors could see the remains of Tasmanians in the Pitt-Rivers museum in Oxford, the Hunterian museum of the Royal College of Surgeons and the Natural History Museum in London. In the 20th century what was believed to be 'King Billy's Skull' was displayed at the Anatomy Museum at the University of Edinburgh. The Natural History Museum in particular had an important cultural presence. Its acquisition of the remains of Tasmanians was reported in the press[80] and it commanded over 400,000 visitors a year.[81] From 1899 those visiting the zoological mammals gallery would have seen a variety of representations of Tasmanians, including skulls displayed to demonstrate the smaller brain capacity of the 'lower type' of man, and a full skeleton. Adopting a Darwinian monogenist approach to racial science, the Natural History Museum left its visitors in no doubt what had happened to the 'aboriginal inhabitants of Tasmania ... now unfortunately exterminated'.[82]

Despite the cultural presence of Indigenous Tasmanians and the utility of memories of their genocidal decline in the 19th century, in the 20th-century memories of the Tasmanian genocide faded. The sense of imperial crisis at

---

79   Charles Darwin, *The Descent of Man and Selection in Relation to Sex* (London: Penguin, 2004), 212–221.

80   *The Times*, 28 July 1899.

81   William Stearn, *The Natural History Museum at South Kensington* (London: Heinemann, 1981), 393.

82   *Guide to the Specimens Illustrating the Races of Mankind* (London: Natural History Museum, 1908), 33.

the *fin-de-siècle* certainly meant that destruction in Van Diemen's Land could no longer be used as evidence of the providential mastery of an imperial race. By the 1930s a new narrative had been constructed that suggested the 'Tasmanian natives' had died 'out of sight and out of mind' of the British government.[83] After the Second World War, and the recharacterisations of race in the aftermath of Nazi destruction, Tasmanian remains were removed from display in the Natural History Museum, for example, as ideas of racial hierarchy were revisited. Although debates on the return of those remains to Tasmania in the late 1990s and early 21st century would force the Tasmanian genocide back into public discourse, it has remained a more marginal affair. In some places 19th-century narratives of the meaning of destruction in Van Diemen's Land do resurface, however. Niall Ferguson, a historian who is campaigning for a more prominent role for the history of the empire in the formation of 21st-century British identities, did acknowledge genocide in Tasmania in his book *Empire*. Ferguson described 'one of the most shocking of all chapters in the history of the British Empire' in which 'the Aborigines in Van Diemen's Land were hunted down, confined and ultimately exterminated'. But Ferguson ascribed a rather familiar significance to the episode: 'All that can be said in mitigation is that, had Australia been an independent republic in the 19th century, like the United States, the genocide might have been on a continental scale rather than just a Tasmanian phenomenon'. He continues, 'One of the peculiarities of the British Empire was the way that the imperial power at the centre endeavoured to restrain the generally far more ruthless impulses of the colonists on the periphery'.[84] Ferguson's words could have been spoken by a member of the Aborigines' Protection Society in the 1840s and are an eloquent reminder of how an understanding of the genocide of Indigenous Tasmanians could translate into support for and faith in Empire in British culture. After the middle of the century, with Britain's moral and imperial ascendancy apparently growing, the erasure of Indigenous Tasmanians appeared simply to confirm, from whichever direction it was viewed, that ascendancy.

Such conclusions might be surprising when viewed from the Holocaust-conscious present. Britons live with and learn about genocide continually. But the genocides that they confront in their schools, museums and cinemas are perpetrated by others, with the Holocaust at the very centre of those memories. The critics of Holocaust memory often dismiss its role in identity

---

83   *The Times*, 26 January 1938.
84   Niall Ferguson, *Empire: How Britain Made the World* (Penguin: London, 2003), 108.

as a modish indulgence, at the same time as calling for a return to a time when Britain's historical memories were dominated by British achievement in empire. It should be salutary to remember that one of those achievements of empire was the destruction of Indigenous peoples. In the case of Tasmania this was not a destruction somehow shrouded in silence, or kept away from the metropolitan observers. It was written, re-written and remembered, and indeed both regretted and celebrated. But even where genocide appeared to be identified as a national disgrace, it never undermined the sense of Britain's colonial mission and more and more frequently became understood as evidence of that mission's providential purpose.

Chapter 2

SETTING THE PICTURE STRAIGHT

The ordinary women of Nazi Germany and Rwanda
who participated in genocide

Kimberly Allar

'Sadistic female guard brought to justice';[1] 'Danger women';[2] 'Nazi she-devils';[3] 'The bitches of Buchenwald';[4] 'Mother of Atrocities';[5] *The Beautiful Beast;*[6] *Ilsa: She Wolf of the SS.*[7] These headlines and titles come from media outlets and academic publications. Their purpose is to shock and attract the public, stirring prurient interest and grabbing attention with the horror of the crimes, the terror of the genocidal regimes and the gender of the actors involved – but they send other messages as well. While male violence is frequently normalised and even expected in certain situations, female violence both repels and attracts since it contradicts the traditional view of women as peacemakers and life-givers.[8]

1   Michael Leidig, 'Sadistic female guard brought to justice', *Sunday Express*, 25 September 2005.
2   Yvonne Roberts, 'Danger women', *Evening Standard*, 1 February 2006.
3   Clare Raymond, 'Nazi she-devils', *Mirror*, 11 November 2005.
4   Tony Rennell, 'Bitches of Buchenwald', *Daily Mail*. 24 January 2009.
5   Carrie Sperling. 'Mother of Atrocities: Pauline Nyiramasuhuko's role in the Rwandan Genocide', *Fordham Urban Law Journal*, Vol. 33 (Jan 2006).
6   Daniel Patrick Brown, *The Beautiful Beast: The Life and Crimes of SS–Aufseherin Irma Grese*, (Ventura, Cal.: Golden West Historical Publications, 1996).
7   *Ilsa, She Wolf of the SS*, DVD, directed by Don Edmonds, (Hollywood: Cambist Films, 1975).
8   Georgie Ann Weatherby, Jamie Blanche, Gonzaga Rebecca Jones, 'The Value of Life: Female killers and the feminine mystique', *Journal of Criminology and Criminal Justice Research and Education*, Vol. 2; 1, 2008.

Study of the participation of women in militarised positions and the perpetration of genocide has grown during the last few decades, capturing the attention of academic, legal and media circles, a combined outgrowth of surging interest in women's and genocide studies. This is certainly a welcome development, but what exactly are the messages they are communicating? Furthermore, what are the repercussions of these portrayals? Do they generate further discourse and understanding of female perpetrators? Or do they impede further consideration and study due to their reliance on preconceived notions that determine portrayals and understanding?

Unlike male perpetrators, who have been the focus of intensive social, psychological and historical investigations, women are generally overlooked or even relegated to the sidelines.[9] Nearly every major study has focused on men, leaving unclear any understanding of how women respond to the militarisation and brutalisation associated with genocide.[10] While the press and public consciousness frequently return to themes of diabolism and sadism when confronting female perpetrators, legal and academic standpoints have developed their own rhetoric, which typically engages a broader, though also flawed, interpretation of women's roles by suggesting a lack of agency or inherent character flaws. Within both domains extraordinary figures garner the attention, becoming the de-facto representatives for all female

---

9   There is a voluminous amount of literature dedicated to this subject from the past 70 years. Some of the studies, in order of their publication, that have most influenced the perception of male perpetrators include: Eugon Kogon, *Der SS-Staat: Das System der deutschen Konzentrationslager*, (Munich: Alber, 1946); Theodor W Adorno, Else Frenkel-Brunswik, Daniel J Levinson, R Nevitt Sanford, *The Authoritarian Personality* (New York: Harper Collins, 1950); Hannah Arendt, *Eichmann in Jerusalem: A Report On The Banality Of Evil* (New York: The Viking Press, 1963); Stanley Milgram, *Obedience to Authority: An Experimental Overview* (New York: Harper & Row Publishers Inc., 1974); Phillip G Zimbardo, *The Lucifer Effect: Understanding How Good People Turn Evil* (New York: Random House, 2007); Christopher Browning, *Ordinary Men: Reserve Police Battalion 101 and the Final Solution in Poland* (New York: Harper Collins, 1992); Daniel Goldhagen, *Hitler's Willing Executioners: Ordinary Germans and the Holocaust* (New York: Vintage Books, 1997).

10   Notable exceptions to this trend are found in recent studies focusing particularly on Nazi Germany. See Wendy Lower, *Hitler's Furies: German Women in the Nazi Killing Fields* (New York: Houghton Mifflin Harcourt, 2013) and Kathrin Kompisch, *Täterinnen: Frauen im Nationalsozialismus* (Köln: Böhlau Verlag, 2008). Simon Erpel, Jane Caplan, and Irmtraud Heike have also been instrumental in re-integrating female perpetrators back into the history and understanding of the Holocaust with their separate works on the Aufseheinnen. In particular see the edited volumes: *Im Gefolge der SS. Aufseherinnen des Frauen-KZ Ravensbrück*, Ed. Simone Erpel (Berlin: Metropol, 2011), and Claus Füllberg-Stolberg and Martina Jung, ect. al, *Frauen in Konzentrationslagern, Bergen-Belsen, Ravensbruck* (Bremen: Edition Temmen 1994).

perpetrators. This is likely due to the relatively small number of cases and the dearth of information currently available. The result is skewed towards the extreme and thus inhibits further exploration and understanding of why and how females become perpetrators, leading to miscarriages of justice and historical inaccuracies. Extraordinary figures have thus come to represent all cases of female perpetrators, omitting the 'ordinary' majority from the historical record, and excusing them, as well as their societies, from having to account for their actions.

The images produced by both popular and academic discourses are often the product of gendered stereotyping, which shares a high degree of similarity across time and cultures.[11] This chapter deconstructs these images and identifies patterns of public perception in order to confront the barriers that have thus far limited our understanding of female perpetrators. When women break traditional gender boundaries by crossing into the masculine realm of violence, the response is polemical, from allegations of unfortunate, uncontrollable madness and hysteria to charges of inherent evil. Both distorted perceptions damage our understanding of who these women were and how they were mobilised to participate in genocide. They adopt a dispositional position, rather than considering the context and situation of their crimes, which is paramount to understanding the warped universe of genocide.

This chapter will examine two different cases in which women played significant roles in the perpetration of genocide or in crimes against humanity: the Aufseherinnen of Nazi Germany and the female genocidaires of Rwanda. While it will briefly consider who these women were, what they did and the context surrounding their behaviours and actions, its primary purpose is to examine how these women are portrayed, considered and remembered in the media and the public consciousness. Their experiences, training, backgrounds and the contexts of their crimes were different, as were the crimes themselves, yet their societies' responses in both a legal and a media framework remained similar. With a comparative analysis of case studies spanning 50 years and two continents, I demonstrate that societies often create similar images and hold particular discourses in order to address transgressing women who participate in the 'crime above all crimes'. Ultimately, these discourses indicate more about the popular reception of violated gender norms than the psychology of female perpetrators.

---

11   John E Williams and Deborah L Best, *Measuring Sex Stereotypes: A Thirty Nation Study* (Beverly Hills, Cal.: Sage Publications, 1982); Todd D Nelson, *The Psychology of Prejudice*, 2nd ed. (New York: Pearson Education, Inc. 2006), 201.

They apply a dispositional explanation, while further relying on extra-ordinary cases to represent all female perpetrators. Female perpetrators are considered unnatural, and are denied the assertion that they are ordinary persons who exercised agency and rationally participated in genocide.

It is important to note that this chapter limits its scope to examining active participants who, in various ways, physically contributed to the genocidal campaign through their *active* involvement and participation. It will not investigate bystanders and passive defenders, referring to the millions of women who supported the regime or stood by the men who orchestrated and carried out the genocide. Though their support certainly contributed to the resulting tragedy by enabling it to unfold, their experiences and involvement require a different examination.[12]

'When women become killers'

Females have historically been, and will unfortunately continue to be, a target in war and genocides. What has changed during the past century, however, is the role of women in campaigning and participating in the humiliation and destruction of other females within this realm. One year after the defeat of the genocidal Hutu regime by the Rwandan Patriotic Front in mid-July 1994, a devastating report was released by African Rights, a London-based human rights organisation.[13] Before the regime capitulated it had spawned a civil war and sponsored a genocidal campaign in Rwanda, claiming the lives of nearly 900,000 Tutsis, or roughly 20 per cent of the small country's population in a period of 100 days.[14] The 264-page report, titled 'Rwanda – not so innocent: When women became killers', included shocking accounts of the atrocities and revealed that thousands of women had actively participated and encouraged the genocide which had ravaged the nation. This came as a startling surprise due to the international outcry over, and prevalence of, rape and violence by Hutus against Tutsi women during the genocidal campaign. In other words, while Tutsi and moderate Hutu men were primarily targeted for death during the brutal slaughter in the country, females were often subjugated to violent rape(s) and then

---

12 One such study on German women in the Third Reich includes Gundrun Schwarz, 'Eine Frau an seiner Seite: Ehefrauen in der "SS-Sippengemeinschaft"' (Hamburg: Hamburger Edition, 1997).

13 Chris McGreal, 'Women turned killers: Chris McGreal in Bujumbura reports on new evidence of orchestrated genocide', *The Guardian*, 26 August 1995.

14 'Leave none to tell the story: Genocide in Rwanda', *Human Rights Watch*, 1 April 2004.

maimed or killed afterward.[15] The role of rape within the recent conflicts in Bosnia and Darfur has also received a good deal of attention, leading to the perpetration of rape being recognised internationally as a war crime.[16] This report by African Rights pointed to an entirely different situation, in which females were implicated in the genocidal process, a situation that clearly contradicted social norms and also challenged the dominant image of females as targets and victims. Yet this dispatch, which generated a great deal of press after its release in August 1995, has been largely eclipsed by the sensational and cruel episode of one single individual, the former Rwandan minister for women and family affairs, Pauline Nyiramasuhuko. Nyiramasuhuko, tried alongside her son, is the first woman to be tried for the crime of genocide;[17] she was sentenced to life in prison in June 2011 at the International Criminal Tribunal for Rwanda.[18] She is unusual, for not only did she hold a position of power in pre-genocide Rwandan society,[19] but she also played a very prominent and public role in instigating the genocide, including handing out cans of gasoline to burn Tutsis alive and ordering the *Interahamwe* soldiers, a Hutu paramilitary organisation responsible for countless atrocities,[20] to rape the women before killing them. Nyiramasu-huko, as remembered by many survivors and fellow perpetrators, was often dressed in military fatigues while shouldering a machine-gun. She was often accompanied by her similarly dressed 24-year-old son Arsene, who

---

15   'Case study: Genocide in Rwanda, 1994'. *Gendercide Watch*, http://www.gendercide. org/case_rwanda.html, accessed 10 May 2011.

16   Rhonda Copelon, 'Surfacing gender: Reconceptualizing crimes against women in time of war', in Alexandra Stiglmayer, ed., *Mass Rape: The War Against Women in Bosnia-Herzegovina* (Lincoln, Neb.: University of Nebraska Press, 1994), 197–218, 205; Andrew Osborn, 'Mass rape ruled a war crime', *The Guardian*, 23 February 2001.

17   Peter Landesman, 'A woman's work', The New York Times Magazine, Section 6; Column 1; Magazine Desk; (15 September 2002), 82.

18   Josephine Hazeley, 'Profile: Female Rwandan killer Pauline Nyiramasuhuko', *British Broadcasting Corporation, BBC African Service*, 24 June 2011.

19   In 1992 there were only three female government ministers and women represented 1% of local-level leadership positions.

      Nichole Hogg, 'Women's participation in the Rwandan genocide: Mothers or monsters?' *International Review of the Red Cross*. Vol. 92, No. 877 (March 2010), 69–102, 74.

20   'Interahamwe' is translated as 'those who work together' in Kinyarwanda, one of the primary languages spoken in Rwanda. The Interahamwe carried out the genocide of the Tutsis in Rwanda during April–July 1994.

      Chris Simpson. 'World: Africa Interahamwe – a serious military threat'. *BBC News*, 2 March 1999.

had explicit 'permission' from his mother to rape and kill Tutsi women, particularly virgins.[21]

This particular mother embodies a terrifying position against the historical cross-cultural ideal of a mother as a nurturing and loving body. The feminist political scholars Laura Sjoberg and Caron E Gentry point out that Nyiramasuhuko 'was the linchpin of the atrocities in Rwanda' due to her political position as a guardian for females and the family as well as her relationship with her son, and state that 'when we lose the *mothers* to the dark side, all is lost'.[22] As a result, Nyiramasuhuko captivated the public's attention and has been branded the 'Mother of Atrocities' for her personal involvement in the genocide.[23]

Nyiramasuhuko was not alone either as a mother or an educated woman who willingly and even enthusiastically participated in the genocide; nevertheless, she has become one of the centrepieces of current media and scholarly focus.[24] Attention has centred not only upon her criminal activities, but also upon her appearance during the trial, during which descriptions of her ranged from wild and exotic[25] to a 'dear great-aunt, with glasses and hair neatly pulled back, wearing a flowery green dress'.[26] Her controversial image is further outlined by insinuations that the mother-son relationship was perverse and even incestuous.[27]

By focusing on Nyiramasuhuko, society has essentially relieved itself of the burden of confronting the notion of violent female genocidaires[28] by highlighting a singular case, which, at least today, dominates ideas concerning female participation in genocide. In other words, by focusing on one arguably extraordinary case, we bypass the uncomfortable idea that ordinary women,

---

21   Landesman, 'A woman's work', 82.
22   Laura Sjoberg and Caron E Gentry, *Mothers, Monsters, Whores: Women's Violence In Global Politics* (New York: Zed Books, 2007), 169.
23   Sperling, 'Mother of Atrocities', 637.
24   While other instances of female perpetrators in Rwanda have garnered international attention, particularly the cases of the Catholic nuns, Sisters Julienne Kizito and Gertrude Mukangango, thus far, Nyiramasuhuko remains at the forefront of research. Nearly every study and report examining female perpetrators references her in some way.
25   Landesman, 'A woman's work', 82
26   Miranda Devine, 'The rise of the women warriors', *Sydney Morning Herald*, 9 September 2004.
27   Sjoberg and Gentry, *Mothers, Monsters, Whores*, 169
28   This French term means 'those who commit genocide', but typically refers to perpetrators of the Rwanda 1994 genocide. As a former colony of Belgium, French remains widely spoken throughout the country.

like men, are also capable of orchestrating and committing atrocities against other people. They, too, can be influenced by social, economic, political and ideological powers that can shape their behaviour yet also leave them with agency to make their own decisions. By highlighting the extraordinary, we divert ourselves from and lose sight of the commonplace: thousands of other women were also actively involved in committing atrocities.

The prevailing image of the extraordinary female

Focusing on singular cases and using them as the model for female perpetrators began in the aftermath of the Holocaust with the picture of the healthy and beautiful young Nazi Frau. The stories and biographies of Irma Grese, Maria Mandel, Herta Bothe, Ilse Koch and a few other female leaders and accused sadists captivated public attention following their public trials in the aftermath of the Second World War. Their profiles have tended to dominate the image of the Nazi woman, creating and supporting a depiction of Nazi female perpetrators as notoriously vile, unfeminine, and even depraved in their dispositions and behaviours. Their images were not only plastered across newspaper headlines in the postwar years, but also led to the creation of songs, movies and pornography featuring the seductive, sadistic female SS guard.[29] While it would be another 50 years until a new female perpetrator captured international attention in the persona of Nyiramasuhuko, the response to her and other female perpetrators of the Rwandan genocide was similar to reactions to female Nazi perpetrators.[30]

29　For more information on female Nazi exploitation within the film and pornography industries see: Marcus Stiglegger, 'Beyond good and evil: Sadomasochism and politics in the cinema of the 1970s', trans. Kathrin Zeitz. Paper held February 9, 2007, at FU Berlin conference 'Performing and Queering Sadomasochism'. See also Isabel Kershner, 'Israel's unexpected spinoff from a holocaust trial', *Jerusalem Journal*, 6 September 2007.

30　Women were active in other genocides throughout the 20th century, such as the Cambodian and Bosnian genocides. The individual cases of Biljana Plavšić of Bosnia and Leng Thirith of Cambodia are particularly prominent. (Biljana Plavšić, the 'Serbian Iron Lady', was the first woman charged with crimes against humanity in an international court, later released on a plea deal in 2009; Leng Thirith was tried in 2007 with her husband for crimes against humanity during the Khmer Rouge genocide, 1975–1979. Her case was recently dismissed in August 2012 due to her advanced stage of dementia.) These women both held positions of power and privilege before the genocide. For a myriad of reasons, from politics to culture, at this time the extent of female participation 'on the ground' is not known, nor are the various roles that women undertook within the genocidal regime.

The emergence of academic inquiry and feminist discourse concerned with women's roles during the Third Reich eventually developed during the 1980s. Gisela Bock and Claudia Koonz opened up the field through their disagreement concerning the position and guilt of females in Nazi Germany. While Koonz argued that German women were complicit and responsible for the genocide by supporting their men and maintaining a sense of comfort and normality at home, Bock asserted that all women were victims of Nazi terror due to the regime's policies that strictly regulated women's reproductive roles and movements in the public sphere.[31]

These arguments can be tentatively applied to Rwandan women as well. On the one hand, women's opportunities and positions in society were suppressed and limited under a strong patriarchal tradition. Nevertheless, many women who participated and even led massacres enjoyed an elevated status as mothers, receiving male support and extra supplies of ammunition.[32] In both 1994 Rwanda and 1944 Nazi Germany, women were offered an unprecedented opportunity to exert power and join males in 'fighting' for the warped ideals of their respective regimes. Gender boundaries, while still existing, became temporarily more flexible during the war, providing opportunities that some, but certainly not all, women took advantage of, for whatever reason, to commit terrible atrocities. Following the carnage, former gender expectations were reinstated through portrayals in the media and legal sentencing by various courts.

While similarities exist concerning the opportunities available to women in Nazi Germany and Rwanda, these two cases are characterised by remarkable differences, stemming from the situational context leading to their participation, as well as geography, time period and training. Nevertheless, it should not be overlooked that both situations led to women directly contributing to a genocide that decimated their countries despite their subordinate roles within their society at the time.[33] In both cases, most of the implicated women simply slipped back into society and assumed their usual roles as mothers and wives, eluding attention, punishment and stigma both internationally and domestically.[34] These women were essentially able to

---

31   Gisela Bock, 'Racism and sexism in Nazi Germany: Motherhood, compulsory sterilization, and the state', in Carol Rittner and John K Roth, eds, *Women in the Holocaust: Different Voices* (St. Paul, Minn.: Paragon House, 1993), 177.

32   African Rights, 'Rwanda: Not so Innocent', 2.

33   Reva N Adler, Cyanne E Loyle, Judith Globerman. 'A calamity in the neighborhood: Women's Participation in the Rwandan Genocide', *Genocide Studies and Prevention* 2.3 (November 2007), 209–234; 226.

34   African Rights, 'Rwanda: Not so innocent', 136–138.

escape attention and hide under the branding and prosecution of a few extra-ordinary females who caught the attention of governments and the media through their former positions of power or their extremely cruel behaviours. Estimates of the number of female perpetrators continue to grow,[35] but thus far we have little understanding of how women *become* perpetrators. The cases of Rwanda and Nazi Germany demonstrate that further study is often hindered by reverting to preconceived frameworks of interpretation. This chapter addresses the issue by providing a brief background of the women and the discourses, thereby elucidating the problems and barriers that future research needs to avoid.

Profiles of female perpetrators

The Aufseherinnen of Ravensbrück

Frauenkonzentrationslager Ravensbrück was established in 1939 to address the increasing numbers of female prisoners incarcerated under the Nazi regime. As the only entirely female camp, which was also run by females, Ravensbrück allowed German women their own realm to rule over a vulner-able prisoner population and also serve National Socialist values. The camp was also the official and primary training centre for all *Aufseherinnen* (female overseers, or guards), many of whom eventually worked within the camp, though others were transferred to smaller female sub-camps that opened throughout the Reich during the last years of the war.[36]

At Ravensbrück ordinary women were transformed into efficient perpet-rators through deliberate indoctrination and hands-on learning, conducted through a specialised, hate-filled rhetoric. These Aufseherinnen could typically be described as average in every way, including social class, occ-upation and physical appearance. They tended to be single and to hail from lower-middle-class families in rural areas and generally had only rudi-mentary schooling.[37] After the war their neighbours and peers generally described them as 'pleasant' and 'friendly' though 'not remarkable in any

---

35 Sjoberg and Gentry, *Mothers, Monsters, Whores*, 159.

36 For more information on the organisation and history of Ravensbrück, see Bernhard Strebel, *Das KZ Ravensbrück, Geschichte eines Lagerkomplexes* (Munich: Ferdinand Schöningh, Paderborn, 2003).

37 Daniel Patrick Brown. *The Camp Women: The Female Auxiliaries who Assisted the SS in running the Nazi Concentration Camp System* (Atglen, Penn.: Schiffer Military History, 2002), 237, 242.

way'.[38] Many claimed that there 'was certainly no cruelty' or depravity in the young women's pre-war dispositions;[39] however, due to the nature and demands of their position, one can possibly assume that some of the women were quite ambitious and even adventurous. After all, becoming a guard in a concentration camp offered opportunities for females that were unparalleled in normal civilian life during the Third Reich, including career advancement, privileged living conditions, and clandestine opportunities to meet men.[40]

Initially the Aufseherinnen were almost entirely volunteers; however, by 1943, the majority of new members were conscripted into their positions at the camps.[41] This change was due to many reasons. Women were prohibited from joining the *Schutzstaffel* (SS), Himmler's elite Praetorian Guard, which was the principal supplier for camp guard employees. After the outbreak of war in 1939, more women, particularly from outside of Germany, were incarcerated under the SS, requiring more guards and more facilities to incarcerate them as under Nazi ideology women and men were to inhabit separate realms.[42] Under the pressure of labour shortages due to the mass deployment of able-bodied men to the front, the government had to reconsider its position on the role and place of women within the structure of the Third Reich. The practical need for women in the workforce and in the camp system trumped party ideology, leading to the aggressive recruitment of females in traditionally 'male-appointed' realms.[43]

---

38 Leonora Zimmerman and other unidentified former neighbours as quoted in Sarah Helm's investigative report, 'The Nazi guard's untold love story', *The Sunday Times*, 5 August 2007.

39 ibid.

40 For more information on the motivations of Aufseherinnen for joining the SS-Auxiliaries, see Fotini Tzani, *Zwischen Karrierismus und Widerspenstigkeit: SS Aufseherinnen im KZ-Alltag* (Lorbeer Verlag, 2011), 53–56.

41 Bernhard Strebel, *Das KZ Ravensbrück*, 82–84. The largest numbers of recruits came in 1944, accounting for two-thirds of the total number of Aufseherinnen. Strebel estimated that out of the total number of Aufseherinnen at the end of the war, 10% were volunteers, 20% were sent through employment agencies and nearly 70% were conscripted.

42 Brown, *The Camp Women*, 16. Also see Joseph Goebbels, 'Deutsches Frauentum', *Signale der neuen Zeit. 25 ausgewählte Reden von Dr. Joseph Goebbels*, (Munich: Zentralverlag der NSDAP., 1934), 118–126. Also see Jack G Morrison, 'Chapter 1: National Socialism and women', *Ravensbrück: Everyday Life in a Women's Concentration Camp, 1939–1945* (Princeton, NJ: Wiener, 2000); and Kathrin Kompisch, *Täterinnen: Frauen im Nationalsozialismus* (Boehlau Verlag, 2008), 155.

43 The position of German women in the Third Reich is explored in Claudia Koonz, *Mothers in the Fatherland: Women, the Family and Nazi Politics* (New York: St. Martin's Press, 1987).

By 1943 the German Labour Service, the *Reichsarbeitsdienst*, required all single women between the ages of 17 and 45 to work for the 'greatness' of the Reich.[44] This was followed in August 1944 by the order of Propaganda Minister Joseph Goebbels for *totaler Kriegseinsatz* (mobilisation for total war), which included the forced conscription of all factory workers within the Reich into the Waffen-SS.[45] Nevertheless, service within camps was not particularly appealing to many women. Auschwitz Commandant Rudolf Höss reported in his postwar autobiography, 'In spite of the keen recruiting … very few candidates volunteered for concentration camp service, and compulsion had to be used to obtain the ever-increasing numbers required.'[46] Eventually, the practice of forcibly drafting women from factories or intimidating them into the auxiliary forces became commonplace.[47]

While Reichsführer Heinrich Himmler required SS men to regard auxiliaries and females as 'equals and comrades',[48] disputes and affairs nevertheless arose between the sexes. No matter what position a female held within the camp, she was always subordinated to an SS man and her opportunities for advancement remained limited when compared to her male counterparts.[49] Himmler insisted that a women's camp be run by a female in conformity with his rigid convictions of separate gender spheres, yet this often generated friction and in-fighting between male and female officers. Oberaufseherin Johanna Langefeld, the head overseer of the female guards at Ravensbrück and later Auschwitz-Birkenau, was transferred to different camps multiple times and was eventually released from her duties following her constant feuding with male officials and camp commandants.[50] Commandant Höss held many of the female guards at Auschwitz in disdain, referring to them as

---

44   Morrison, *Ravensbrück*, 24.

45   Brown, *The Camp Women*, 238.

46   Rudolf Höss, *Commandant of Auschwitz: The Autobiography of Rudolf Höss*, trans. Constantine FitzGibbon (London: Phoenix Press, 2000), 138.

47   Brown, *The Camp Women*, 16. One such government 'proposition/coercion' illustrates the position that many poor young women were faced with: 'Today we have a job for you, where you don't have to physically work and if you don't take this job, then you will end up as one who refuses to work and you, yourself, will be in the camp together with the *arbeitscheuen Gesindel*, "work-shy riff-raffs".' See also Stefanie Oppel, *Die Rolle der Arbeitsämter bei der Rekrutierung von SS-Aufseherinnen* (Fordergemeinschaft Wissenschaftliche Publikationen, 2006).

48   Brown, *The Camp Women*, 14–15.

49   Heike, 'Johanna Langefeld: Die Biographie einer KZ-Oberaufseherin', *WerkstattGeschichte*, 12 (Hamburg: Verlag Ergebnisse, 1995), 7–19, 11.

50   Höss, *Commandant of Auschwitz*, 137–138; Margarete Buber-Neumann, *Under Two Dictators: Prisoner of Stalin and Hitler*, Trans. Edward Fitzgerald (London: Pimlico, 2008), 233.; Kompisch, *Täterinnen*, 157.

'a lot of flustered hens' with 'extremely low' morals.[51] Höss later put the situation more bluntly, lamenting that none of his men would ever take orders from a woman.[52] While women may have been begrudgingly acknowledged in their positions at the camps, expecting men to take orders from them was taking things too far.

The training period for female guards varied throughout the war, from well organised in the beginning to haphazard in the later years.[53] The initially required curriculum for guard education was three to six weeks and could roughly be divided into three parts: ideological training, systematic instructions and an internship. A prominent aspect of female (as well as male) training programs was its military-like composition. Konzentrationslager Dachau, which opened in 1933, served as the prototype for all future concentration camps. It was also the primary training centre for the male SS camp guards, known as the *Totenkopfverbände*. Ravensbrück followed the Dachau example in its organisation of the camp and the administration of the guards. Trainees were housed in barracks, wore smart uniforms complete with recognised insignia, attended daily drills and had to respect military hierarchies of rank. Obedience was stressed and could even be considered synonymous with loyalty – to the group, the administration, and above all else to National Socialism and the Third Reich.[54]

Throughout the training period, candidates were subjected to rigorous military discipline similar to their male counterparts.[55] Punishments were inflicted for minor infractions during training. Discipline and behaviour were tightly regulated and controlled down to the most minute detail.[56] The conditioning process and training regimen were both 'grueling and demanding'.[57] Violence was dispensed through the ranks and as it passed from the higher administration to guard to prisoner, brutality grew and intensified in both nature and scope. According to one former prisoner who worked within the camp administration, new recruits were assigned to 'accompany the worst of the old wardresses, all brutal, bullying, reporting, ear-boxing types ... Again and again one could observe the same transformation: these young working

---

51   Höss, *Commandant of Auschwitz*, 137, 139.

52   ibid, 137.

53   Brown, *The Camp Women*, 17.

54   Tom Segev, *Soldiers of Evil: The Commandants of the Nazi Concentration Camps*, trans. Haim Watzman (New York: McGraw-Hill, 1988), 95–97.

55   Brown, *The Camp Women*, 17.

56   Wolfgang Sofsky, *The Order of Terror: The Concentration Camp*, trans. William Templer (Princeton, NJ: Princeton University Press, 1993), 112.

57   Brown, *The Camp Women*, 17.

women were soon every bit as bad as the old hands, ordering the prisoners around, bullying them and shouting as though they had been born in a barracks.'[58] Superiors and higher-ranking officers punished trainees or lower-ranking guards, who in turn vented their anger and frustrations onto the prisoners under their supervision, thus ensuring a cycle of escalating violence.

Most female guards were employed as overseers, which entailed guarding prisoners and enforcing camp regulations. They guarded prisoners on their way to and from work, supervised inmates during work and policed the camp around the clock. Their primary concern was to maintain discipline amongst the prisoners, though some duties were strictly reserved for males. For instance, execution squads, even in Ravensbrück and other female camps, were exclusively composed of SS men.[59] External guard units, whose cohort became increasingly non-German in the later years of the war, were also completely male.[60] Female guards were relegated to duties inside or in the immediate vicinity of the camp. When an Aufseherin was assigned to guard an external work group, she was often accompanied by an SS man, another Aufseherin or a dog trained for the purpose.[61] In other words, females were rarely found alone with prisoners, because they were considered incapable of inflicting the necessary force and intimidation needed for certain positions.

While Aufseherinnen were restricted in their activities and movements within the camp, this is not to say that they did not engage in cruel and inhumane actions. Violence and brutality were the order of the concentration camp – and the Aufseherinnen were responsible for maintaining this atmosphere of suffering and horror. Beatings and excessive violence were everyday occurrences in the lives of the prisoners. One survivor recorded: 'Punishments were the order of the day in the camp. The *Aufseherki* [Polish alteration for Aufseherinnen] would often burst in, kicking us, pushing us they would rush us "ahead".'[62] Another testimony relayed:

> Two especially severe and brutal *aufseherki* were sent to our camp from Oświęcim [Auschwitz]. They beat us every chance they got, hitting us in the face with their fists, or with rubber batons. They would often take

---

58 Buber-Nuemann, *Under Two Dictatorships*, 233.
59 Buber-Neumann, *Under Two Dictatorships*, 210.
60 Heike, 'Langerverwaltung und Bewachungspersonal', 222.
61 Kompisch, *Taterinnen*, 159.
62 Polski Instytut Źródłowy w Lund (PIZ), Vol. 4, Record of Witness Testimony no. 117, taken by Institute Assistant Luba Melchior at the Polish Documentary Institute in Lund, Malmö, on January 13, 1946.

prisoners to the toilets, where for the slightest infraction they tortured them, often until the victims lost consciousness.[63]

Few limits were imposed to curtail the brutal mistreatment of the inmates. Overseers ruled with an iron fist and could react on a whim.[64] The ruling principle and overall objective was to instil and maintain terror within the prisoner population.

Along with guard details, Aufseherinnen were responsible for overseeing the administration of disciplinary infractions. There were numerous punishments that could be officially meted out to prisoners. In Ravensbrück one of the most common was *Strafstehen*, or 'punishment standing', consisting of standing at attention for an unspecified amount of time, which could be hours or even days. Other punishments included withholding of food and mail; confinement to the 'Idiots' Room', where inmates were imprisoned in a barracks and left to die; or assignment to the *Strafblock*, the 'prisoner block', where inmates were required to do the hardest manual labour under the harshest conditions. The worst punishment occurred within 'The Bunker', where inmates were placed in solitary confinement and often subjected to harsh punishments, which included receiving 25 lashes on their bare backside.[65]

In spite of the background of extreme evil and little good, most female guards were neither overly brutal nor particularly kind, and instead did their jobs indifferently because they wanted to conform and belong to the group, or simply did not care.[66] Brutal and sadistic women obviously overshadowed their 'ordinary' peers, then and now. They not only commanded attention among the prisoners who were on the receiving end of their cruelty; they also attracted the notice of their superiors and were duly rewarded for their 'efforts.' These were the women who were assigned nicknames by the prison population, and thus became singled out and separated from the homogenous group of female overseers.

Within the camps, Aufseherinnen were addressed by their official titles and not their individual names, leaving their identities largely unknown, in contrast to SS men who were typically referred to by both their rank

---

63   PIZ, Vol. 9, Record of Witness Testimony no. 357, taken by Institute Assistant Helena Dziedzicka at the Polish Documentary Institute in Lund, Malmö, on March 20, 1946.

64   Sofsky, *Order of Terror*, 32.

65   Morrison, 'Crime and Punishment', 221–238.

66   Germaine Tillon, *Ravensbrück*, trans. Gerald Satterwaite, (Garden City, NJ: Doubleday, 1975), 70. Tillon's testimony is supported by psychological observations made by Roy Baumeister, 'The Holocaust and the four roots of evil', in Leonard S Newman and Ralph Erber, eds, *Understanding Genocide: The Social Psychology of the Holocaust* (Oxford: Oxford University Press, 2002), 254.

and last name.[67] As a result, female guards did not elicit attention from Allied governments seeking postwar justice, nor did they feature in survivor memoirs.[68] Instead, they remained known simply as 'Frau Aufseherin' to the inmates they terrorised as well as in the historical memory of the Holocaust, which has largely overlooked them. Interestingly, as one study has demonstrated, the tradition of retaining the individuality of SS men while referring to 'SS' women as an anonymous mass continued in some postwar trials. During the Majdanek trials of the 1960s and 1970s, reporters referred to male defendants by their given names, while female defendants were often called by their adopted nicknames or titles.[69]

After the war the Allies caught and tried only a handful of female overseers, as the majority simply returned home and were absorbed back into their communities. Less than ten per cent of Aufseherinnen were tried after the war, which can be attributed to a variety of factors including the chaotic conditions after the war, the reluctance of governments to try and execute women and the anonymity among female guards within the camp system.[70] For the women who were apprehended during the final weeks and months of the war, only a small percentage were actually tried and found guilty.

It is difficult to establish a pattern or even generalise about the treatment of the Aufseherinnen by postwar courts due to the multiple jurisdictions and long time span involved.[71] Studies have demonstrated that both the media and the courts viewed former overseers with a gender bias. Unlike the

---

67   Elissa Mailäner Koslov, 'Täterinnenbilder im Düsseldorfer Majdanek-Prozess (1975–1981)', *Im Gefolge der SS: Aufseherinnen des Frauen KZ-Ravensbrück*, ed. Simone Erpel (Berlin: Metropol, 2011), 211–217; 218.

68   In addition to the more personal means of addressing male guards, men were also tattooed with their blood-type on their upper-left arm, signifying their membership to the SS; this practice was never extended to women. These two factors made identifying SS men in the post-war period easier.

69   Sabine Horn, '"… ich fühlte mich damals als Soldat und nicht als Nazi" Die Majdanek-Prozess in Fernshen- aus geschlechtergeschichtlicher Perspektive betrachtet', *'Bestien' und 'Befehlsempfänger': Frauen und Manner in NS-Prozessen nach 1945*, ed. Weckel, Ulricke, Edgar Wolfrum (Gottingen 2003), 222–249.

70   Irmtraud Heike, 'Female concentration camp guards as perpetrators: Three case studies', in Olaf Jensen and Claus-Christian W Szejnmann, eds, *Ordinary People as Mass Murderers: Perpetrators in Comparative Perspectives* (New York: Palgrave Macmillan, 2008), 137.

71   The British military court held the first Belsen trial that tried a number of former Aufseherinnen and female kapos on 17 September 1945. During the next ten years trials were held by all major Allied nations, often taking place at the sites of the former concentration camps. Eventually, trials were held before German courts, both in the Federal Republic of Germany and the German Democratic Republic. To date, the last trial involving a former Aufseherinnen, Luise Danz, took place in Germany in 1996. The case was dismissed due to her ill health.

treatment of her male defendant counterparts, the media often held her to a higher moral standard, while at the same time denying her agency and independent initiative.[72] Her 'character' was as much on trial as her crimes, often leading to meticulous attention to her background, psyche and appearance. Newspapers reported on female defendants' clothes and hairstyles, while upbringing, lifestyles and personal choices unrelated to their crimes were minutely examined and judged.

The courts often interpreted and handed down sentences according to supposed gender norms.[73] Some women received harsher sentences, as their behaviour was interpreted as dangerous for violating their traditional roles as women, while others were exonerated because, due to their position as employees and women, they were supposedly not responsible for the actions.[74] To a great extent, the different needs of societies were reflected in the judgements and sentences handed down to female defendants. The need for reconciliation and rebuilding brought lighter sentences for some women, while the desire to restore gender boundaries produced harsher punishments for others. Ultimately, extraordinary defendants, those women who behaved particularly cruel, came to represent all female perpetrators. These particular cases carried the blame while constructing the story of female involvement within the genocide. The accounts of the majority were thus superseded and ultimately ignored or omitted from the post-genocide social consciousness and the historical record. This miscarriage ultimately allowed society to reconcile female involvement by pointing out and punishing the extraordinary, therefore avoiding uncomfortable introspection of the role of 'ordinary' women during the genocide.

It is difficult to ascertain how influential postwar trials were in the formation of the image of the aberrant, 'unnatural' female perpetrator prevailing today. Most trials were generally ignored or went unreported by the press and other media outlets, though a few trials did capture the public's

---

72 Kathryn Meyer, 'Die Frau ist der Frieden der Welt: Von Nutzen und Lasten eines Weiblichkeitsstereotypes in Spruchkammerentscheidungen gegen Frauen', in Ulrike Weckel and Edgar Wolfrum, eds, *'Bestien' und 'Befehlsempfanger': Frauen und Manner in NS-Prozessen nach 1945* (Gottingen 2003), 117–138; 131.

73 Claudia Kuretsidis-Haider, 'Täterinnen vor Gesricht. Die Kategorie Geschlecht bei der Ahndung von nationalsozialistischen Tötungsdelikten in Deutschland und Osterreich', *Sie waren dabei: Mitlauferinnen, Nutzniesserinnen, Taterinnen im Nationalsozialismus*, Dachau: 8, Dachauer Symposium zur Zeitgeschichte, 2007, 187–210.

   See also Elissa Mailander Koslov, *Gewalt im Dienstalltag: Die SS-Aufseherinnen des Konzentrations- und Vernichtungslagers Majdanek 1942–1944* (Hamburger Edition, 2009).

74 Kathryn Meyer, 'Die Frau ist der Frieden der Welt', 131.

attention and imagination, just as these same few women captured the attention of their superiors and their inmates during the war. The public was fascinated by postwar stories of Irma Grese and Ilse Koch.[75] These women, along with a few others, and the atrocities they committed became infamous within Holocaust literature. Their stories were sensationalised, broadcast on newspaper headlines and have become the subjects of myth. One specific example was Ilse Koch, the wife of Commandant Karl Otto Koch, who was accused of using prisoners' skins for lampshades in her home as well as committing perverse sexual acts against prisoners (the former accusation has largely been disproven).[76] While these specific trials received a great deal of attention, Cold War politics and new media headlines quickly overshadowed international attention to them.

The role and demeanour of the female guards who carried out the Holocaust were unusual in that their actions unfolded within a female realm, even though the genocide was originally orchestrated and implemented by males. The Aufseherinnen's position and activities were quite different from the Rwandan case; nevertheless, the results of their behaviour – the terrorisation and slaughter of other females – were the same.

Rwandan female genocidaires

Most Rwandan women who actively participated in the genocide did so through indirect ways, such as looting victims' property, pointing out the hiding places of potential victims and supporting their menfolk by providing food, housing and emotional encouragement.[77] As many studies have pointed out, these activities not only conform to expected gender roles, but were also frequently encountered during other international and domestic conflicts throughout history, including in Eastern Europe under Nazi occupation.[78] Nevertheless, women did act outside of traditional gender roles

---

75 For more information on the biographies and cases of these two notorious women, please consult, Daniel Patrick Brown, *The Beautiful Beast: The Life and Crimes of SS-Aufseherin Irma Grese* (Ventura, CA: Golden West Historical Publications, 1996); and Arthur LJ Smith, *Die Hexe von Buchenwald: Der Fall Ilse Koch* (Bohlau Verlag GmbH & Cie, 1983). Note that Ilse Koch was not an Aufseherinnen, nor employed through the SS in any way. She was, however, the wife of Commandant Koch and both husband and wife openly and flagrantly ruled and committed many atrocities during their reign in KL Buchenwald and Majdanek.

76 Dan Alban, 'Books bound in human skin; lampshade myth?" *The Harvard Law Review*, 11 November 2005.

77 Hogg, 'Women's participation', 78.

78 Adler, Loyle, Globerman, 'A calamity in the neighborhood', 226.

as well as outside the acceptable boundaries of human behaviour.[79] In other words, while wives, sisters and mothers might have privately assisted and encouraged their male kin who participated in the genocide, a significant number of women perpetrated the genocide within the public sphere, even if they allegedly committed fewer violent acts than men.[80] In fact, thousands of women were directly responsible for horrible atrocities, including instigating kidnap, rape and murder.

The African Rights Report documented that many women indulged in 'extraordinary cruelty' in which they slaughtered hundreds of baby boys, doused victims with gasoline and then lit them on fire, robbed corpses, threw grenades into crowds of Tutsis seeking refuge, and accompanied their husbands and sons in execution-style shooting sprees.[81] Women were also observed at roadblocks in which they assisted the Interahamwe in checking identification cards and arresting any Tutsis they identified. These episodes of violence were not unique, nor were they carried out by a specific demographic of females.

While Aufseherinnen typically hailed from uneducated, rural backgrounds, Rwandan female perpetrators came from all walks of life, from the very young to the elderly, from the educated to the illiterate, and from the coerced to the ideologically driven.[82] In fact, some of the most privileged, educated females were the most active in targeting victims and providing the means for their destruction. Teachers who assisted in organising killing squads, pointing out potential victims (including their former pupils) and rallying support represented one of the largest groups of female perpetrators.[83] They were further backed by women employed in health services and even the church.[84] The official report noted that 'the very women who had access to political power and economic means' were the ones who 'went on killing sprees in the company of their children' and 'made lists of people to be killed which they gave to soldiers' in charge of carrying out the genocide.[85]

---

79   It should be noted that under Rwandan Gacaca Law, people who in any way assisted the killers during the genocide are subject to the same punishment as the actual killers. Hogg, 'Women's participation', 81. This is different from post-Holocaust justice in which very few indirect perpetrators were ever held accountable for their actions. (Most cases were either held in civil court, and many ultimately resulted in acquittals.)

80   Hogg, 'Women's participation', 69–102, 78.

81   African Rights, 'Rwanda: Not so innocent', 2, 14.

82   ibid., 1–2; 136–137.

83   ibid., 105.

84   ibid., 112.

85   ibid., 1–3.

Nevertheless, thousands of other women also took advantage of the chaotic situation to engage in brutal acts, from shooting refugees to hacking other women and children to death.[86]

It is difficult to provide a clear picture of who the Rwandan female genocidaires were. Postwar fact-finding missions are hindered by the population's high illiteracy rates and low percentage of telephone ownership. Records were rarely kept or retained during the chaotic conditions of the genocide.[87] Nevertheless, due to the often extremely intimate nature of the killings, individuals could be identified and singled out after the carnage. Information has also been obtained through testimonies, Gacaca courts[88] and the few investigations by outside organisations, most notably, the 1995 African Rights report. While data are not exact, most sources cite that thousands of women participated from every class, age demographic and occupation.[89]

While it is unclear what precise motivations encouraged women to participate in the genocide, a few studies have categorised some of the most likely reasons leading to involvement. In the case of Rwanda, Nicole Hogg identifies three primary motives falling under the categories of fear, greed and propaganda.[90] Other motivations played a role as well, many of which were similar to the Aufseherinnen, including unprecedented economic and occupational opportunity; political propaganda; and peer pressure from husbands, friends, and the community.[91] Despite the multiple and complex reasons for becoming involved, the fact is that many women did participate even without overt threats and lucrative incentives.

One of the most alarming roles of women in the Rwandan genocide was advocating and encouraging fellow militants to use rape against women as a weapon for terrorising, humiliating and ultimately destroying the targeted enemy.[92] African Rights reported that 'women particularly excelled as "cheerleaders" … singing and ululating the killers into action' while men

---

86   ibid., 15.

87   Adler, Loyle, Globerman, 'A Calamity in the Neighborhood', 213.

88   Gacaca courts refer to the justice system established in Rwanda after the genocide in order to handle the large numbers of perpetrators. Gacaca were courts of law that embraced traditional transitional local justice intended to include the community and create healing.

89   African Rights, 'Rwanda: Not so Innocent', 1–2.

90   Hogg, 'Women's participation in the Rwandan genocide: Mothers or monsters?', *International Review of the Red Cross*, Vol 92, Nr 877, (March 2010), 69–102, 83.

91   Hogg, 'Women's participation', 86–90.

92   Sjoberg and Gentry, *Mothers, Monsters, Whores*, 166; African Rights, 44.

raped and then slaughtered their victims.[93] Women also singled out victims, often other women and children, but occasionally men as well, for humiliation, torture and death. Thus, women were not only publicly present at massacres during the three-month genocide; they also assisted in deciding who should live and who should die, and then in finishing off the victims by dousing them with gasoline or hacking them to death.[94]

How did Rwandan females come to kill? In Nazi Germany, most female guards were actively recruited and trained in an official, semi-organised manner by the Nazi government; however, in Rwanda, women were not officially recruited, and if they were, it was done on a largely ad-hoc basis. Women were a rare presence in the military and only a few females ever achieved any position of power within the Rwandan army.[95] After the outbreak of the genocide, more women unofficially joined the ranks due to pressure from their husbands, excitement over the events, or even opportunity. One post-genocide study noted that of the extremely small number of female Interahamwe, only one in ten received any military training prior to the genocide. The few females who did receive training were regarded as rebels and were often ostracised from friends and relatives during and after the atrocity. These particular women, who were taught 'civil defence' exercises, were often trained only by their husbands, who were themselves already members of the paramilitary group. In other words, these women were not trained in an official capacity amongst fellow females, as was the case in Germany. Instead, 'instruction' lasted less than a month, if at all, and usually consisted of simple weapon handling in the company of males.[96]

Coming from a traditionally strict patriarchal society in which women had limited opportunities, combined with the chaotic conditions of the genocide, which disrupted and destroyed all spheres of life, Rwandan women were thrust into a stressful situation in which they had to balance traditional roles with new identities. According to bystanders and even the perpetrators themselves, many felt trapped in 'haphazard or situational' positions in which participation in the genocide, in both active and passive ways, was expected or demanded by outside forces.[97] Nevertheless, many women did successfully navigate this complex situation and some did so by actively taking part in the murder of Tutsis. While the pressure and threat

---

93   African Rights, 'Rwanda: Not so innocent', 39, 44–45.
94   ibid., 31–36.
95   Hogg, 'Women's participation', 95.
96   Adler, Loyle, Globerman, 'A calamity in the neighborhood', 223–224.
97   ibid., 221–222.

that women may or may not have experienced at the hands of males during the genocide should not be dismissed,[98] some evidence exists that women captured the attention and admiration of male perpetrators and even became leaders, encouraging and carrying out massacres.[99]

Immediately following the genocide, most women, like their male counterparts, were not prosecuted; they simply resumed their normal lives in both the private and public spheres or managed to successfully flee the country.[100] Nevertheless, nearly 3,000 women were charged with genocide-related crimes and tried in Gacaca courts, resulting in their eventual incarceration.[101] It is unclear whether there was any gender bias influencing Gacaca courts. In other words, were women judged more harshly for violating traditional female roles? Were they given more lenient sentences? How did their communities and legal systems view and handle their pasts?[102]

Despite the difference between Nazi organisation and training of female perpetrators and the ad-hoc, unorganised involvement characterising Rwandan female perpetrators, both groups produced female killers whose active and violent participation contributed to the genocide. While the Aufseherinnen were trained according to military regulations in a relatively controlled environment, Rwandan female killers were rarely trained, and if they were, it occurred alongside male recruits outside of a military capacity. Nevertheless, both groups of women appeared to adapt successfully to their unfamiliar positions of power by following and executing their orders, thus making the transition from a civilian to a supporter of a genocidal regime.

---

98   Hogg, 'Women's participation', 80, 72.
99   Nyiramasuhuko is the most famous case, yet others exist, as outlined in the African Rights report, 15–24.
100 Cyanne E Loyle and Christian Davenport, 'Some left to tell the tale: Finding perpetrators and understanding state-sponsored violence'. Paper presented at the Politics and Protest Workshop, City University of New York, 13 October 2011.
101 Adler, Loyle, Globerman, 'A calamity in the neighborhood', 212.
102 Some studies have broached this issue from both a legal and a social standpoint, in particular, the psychological study undertaken by Adler, Loyle, Globerman, 'A calamity in the neighborhood: Women's participation in the Rwandan genocide', and Nichole Hogg, 'Women's participation in the Rwandan genocide: Mothers or monsters?'; both which have been used extensively throughout this chapter. In addition, Jean Hatzfeld's journalistic report on the Rwandan perpetrators also offers some commentary on the role women played, as well as their reception by their society during and after the genocide. Jean Hatzfeld, Machete Season: The Killers in Rwanda Speak, trans. Linda Coverdale (New York: Picador 108-113). Their findings largely conform to many of the same gendered biases that the German case presents in which women were either demonised by their communities or granted impunity for their alleged powerlessness. However, more studies need to be conducted.

Female perpetrator image, pigeon-holed perceptions and biased discourses

While the two cases of Rwanda and Germany were quite different, along with the experiences of the female perpetrators within the regimes, perhaps the most striking similarity is the societal emphasis and resulting images emerging after the genocide. Despite evidence that thousands of ordinary women were participants in the genocide in both situations, society, and to some extent academia, has fixated on the sensational story. This is not too surprising considering the fascination their specific cases present and the media's emphasis on and dramatisation of their stories in order to sell within their media outlets. Yet it is perhaps revealing that although cases involving extraordinary or sadistic males certainly exist and are well known, male perpetrators are still largely regarded as 'normal' people who reacted to situational pressures and even acted under normalised behavioural expectations.[103] Female perpetrators, on the other hand, continue to shock and confound. Instead of interpreting their behaviours as the product of extraordinary situations and the ultimate result of human agency, portrayals tend either to cast them as deviants and aberrations or to quietly grant them impunity for their perceived powerlessness concerning the events.

The psychologist Steven Baum concluded, '[M]ost evil is the product of rather ordinary people caught up in unusual circumstances.'[104] His findings largely support the theory that cultural influences, rather than character traits or mental deficiencies, contribute to the participation and escalation of genocide, but this analysis has not been extended to female involvement. While studies of male Nazi perpetrators have tended to focus on situational circumstances or a combination of situational and dispositional influences, rather than simply dispositional forces, to understand and explain perpetrator behaviour, the current discourse concerning female perpetrators has relied almost entirely upon dispositional understandings. While social and historical discourses have tended to present SS men as complex characters influenced by a variety of factors and motivations, SS women have been

---

103   For more information on the historiography concerning Nazi male perpetrators, see Claus-Christian W Szejnmann, Perpetrators of the Holocaust: A historiography', in Olaf Jensen and Claus-Christian W Szejnmann, eds, *Ordinary People as Mass Murderers: Perpetrators in Comparative Perspectives* (New York: Palgrave Macmillan, 2008), 25–54. For a social-psychological perspective, see Leonard S Newman and Ralph Erber, eds, *Understanding Genocide: The Social Psychology of the Holocaust* (Oxford: Oxford University Press, 2002), 43–67.

104   Steven K Baum, *The Psychology of Genocide: Perpetrators, Bystanders, and Rescuers* (New York: Cambridge University Press, 2008), 170.

portrayed as sexually depraved monsters or wayward, easily manipulated females. In a similar fashion, male participants in the Rwandan genocide have also largely been deemed to be ordinary men caught up in an extreme situation.[105] The image of a singular crazed, sexually driven male Hutu soldier simply does not exist, despite evidence that particular individuals certainly did behave that way. Instead, the Interahamwe frequently are portrayed as a group,[106] and are rarely singled out and defined as individual cases, unlike their female counterparts.

While academic fields have made strides in addressing and correcting the situation, popular culture still struggles with the portrayal of an 'ordinary' female perpetrator. In the 2008 film *The Reader*, based upon the 1995 novel published under the same name by the German law professor and judge Bernhard Schkink, an ordinary, illiterate female concentration camp guard meets and attracts a teenage boy in postwar West Germany. The film concludes with her trial, guilty verdict and subsequent suicide, which occur decades after the crimes. The movie is notable in that it features and centres upon an ordinary female perpetrator – a stark departure from previous Hollywood films focusing solely on male Nazis or the sexually perverse and sadistic female Nazi.[107] Despite this Hollywood novelty of a 'Holocaust film' starring a female Nazi, and the fact that the film portrays a nameless, 'ordinary' female perpetrator, the story still presents a very sexual and sensual being who seduces an innocent adolescent. In other words, she might have been undereducated, poor and desperate, but she was still oversexed and immoral.

By studying examples of scholarship and media stories, I have identified three prominent discourses that many authors and audiences turn to in order to explain female perpetrators. These theories, or patterns of discourse, are powerful influences shaping the image, perception and overall social identity of this distinct group, which in turn inspire societal reception and understanding.

---

105 Lee Ann Fujii. *Killing Neighbors: Webs of Violence in Rwanda.* (Ithaca, NY: Cornell University Press, 2009).

106 Simpson, 'Africa Interahamwe',1999.

107 For more information on Hollywood and Nazism, see my paper 'Normal men or sadistic killers: An examination into the rise of the evil Nazi in Hollywood during the 1990s', presented in part along with Michael Geheran and Jan Taubitz at the public symposium 'Holocaust Memory Legacies of Disaster or Lessons of Cosmopolitanism, at Clark University on April 29, 2010.

Also see David Sterritt's article, 'The one serious subject Hollywood doesn't avoid'. *The Christian Science Monitor.* November 22, 2002.

The first stresses the 'ordinariness' of the women, arguing that all humans, regardless of gender, are capable of evil due to various social and psychological pressures.[108] Nearly every study that has promoted this thesis has focused on males, leaving only brief remarks concerning females. While the genders are not complete opposites, they are also not identical, as women approach and respond to similar situations differently from their male counterparts. This difference in response does not make them mad or 'unordinary'; rather, it highlights the fact that we currently have little understanding of how women, due to both social constructions and biology, respond to violence and the unregulated use of violence.[109] How did women in Nazi Germany and Rwanda interpret and navigate their new positions and access to violence and power? Did women feel the need to 'prove' themselves in front of male audiences and a patriarchal administration? Were they ashamed and conflicted about the transgression of traditional gender roles? Did they embrace the freedom and power provided by the situation? The current focus on the disposition of women severely limits inquiry into these pertinent questions.

The second discourse asserts that female perpetrators were manipulated, used and then scapegoated by their male counterparts in order to support the status quo of a patriarchal society in which females and males have separate (and largely unequal) roles within that society. Some scholars claim that women perpetrators 'served mainly as instruments of masculine aggression, pawns in the game, responding to orders and encouragement by men who often held positions of authority over them.'[110] When females did partake in violence, it was often merely an attempt to join the dominant community of males. Thus, during extraordinary situations, such as outbreaks of genocide and war, females who wanted or were pressured to participate were required to 'join in a macabre male-bonding ritual in which cohesion was established

---

108 Feinman, 'Shock and Awe: Abu Ghraib, Women Soldiers, and Racially Gendered Torture', in Tara McKelvey, ed., *One of the Guys: Women as Aggressors and Torturers* (Emeryville, Cal.: Seal Press, 2007), 57–80, 63.

109 For more information concerning cases that have touched upon this issue, see Susanne Heschel, 'Does Atrocity Have a Gender? Feminist Interpretations of the Women in the SS', in JM Diefendorf, ed., *Lessons and Legacies VI. New Currents in Holocaust Research*, (Evanston, Ill.: Northwestern University Press, 2004); and Jana L Pershing, 'Men and Women's Experiences with Hazing in a Male-Dominated Elite Military Institution', *Men and Masculinities*, Vol. 8, No. 4, 470–492 (2006).

110 Barbara Finlay. 'Pawns, Scapegoat, or Collaborator?" *One of the Guys: Women as Aggressors and Torturers*. Ed. Tara McKelvey. (Emeryville, CA: Seal Press, 2007), 199–213, 204.

through acts of violence and humiliation' toward the enemy-other.[111] This explanation supports the argument that many feminists have long supported which 'saw men as the perpetual perpetrators, women as the perpetual victims, and the male sexual violence against women as the root of all injustice.'[112] Indeed, many women attested to feeling intimidated in both Nazi Germany and 1994 Rwanda. Both groups came from traditionally patriarchal societies in which women's roles were limited. These women were conscious of their new opportunities and positions within a traditionally male realm and they likely experienced some feelings of trepidation or fear for breaching these gendered boundaries.[113] Furthermore, many women were threatened, or felt threatened, into participation.

This discourse also incorporates the allegation that women, due to their sex, are viewed as 'destabilising forces' within male communities such as military environments, because they are unable to control their passions and their reproductive, biological needs.[114] Women who indulge in violence are seen as being corrupted by their recently recognised sexual freedoms.[115] In turn, not only are the women's actions interpreted as sexually driven, but the women themselves are viewed as sexually depraved. This idea, which has been popularly supported by the media, has also been adopted and indulged by many pornographic representations leading to an underworld culture of perverted misogynistic images of sexy female SS officers and other violent females appearing in pornographic films and in adult costume shops.[116]

This discourse not only objectifies women, but it completely denies their independent human agency. Instead, it reverts back to historically constructed gender roles in which women are merely fragile vessels that can be used by males as instruments to do their bidding.[117] After the carnage is over and the atrocities are made public, those in power (through force or reinstatement) are able to point to specific 'out-of-control' females as the cause and root

---

111　Finlay, 'Pawn, scapegoat, or collaborator?" 204.

112　Tara McKelvey, 'Introduction', *One of the Guys: Women as Aggressors and Torturers*, ed. Tara McKelvey, (Emeryville, CA: Seal Press, 2007), 12.

113　Nelson, *The Psychology of Prejudice*, 230.

114　Barbara Ehrenreich, 'Foreword: Feminism's assumptions upended', *One of the Guys: Women as Aggressors and Torturers*, ed. Tara McKelvey. (Emeryville, CA: Seal Press, 2007), 7–16, 2.

115　Sjoberg and Gentry, *Mothers, Monsters, Whores*, 147.

116　Lynn Rapaport. 'Holocaust pornography: Profaning the sacred in Ilsa, She-Wolf of the SS'. *Shofar: An Interdisciplinary Journal of Jewish Studies*. Vol. 22, No 1, (Fall 2003), 53–79. Also refer to footnote 26.

117　Finlay, 'Pawn, scapegoat, or collaborator?' 210.

of the abuse.[118] In doing so they are able to disparage the threat of female encroachment into the male realm, while simultaneously re-establishing the status quo. Intractable women are singled out, allowing societies to re-establish under 'the blanket cover of innocence' that women at home provide and maintain.[119] The nation's alibi is fashioned, conventional order is tentatively restored and a façade of healing and reconciliation is installed, while blame is dumped at the feet of the wayward few. In the cases of both Rwanda and Germany, societies were somewhat successful at hiding behind the traditional image of the innocent wife and mother who had not sullied her hands partaking in the carnage. This situation not only identifies gender transgressions, but also supports the notion that male violence is considered normal, while female violence is attributed to misconstrued social roles or manipulation by males. In either case, the female's actions are interpreted as disruptive and threatening to the traditional understanding of the world.

The final discourse labels these women as extraordinary individuals whose characters are deficient and flawed. This path tends to be the most common rhetoric indulged in by the popular media to approach and understand these women. It is also the simplest and perhaps least distressing explanation for people to see and to accept. By labelling these women as freaks, society somewhat alleviates the 'deep revulsion felt towards women who step out of a nurturing role by behaving in a violent manner'.[120]

The image of the extraordinary female is not only interpreted as awry, flawed and dangerous, but has also become representational of any and all female perpetrators. Female genocidaires are not *real* women; they are wrong and outside of humanity, leaving *true* women pure and unscathed. This interpretation allows us to ignore the phenomenon of female perpetrators because they are not considered normal, ordinary occurrences worthy of deeper investigation.

Conclusion

The prevailing image of the female perpetrator hinders further studies by engaging and binding us to particular patterns of discourse. This chapter not only identified the most prominent critiques, but also demonstrated that they are not limited to particular groups or cases in history. The image of the sexually depraved, sadistic and transgressive woman appeared after 1945

---

118   ibid., 205.
119   African Rights, 'Rwanda: Not so innocent', 3.
120   McKelvey, *One of the Guys*, 8.

and again in 1994. This chapter has looked beyond these images in order to present an accurate account of the 'ordinary woman' involved in genocide. While popular culture and the media play a large role in shaping and publicising these images, often in order to shock and sell, their effects are felt through all layers of society. Justice attempts to be 'blind' and academics strive for objectivity, yet social norms and pressures still manage to trickle in and determine the treatment of subjects and outcomes of study. The desire to explain female perpetrators' dispositions, rather than to examine the situational and social pressures influencing their behaviours, severely limits scholarship and understanding of how women come to actively support and participate in genocide.

Chapter 3

'A HOLOCAUST THE WEST FORGOT'?

Reflections on genocide narratives of the Ukrainian Holodomor

Rebekah Moore

Between 1932 and 1933, a vast famine spread across several regions of the Soviet Union. Generally understood as an outgrowth of the Soviet agricultural policy of collectivisation, the number of people who died as a result of the famine has been variously estimated to be between 4.5 and upwards of 8 million.[1] Although its effects were felt in differing degrees across the Soviet Union, it has been the narratives about the Ukrainian experience of the famine – which has come to be known in Ukraine and elsewhere as the

---

1   This figure range for famine deaths is cited by RW Davies and Stephen Wheatcroft in their 2004 study *The Years of Hunger*. Their own figure for the death toll from the famine is 5.5 to 6.5 million people. See RW Davies and SG Wheatcroft, *The Years of Hunger: Soviet Agriculture 1931–1933* (Basingstoke: Palgrave Macmillan, 2004), 400–401. For their discussion of other figures, see ibid., 412–420. For other varying estimations see, for example, R Conquest, *The Harvest of Sorrow: Soviet Collectivization and the Terror-Famine* (New York: Oxford University Press, 1986), 303, 306; A Karatnycky, 'Forced famine in the Ukraine: A holocaust the West forgot', *The Wall Street Journal*, 7 July 1983, 22; H Kuromiya, 'The Soviet famine of 1932–1933 reconsidered', *Europe-Asia Studies*, vol. 60, no. 4, 2008, 665; LY Luciuk, 'Foreword: Reaping what they once sowed', in LY Luciuk, ed., *Holodomor: Reflections on the Great Famine of 1932–1933 in Soviet Ukraine* (Kingston: The Kashtan Press, 2008), v; JE Mace 'The man-made famine of 1933 in the Soviet Ukraine: What happened and why?', in IW Charny, ed., *Toward the Understanding and Prevention of Genocide: Proceedings of the International Conference on the Holocaust and Genocide* (Boulder: Westview Press, 1984), 67; and C Young, 'Remember the Holodomor', *The Weekly Standard*, 8 December 2008.

CHAPTER 3

Holodomor – that have emerged as particularly controversial in subsequent historiographical and public discourse.

Much of the discussion about the Holodomor has been dominated by questions concerning its genocidal nature, and a long-running historiographical debate, largely confined to historians outside of Ukraine, has persisted on this point. Even though much of the scholarship on the famine concludes it was not a genocide, those who argue in favour of a genocidal interpretation have produced a large literature, and within post-Soviet Ukraine itself, much of the public discussion and commemoration has been built upon this particular classification.

In arguing for this famine-as-genocide interpretation, distinct narratives surrounding the Holodomor have emerged. Their creation, however, has drawn heavily on comparisons with other genocides, particularly the Holocaust. This chapter argues that the genocide discourses surrounding the Holodomor, both in and outside of Ukraine, have been purposefully formed through comparisons with the Holocaust, adopting both the terminology and mechanisms of commemoration normally associated with the latter. It will explore the implications of these comparisons for our understandings of the Holodomor, and how we address past atrocity more generally.

The development of scholarly and public discourse about the famine is a relatively recent phenomenon, as for many years it received little attention and recognition. This state of affairs was undoubtedly influenced by the official Soviet line of denying that the famine had ever occurred. At the time it was taking place, a few foreign journalists and officials, such as Gareth Jones and Malcolm Muggeridge, managed to report what they had witnessed in the areas affected.[2] It was, however, the accounts of other foreign correspondents, perhaps most notably those of *The New York Times*'

---

2   Examples of Muggeridge's reports include a three-part series entitled 'The Soviet and the peasantry: an observer's notes', the individual articles of which were 'Famine in North Caucasus', *Manchester Guardian*, 25 March 1933, 13–14; 'Hunger in Ukraine', *Manchester Guardian*, 27 March 1933, 9–10; and 'Poor harvest in prospect', *Manchester Guardian*, 28 March 1933, 9–10. For discussion of Muggeridge and his reporting on the famine, see, for example, DG Dalrymple, 'The Soviet famine of 1932–1934', *Soviet Studies*, vol. 15, no. 3, 1964, 250–284; and I Hunter, 'A tale of truth and two journalists: Malcolm Muggeridge and Walter Duranty', in WL Hewitt, ed., *Defining the Horrific: Readings on Genocide and Holocaust in the Twentieth Century* (Upper Saddle River, NJ: Pearson Prentice Hall, 2004), 134–135. For Jones' reporting, see 'Famine in Russia', *Manchester Guardian*, 30 March 1933, 12. For more on the famine reports of Muggeridge and Jones, see, for example, S Colley, 'A curtain of silence: An essay in comparison', *Canadian-American Slavic Studies*, vol. 42, no. 3, 2008, 297–319.

Walter Duranty, that downplayed and covered up the extent of the famine and came to dominate understandings of it in the West.[3] Discussion of the Holodomor, then, as one historian has recognised, began as a 'history in exile'.[4] Prior to a 'rediscovery' of the famine in the early 1980s, the majority of publications on the subject resulted from the efforts of the Ukrainian diaspora. Nonetheless, these publications remained largely marginal, and, while some Western scholars of the Soviet Union made brief references to a 'man-made famine' in their work, for a long time it did not command serious or extensive attention in Western scholarship.[5] Several initiatives in the early 1980s worked to change this situation. Between 1982 and 1983, commemorating the 50th anniversary of the famine, the Harvard Ukrainian Research Institute (HURI) launched the Famine Project, and in 1983 the first international conference on the famine was held in Montreal. With this new attention, however, came a new conception of events. It was presented not as a terrible catastrophe brought about by unwise policy decisions and governmental negligence, but as a premeditated attack specifically targeting the Ukrainian people, and in this sense, an attempted genocide.

As the 1980s wore on, attention to the famine in both scholarly and public contexts increased. In 1984, Ukrainian émigrés in Canada produced a documentary film entitled *The Harvest of Despair*, which was widely screened in North America and thus served to introduce the famine to a wider public. In this same year, James Mace, at the time a junior research fellow at HURI, first described the famine as 'an act of genocide' in two separate academic

---

3   For examples of Duranty's selective reporting on the famine, see W Duranty, 'Soviet acts to spur basic industrialization', *The New York Times*, 4 October 1932, 11; 'Soviet in 16th year: Calm and hopeful', *The New York Times*, 13 November 1932, E4; 'All Russia Suffers shortage of food: Supplies dwindling', *The New York Times*, 25 November 1932, 1; and 'Food shortage laid to Soviet peasants', *The New York Times*, 26 November 1932, 9. Duranty remains a highly controversial figure, heightened by the increased research into the famine in recent times. For biographical accounts, see, for example, JW Crowl, *Angels in Stalin's Paradise: Western Reporters in Soviet Russia 1917–1937, A Case Study of Louis Fischer and Walter Duranty* (Washington: University Press of America, 1982); and SJ Taylor, *Stalin's Apologist: Walter Duranty, the New York Times's Man in Moscow* (Oxford: Oxford University Press, 1990). In 2003 an ultimately unsuccessful campaign was launched to have Duranty's Pulitzer Prize revoked. See Young, 'Remember the Holodomor'.

4   M Edele, *Stalinist Society 1928–1953* (Oxford: Oxford University Press, 2011), 236.

5   See, for example, Dalrymple, 'The Soviet famine of 1932–1934', 250–284; DG Dalrymple, 'The Soviet famine of 1932–1934: Some further references', *Soviet Studies*, vol. 16, no. 4, 1965, 471–474; M Lewin, 'Taking grain: Soviet policies of agricultural procurements before the war', in C Abramsky, ed., *Essays in Honour of E. H. Carr* (London: Macmillan, 1974), 291–296; and A Nove, *An Economic History of the USSR* (Harmondsworth: Penguin, 1972), 177–181.

publications.[6] By 1986, a major turning point was reached in famine histor-iography with the publication of Robert Conquest's *The Harvest of Sorrow: Soviet Collectivization and the Terror-Famine*, which represented the first full-scale scholarly study of these events. Like Mace, Conquest also presented the famine as planned on the part of Soviet authorities, and alluded to the idea that it was a genocide against Ukrainians. He declared that '[i]t certainly appears that a charge of genocide lies against the Soviet Union for its actions in the Ukraine,' but nonetheless noted that 'whether these events are to be formally defined as genocide is scarcely the point. It would hardly be denied that a crime has been committed against the Ukrainian nation.'[7]

Following the publication of *The Harvest of Sorrow*, attention to the famine rapidly increased and the genocidal interpretation began to enjoy considerable support from various groups and bodies. Beginning in 1985, the famine appeared in American public high school history curricula as part of studies of genocide and human rights.[8] Furthermore, in April 1988 the United States Commission into the Ukrainian Famine submitted its report to Congress. This commission, led by Mace as its executive director, had been established a few years earlier following lobbying by the American Ukrainian community.[9] Having argued that the famine was man-made, preventable and widely known to Soviet authorities, the 16th finding of the report declared that 'Joseph Stalin and those around him committed genocide against Ukrainians in 1932–1933.'[10]

Two years later, the final report of the International Commission of In-quiry into the Ukrainian Famine was published. The establishment of this inquiry was, like the United States Commission, the result of efforts from the Ukrainian émigré community, having being created and funded by the World Congress of Free Ukrainians.[11] The report revealed that all seven

---

6   See JE Mace, 'Famine and Nationalism in Soviet Ukraine', *Problems of Communism*, vol. 33, no. 3, 1984, 37; and Mace 'The Man-Made Famine of 1933 in the Soviet Ukraine', 67–83.

7   R Conquest, *The Harvest of Sorrow: Soviet Collectivization and the Terror-Famine* (New York: Oxford University Press, 1986), 272.

8   J Coplon, 'In search of a Soviet holocaust: 55-year-old famine feeds the right', *Village Voice*, 12 January 1988, 32.

9   SG Wheatcroft, 'Towards explaining soviet famine of 1931–3: Political and natural factors in perspective', *Food and Foodways*, vol. 12, nos. 2–3, 2004, 117.

10   United States Commission on the Ukrainian Famine, 'Executive summary: Commission efforts and accomplishments', in *Investigation of the Ukrainian Famine, 1932–1933: Report to Congress* (Washington: United States Government Printing Office, 1988), vii.

11   IA Hunter, 'Putting history on trial: The Ukrainian Famine of 1932–1933', *Journal of Ukrainian Studies*, vol. 15, no. 2, 1990, 47.

commissioners were unanimous in their view that 'it is beyond doubt that the immediate cause of the 1932–33 famine lay in the grain procurements imposed upon Ukraine from 1930 onwards' believing that 'the Soviet authorities, without actively wanting the famine, most likely took advantage of it once it occurred to force the peasants to accept policies which they strongly opposed.'[12] They were not, however, in similar agreement on the question of the famine's genocidal nature, with two commissioners dissenting on this point.[13] In this sense, the international commission's lack of unanimity can be seen as the beginnings of the bifurcation of the current discourse about the genocidal status of the Holodomor.

Of course, this new attention on the famine during the 1980s and into the early 1990s was largely occurring outside of Ukraine itself, where discussion of these events was still strictly limited. With perestroika, however, came a degree of relaxation and the tentative beginnings of a Ukrainian discourse about the famine. It was at this time that the Ukrainian word 'Holodomor' began to be used and popularised, and has subsequently come to be adopted in both scholarly and public discourse on the famine. The word Holodomor comes from the Ukrainian words *holod*, meaning hunger or famine, and *mor*, meaning mass death.[14] In post-Soviet Ukraine, the Holodomor has served as a central element in the creation of new national histories and narratives, even if this process has itself not been without controversy.[15]

---

12   International Commission of Inquiry into the 1932–33 Famine in Ukraine final report, 10 March 1990, as cited in LY Luciuk, ed., *Holodomor: Reflections on the Great Famine of 1932–1933 in Soviet Ukraine* (Kingston: The Kashtan Press, 2008), 268, 271–272.

13   ibid., 282–285.

14   This translation of the term 'Holodomor' is taken from JE Mace, 'Is the Ukrainian genocide a myth?', *Canadian-American Slavic Studies*, vol. 37, no. 3, 2003, 51. Others believe the term can be simply translated as 'death by hunger'. For more on the issues concerning 'naming' the famine, see, for example, CAM Duncan, 'Afterword: Labelling events and selecting contexts in history', in LY Luciuk, ed., *Holodomor: Reflections on the Great Famine of 1932–1933 in Soviet Ukraine* (Kingston: The Kashtan Press, 2008), 227.

15   For discussion of how the Holodomor has featured in political and cultural life in post-Soviet Ukraine, see, for example, J Dietsch, *Making Sense of Suffering: Holocaust and Holodomor in Ukrainian Historical Culture* (Lund: Lund University Press, 2006); DR Marples, *Heroes and Villains: Creating National History in Contemporary Ukraine* (Budapest, Central European University Press, 2007); and C Wanner, *Burden of Dreams: History and Identity in Post-Soviet Ukraine* (State College, Pa.:, Pennsylvania State University Press, 1998). For an examination of the role of Holodomor memory in recent Ukrainian politics, see T Zhurzhenko, '"Capital of Despair": Holodomor memory and political conflicts in Kharkiv after the Orange Revolution', *East European Politics and Societies*, vol. 25, no. 3, 2011, 597–639.

CHAPTER 3

From these tentative beginnings in the 1980s, a large discourse has emerged about the famine, with an extensive debate regarding its genocidal status being one of its key features. For those who argue for the genocidal interpretation, the famine in Ukraine qualifies as an act of genocide in the sense that it was a planned and deliberate attack which, to use Mace's representative argument, aimed to 'destroy the Ukrainian nation as a political factor and social organism, a goal which could be attained far short of complete extermination.'[16] In holding this position, several common arguments are evoked in order to support it, forming what one might term the 'standard' genocidal argument. First, it is maintained that no natural factors played a role in the onset of the famine, as the harvests of those years were actually quite good or at least adequate. Instead, the famine resulted from the impossible grain requisitions imposed by the regime upon the Ukrainian peasantry, and can be tied to a concurrent attack upon Ukrainian nationalism.[17] Additionally, it is argued that the Soviet leaders were well aware of what was occurring, but did nothing to assist the starving and prevented any international aid from reaching them.[18] Despite the fact that grain reserves were available, the Soviet Union continued its exports. Furthermore, the borders of the affected areas were sealed, preventing the starving from moving on in search of food.[19]

Conversely, in rejecting this famine-as-genocide interpretation, those who argue the counterview also advance several common points in support of their position. Many of these historians point to the fact that proportionately speaking, it was the population of Kazakhstan that was affected most severely by the famine.[20] This particular point leads to the second stressed

---

16 Mace, 'The man-made famine of 1933 in the Soviet Ukraine', 67.

17 F Sysyn, 'The Ukrainian Famine of 1932–3: The role of the Ukrainian diaspora in research and public discussion', in L Chorbajian and G Shirinian, eds, *Studies in Comparative Genocide* (London, Macmillan, 1999), 191. Although not a supporter of the famine-as-genocide view, Terry Martin has provided a classic study on the 'national factor' in the famine of 1932–1933. See T Martin, *The Affirmative Action Empire: Nations and Nationalism in the Soviet Union, 1923–1939* (New York: Cornell University Press, 2001).

18 See, for example, R Conquest, D Dalrymple, J Mace and M Novak, *The Man-Made Famine in Ukraine* (Washington, DC, American Institute for Public Policy Research, 1984), 6–7; and Mace, 'Famine and nationalism in Soviet Ukraine', 38.

19 See also N Werth, 'A state against its people: Violence, repression, and terror in the Soviet Union', in S Courtois and others, eds, *The Black Book of Communism: Crimes Terror Repression*, trans. J Murphy and M Kramer (Cambridge: Harvard University Press, 1999), 164. Werth, however, ultimately comes down in favour of the non-genocide argument. See Werth, 'A state against its people', 168.

20 See Kuromiya, 'The Soviet famine of 1932–1933 reconsidered', 667; and A Nove, 'When the head is off', *The New Republic*, 3 November 1986, 37.

by scholars, namely that the famine stretched far beyond the geographical borders of Ukraine into other areas, meaning that it cannot necessarily be construed as a singular attack against only Ukrainians as other ethnic groups felt its effects. Additionally, many emphasise the differences between the rural and urban experience of the famine, in that Ukrainian (and other) peasants starved while Ukrainian (and other) urban workers remained, in relative terms, better provisioned.[21] These factors have generally led most scholars who argue against the genocidal interpretation to see the famine not as an ethnic genocide but as an example of the regime's ruthless attitudes towards the peasantry.[22] If anything, the famine targeted peasants as a group, not a particular national or ethnic identity. Furthermore, some historians have argued for the primacy of environmental causal factors in the onset of the famine,[23] while others have suggested that political elements such as peasant resistance played a crucial role.[24]

One of the most important recent contributions to this ongoing debate has been RW Davies' and Stephen Wheatcroft's 2004 study *The Years of Hunger: Soviet Agriculture 1931–1933*, which was heralded as an authoritative account of the subject. Indeed, one scholar has described the book as '[t]he most notable work in the school of writing that maintains that the famine was not genocide.'[25] In rejecting the genocide interpretation, Wheatcroft and Davies argued that the famine had resulted from a complex interaction of factors. They argued in their conclusion:

> We do not at all absolve Stalin from responsibility for the famine. His policies towards the peasants were ruthless and brutal. But the story which has emerged in this book is of a Soviet leadership which was struggling with a famine crisis which had been caused partly by their

---

21 See J Himka, Review J Dietsch, *Making Sense of Suffering: Holocaust and Holodomor in Ukrainian Historical Culture* and SV Kul'chyts'kyi, *Holod 1932–1933 rr. v Ukraini iak henotsyd/Golod 1932–1933 gg. v Ukraine kak genotsid, Kritika: Explorations in Russian and Eurasian History*, vol. 8, no. 3, 2007, 693; and Kuromiya, 'The Soviet famine of 1932–1933 reconsidered', 668.

22 See, for example, Wheatcroft, 'Towards explaining Soviet famine', 120.

23 See, for example, MB Tauger, 'The 1932 harvest and the famine of 1933', *Slavic Review*, vol. 50, no. 1, 1991, 70–89; and MB Tauger, 'Natural disaster and human actions in the Soviet famine of 1931–1933', *The Carl Beck Papers in Russian & East European Studies*, no. 1506 (Center for Russian and East European Studies, University of Pittsburgh, 2001).

24 See, for example, DR Penner, 'Stalin and the *Ital'ianka* of 1932–1933 in the Don Region', *Cahiers du Monde russe*, vol. 39, no. 1, 1998, 27–67.

25 DR Marples, 'Ethnic issues in the famine of 1932–1933 in Ukraine', *Europe-Asia Studies*, vol. 61, no. 3, 2009, 508.

wrongheaded policies, but was unexpected and undesirable. The background to the famine is not simply that Soviet agricultural policies were derived from Bolshevik ideology, though ideology played its part. They were also shaped by the Russian pre-revolutionary past, the experiences of the civil war, the international situation, the intransigent circumstances of geography and the weather, and the *modus operandi* of the Soviet system as it was established under Stalin. They were formulated by men with little formal education and limited knowledge of agriculture.[26]

Overall, Wheatcroft and Davies suggested the famine was 'a consequence of the decision to industrialise this peasant country at breakneck speed.'[27]

In the wake of the publication of *The Years of Hunger*, scholarly interest and discussion about the Holodomor show no signs of slowing. Historians who argue against the genocide interpretation are continuing to advance alternative explanations for the origins, causes and implications of the famine. Of course, those who argue the counterview remain equally active. Publications about the Holodomor continue to appear with regularity and in 2009 the academic periodical *Holodomor Studies* was founded.[28] Additionally, HURI, so instrumental in bringing the famine to scholarly and public consciousness in the early 1980s, hosted large conferences and events to commemorate the 75th anniversary of the famine in 2008. Outside of the realm of academia, the Holodomor continues to be discussed and presented in more public forums. For example, following several years of production in the United States a feature-length documentary film entitled *Holodomor: Ukraine's Genocide* was released in 2012.[29]

Having considered the development and evolution of the discussion surrounding the Holodomor, important questions remain regarding what it

---

26 Davies and Wheatcroft, *The Years of Hunger*, 441.
27 ibid.
28 For recent publications on the Holodomor which endorse a genocidal view of events, see, for example, A Graziosi, *Stalinism, Collectivization and the Great Famine* (Cambridge: Ukrainian Studies Fund, 2007); H Halyna, ed., *Hunger By Design: The Great Ukrainian Famine and its Soviet Context* (Cambridge: Ukrainian Studies Fund, 2008); WW Isajiw, ed., *Famine-Genocide in the Ukraine: 1932–1933: Western Archives, Testimonies and New Research* (Toronto: Ukrainian Canadian Research and Documentation Centre, 2003); P Kardash, *Genocide in Ukraine*, trans. D Myrna (Melbourne: Fortuna Publishers, 2007); and LY Luciuk, ed., *Holodomor: Reflections on the Great Famine of 1932–1933 in Soviet Ukraine* (Kingston: The Kashtan Press, 2008).
29 See *Holodomor: Ukraine's Genocide*, http://www.holodomorthemovie.com, accessed 8 October 2014.

might suggest for understanding and writing about past atrocity. In particular, the arguments in favour of a genocidal interpretation of the famine are especially illustrative in this regard. What emerges most clearly from a close examination of these narratives is the centrality of the Holocaust in their creation and continued trajectories. Indeed, comparisons between the Holodomor and the Holocaust might be described as a hallmark of the 'famine-as-genocide' argument, and offer several insights into how the Holodomor is understood and how historians might seek to make sense of past atrocity more generally.

The drawing of comparisons and links between the Holocaust and the Holodomor, it has been argued, began with the Ukrainian diaspora, and then later translated into the discussion in Ukraine itself following the collapse of the Soviet Union.[30] The specific form these comparisons have assumed includes the adoption of terminology and mechanisms of commemoration connected with the Holocaust. A particularly illustrative example of these impulses can be observed in Conquest's *The Harvest of Sorrow*. He opened his study with the following invocation of the experience and conditions of the famine:

> Fifty years ago as I write these words, the Ukraine and the Ukrainian, Cossack and other areas to its east – a great stretch of territory with some forty million inhabitants – was like one vast Belsen. A quarter of the rural population, men, women and children, lay dead or dying, the rest in various stages of debilitation with no strength to bury their families or neighbours. At the same time, (as at Belsen), well-fed squads of police or party officials supervised the victims ... In terms of regimes and policies fifty years is a long time. In terms of individual lives, not so long. I have met men and women who went through the experiences you will read of as children or even as young adults. Among them were people with 'survivors' guilt' – that irrational shame that they should be the ones to live when their friends, parents, brothers and sisters died, which is also to be found among the survivors of the Nazi camps.[31]

The appeal to such imagery and the use of direct analogies to the Holocaust and its victims underlie Conquest's opinion (at least at the time of his original writing) that the famine was a genocide akin to that of the

---

30   Marples, *Heroes and Villains*, xii.
31   R Conquest, *The Harvest of Sorrow: Soviet Collectivisation and the Terror-Famine* (1986) (London: Pimlico, 2002), 3.

Nazis' murder of the Jews – in its scope, the number of victims, and their suffering.[32]

Similarly, several writers have frequently employed the term 'Holocaust' in reference to the famine. It has been variously described as 'a Holocaust the west forgot',[33] 'the hidden Holocaust',[34] 'the Ukrainian Holocaust',[35] 'the early Holocaust',[36] and the 'holocaust-famine'.[37] Other phrases and terms commonly associated with the Holocaust have also been applied to the Holodomor, such as Mace's description of it as 'a means used by Stalin to impose a "final solution" on the most pressing nationality problem in the Soviet Union'.[38]

In addition to this adoption of terminology, the discourses surrounding the Holodomor also demonstrate several mechanisms of commemoration and protection of memory which echo those of the Holocaust. Perhaps the most illustrative example of this impulse is the attempted adoption within Ukraine itself of legal structures similar to those which exist in Germany and other countries against Holocaust denial. In November 2006 a law was passed in Ukraine which formally recognised the Holodomor as a genocide, although attempts to criminalise Holodomor denial with this same law were ultimately unsuccessful. Additionally, several national governments,

---

32 With the passing of time, Conquest appears to have altered his opinion on the genocidal nature of the famine. In a 2004 publication, Stephen Wheatcroft cited personal correspondence from Conquest dated August 2003, in which the latter declared he was not of the opinion that 'Stalin purposely inflicted the 1933 famine. No. What I argue is that with the resulting famine imminent, he could have prevented it, and put 'Soviet interests' other than feeding the starving first – thus consciously abetting it.' See Wheatcroft, 'Towards explaining Soviet famine of 1931–3', 134, n. 26. Wheatcroft later claimed that 'Conquest appears to have become concerned about the views that were being attributed to him, and had quite explicitly asked Professor Davies and myself to make clear in our book what his (Conquest's) views were on these matters'. See SG Wheatcroft, 'On continuing to misunderstand arguments: Response to Mark Tauger', *Europe-Asia Studies*, vol. 59, no. 7, 2007, 860. Parentheses in original.

33 Karatnycky, 'Forced famine in the Ukraine', 22.

34 M Dilot, *Execution By Hunger: The Hidden Holocaust* (New York: WW Norton, 1985).

35 S Weatherbe, 'The Ukrainian Holocaust', *Ukrainian Review*, vol. 32, no. 2, 1984, 18–25.

36 F Kapusta, 'The early Holocaust in Europe: Collectivization and the man-made famine in Ukraine, 1932–33', *Ukrainian Quarterly*, vol. 37, no. 4, 1981, 369–382.

37 GV Mylton, 'Books expose famine-genocide', *Ukrainian Weekly*, 8 October 2000. For other examples of the term 'Holocaust' being used to describe the famine, see I Drach, 'To the famine-genocide of 1933', trans. RK Stojko-Lozynskyj, *Ukrainian Quarterly*, vol. 40, no. 4, 1993, 357, 361; and VI Hryshko, *The Ukrainian Holocaust of 1933*, trans. M Carynnyk (Toronto, Bahriany Foundation, 1983).

38 Mace, 'Famine and nationalism in Soviet Ukraine', 37.

including those of Australia, the United States and Canada, have formally recognised the famine as a genocide against the Ukrainian people and a Holodomor Remembrance Day is now observed in Ukraine, Canada and several other countries.[39] Efforts to have the United Nations officially recognise the famine as a genocide, however, have thus far proved ineffective.

Another important point of comparison which has been drawn between the Holodomor and the Holocaust is the number of victims. There are, as outlined previously, wildly varying estimates of the number of deaths from the famine. Wheatcroft and Davies estimated the total number of deaths in the Soviet Union to be between 5.5 and 6.5 million people.[40] More recently, in his 2010 study *Bloodlands*, Timothy Snyder placed the specific Ukrainian death toll from the famine at 3.3 million people.[41] Nonetheless, despite this lingering uncertainty regarding the exact number of deaths, those arguing for the famine-as-genocide interpretation have drawn parallels between the scope of mortality for the Holodomor and the Nazis' destruction of the Jews. Mace, for example, has argued that 'purely in terms of mortality, it was … of the same order of magnitude as the Jewish Holocaust', a view echoed by another scholar who has suggested that the death toll from the famine was 'clearly … of the same order as the catastrophe that struck Europe's Jews'.[42] This line of reasoning has been taken slightly further by historian Lubomyr Luciuk, who has argued that 'the intensity of mortality in Soviet

---

39   For discussion of these various initiatives, see, for example, P Borisow, 'Holodomor: Metagenocide in Ukraine – its origins and why it's not over', *Canadian-American Slavic Studies*, vol. 42, no. 3, 2008, 251, n. 1; S Kulchytsky, 'Defining the *Holodomor* as genocide', in LY Luciuk, ed., *Holodomor: Reflections on the Great Famine of 1932–1933 in Soviet Ukraine* (Kingston: The Kashtan Press, 2008), 129; Luciuk, 'A genocide long ignored', A17; Marples, *Heroes and Villains*, 52; and Young, 'Remember the Holodomor'. For examples of Holodomor legislation both in Ukraine and in Canada, see The Law of Ukraine, No. 376-V, 'On the *Holodomor* in Ukraine, 1932–1933', 28 November 2006, as cited in LY Luciuk, ed., *Holodomor: Reflections on the Great Famine of 1932–1933 in Soviet Ukraine* (Kingston: The Kashtan Press, 2008), 357–359; and Statutes of Canada, Bill C-459, 'The Ukrainian Famine and Genocide ("Holodomor") Memorial Day Act', 29 May 2008, as cited in LY Luciuk, ed., *Holodomor: Reflections on the Great Famine of 1932–1933 in Soviet Ukraine* (Kingston: The Kashtan Press, 2008), 361–363, respectively.

40   Wheatcroft and Davies, *The Years of Hunger*, 401.

41   T Snyder, *Bloodlands: Europe Between Hitler and Stalin* (New York: Basic Books, 2010), 53.

42   See Mace, 'The man-made famine of 1933 in the Soviet Ukraine', 67; and D Rayfield, 'The Ukrainian Famine of 1933: Man-made catastrophe, mass murder, or genocide?', in LY Luciuk, ed., *Holodomor: Reflections on the Great Famine of 1932–1933 in Soviet Ukraine* (Kingston: The Kashtan Press, 2008), 89, respectively.

Ukraine over a duration of less than a year confers upon the Holodomor the unenviable status of being a crime against humanity arguably without parallel in European history'.[43] This emphasis on the importance of 'body counts' in describing and conceptualising an atrocity reflects, as one scholar has observed, a tendency to measure 'the qualitative worth of a genocide by the quantitative figures involved'.[44]

Similarly, in drawing these comparisons between the number of victims of the Holodomor and the Holocaust, some authors have also sought to compare the nature of their suffering. For example, one reviewer of *The Harvest of Sorrow* went so far as to suggest that the gas chambers represented a 'kinder' mode of death than that by starvation:

> Conquest's descriptions of the mass starvations ... rank with the most distressing reading I have ever done. In horror it surpasses anything I have seen in the Nazi literature, even Eugene Kogon's *The Theory and Practice of Hell*, a survivor's account of Buchenwald. Indeed, it makes the Nazi death camps with their clean, quick gas chambers disguised as showers seem almost humane.[45]

It is worth noting that, in addition to the many problems which this argument raises from both historiographical and moral perspectives, it is also reminiscent of the Nazis' own attitudes and approach towards the 'Final Solution'.

The question remains as to what purposes such comparisons between the Holodomor and Holocaust are designed to serve, and what they might tell us about the process of writing about and coming to terms with past atrocity. The answers, it seems, lie with the concept of genocide itself, and the centrality of the Holocaust in discussions of atrocity. While fierce controversy and disagreement have characterised much of the scholarly discussion of genocide, a general consensus that it represents a particularly grave transgression against humanity has nonetheless been achieved. In

---

43   Luciuk, 'Foreword', v. Emphasis in original. Luciuk made the same claim in a November 2008 article in the *Winnipeg Free Press*. See L Luciuk, 'A genocide long ignored: Ukraine's suffering gaining recognition', *Winnipeg Free Press*, 22 November 2008, A17. Along similar lines, another commentator has deemed the Holodomor to be 'the most brutal ethnic genocide in history'. See Borisow, 'Holodomor: Metagenocide in Ukraine', 251.

44   IL Horowitz, *Taking Lives: Genocide and State Power* (1976) (New Brunswick, NJ: Transaction Publishers, 1997), 29.

45   EH Methvin, review of R Conquest, *The Harvest of Sorrow: Soviet Collectivization and the Terror-Famine*, *National Review*, vol. 47, no. 23, 1995, 124.

part, this 'status' of genocide has resulted from its fundamental association with the Holocaust; this connection, as one scholar recognises, has granted the term 'an ineluctable and powerful moral connotation: it [is] synonymous with the apex of human evil'.[46] It is this power of the concept of 'genocide' which is important in discussions of the Holodomor, and goes some way towards explaining why a commitment to this classification persists even when much of the scholarship on the famine concludes it was not genocidal in nature.

Furthermore, the Holocaust looms inescapably large in any discussion of genocide. The Nazis' destruction of the Jews has become the paradigmatic genocidal event, is widely considered to be the apogee of historical atrocity, and continues to command the largest degree of public and scholarly attention, discussion and recognition. In being so widely recognised as a singularly terrible event, drawing parallels with the Holocaust can help to highlight the seriousness and magnitude of the comparative case, in terms which are already understandable to large numbers of people. Indeed, one commentator has noted that 'the Holocaust [has] provided a convenient, highly symbolic, and easily recognizable event many [have] used to draw attention to their own interests'.[47] It seems this impulse has been at work in much of the discussion of the Holodomor and some writers have sought to emphasise its seriousness by suggesting that it was a crime of the same dimension as the Nazis' destruction of the Jews. Additionally, in much of the earlier writing on the famine in the 1980s and early 1990s, comparisons to the Holocaust were used to emphasise and condemn the preceding neglect of the Holodomor in scholarly and public discourse. The implied question of such comparisons was: how could an atrocity of the same magnitude as the Holocaust not have received a greater degree of public attention and commemoration?

There exists, however, an additional dimension to such comparisons. As historian Peter Novick has recognised, the centrality of the Nazis' destruction of the Jews in public and scholarly discussion of atrocity has given rise to

---

46   S Straus, 'Contested meanings and conflicting imperatives: A conceptual analysis of genocide', *Journal of Genocide Research*, vol. 3, no. 3, 2001, 359. Similarly, Jeffrey C Alexander has argued that the Holocaust has come to represent 'a tragic archetype and a central component of moral judgment in our time'. See JC Alexander, 'On the social construction of moral universals: The "Holocaust" from war crime to trauma drama', *European Journal of Social Theory*, vol. 5, no. 1, 2002, 52.

47   GD Rosenfeld, 'The politics of uniqueness: Reflections on the recent polemical turn in Holocaust and genocide scholarship,' *Holocaust and Genocide Studies*, vol. 13, no. 1, 1999, 34.

what he terms 'Holocaust envy'.[48] This 'envy' has often found expression in a persistent urge for comparison amongst those who wish to have their own particular atrocities canonised as genocide. In addition to drawing parallels of a historical nature, many have also sought to make moral comparisons between the Holocaust and various atrocities, aiming to demonstrate that their particular event was 'worse' and the victims suffered 'more'. Some of the discourse on the Holodomor, particularly the emphasis placed on 'body counts' and the nature of the victims' suffering outlined earlier, clearly illustrates this impulse. It is this notion of being a 'worse' atrocity which is most problematic about some of the discussion surrounding the Holodomor and is potentially damaging to our understanding of the famine, and to how we write about such events more generally.

To be sure, drawing parallels between different atrocities can be useful and instructive, but important distinctions between historical and moral comparisons remain.[49] Once one engages on the moral plane and suggests that some death or injustice was 'worse' than another, or that certain modes of murder are somehow 'nicer' than others, it is very easy for the comparative to morph, intentionally or otherwise, into the competitive. Israel Charny, a noted scholar of genocide, has made an important observation on this issue, cautioning:

> Although human thought and speech is oriented, not entirely without reason, to concepts of *more* and *less*, *strong* and *weak*, and so on of polarized comparatives and dichotomies it is proving of the utmost importance to guard against such coins of speech leading to the implications, even if unintentional, that the suffering, tragedy or degree of evil inflicted on any one people was somehow *more* than or *less* than that suffered by another people.[50]

Suffering cannot be quantified and then ranked accordingly, and it is distasteful to try. As one scholar has noted, 'it is dangerously unbecoming for victims to engage in divisive squabbles about whose holocaust is real or whose genocide is worse.'[51] Additionally, as has been pointed out by

---

48   P Novick, *The Holocaust in American Life* (Boston: Houghton Mifflin, 1999), 192.

49   On this point, see NG Finkelstein, *The Holocaust Industry: Reflections on the Exploitation of Jewish Suffering* (London: Verso, 2000), 8.

50   IW Charny, 'Comparative study of genocide', in IW Charny, ed., *Encyclopedia of Genocide: Volume I* (Jerusalem: The Institute on the Holocaust and Genocide, 1999), 9–10. Emphasis in original.

51   Horowitz, *Taking Lives*, 241.

numerous scholars, from the perspective of those who did not survive such atrocities, it is also irrelevant.[52]

Finally, it is open to question how instructive comparisons between the Holocaust and the Holodomor are for our understanding and appreciation of the latter. Whether the Holodomor is considered to be a genocide or not, it is clearly a very different event to the Holocaust in its conception, course and context. Trying to compare them on a moral level, as has occurred in much of the discussion of the Holodomor, and asking which was 'worse' or whose victims suffered more, only serves to obscure an appropriate appreciation of what matters most in trying to make sense of these events. Restoring the humanity of the victims, and adequately acknowledging their suffering, are among our most important tasks as historians of atrocity. The fundamental moral point which should guide this process is that all atrocity and the resulting human suffering are recognised as being equally abhorrent. Many of the explicit comparisons between the Holodomor and the Holocaust have obscured this point, and these comparisons are unfair to the memory of the victims of both atrocities. As one commentator noted in a letter to *The Ukrainian Weekly* of 18 May 2003: 'We should not be piggy-backing off the Jews: it diminishes us both.'[53]

---

52   See, for example, RJ Evans, *In Hitler's Shadow: West German Historians and the Attempt to Escape from the Nazi Past* (London: IB Tauris, 1989), 89; and RG Suny, 'Russian terror/ism and revisionist historiography', *Australian Journal of Politics and History*, vol. 53, no. 1, 2007, 13.

53   GA Nestor, 'Famine terminology is problematic', *The Ukrainian Weekly*, 18 May 2003, 7.

Part II

Perceptions and representations: Past

Chapter 4

'THEY ARE KILLING ALL
OF US JEWS'

Australian press memory of the Holocaust

Fay Anderson

On 4 March 1943, Godfrey Blunden, a journalist accredited with the Sydney *Daily Telegraph*, reported from Kharkov on the Eastern Front. His dispatch described a massacre. 'They are killing all of us Jews', an elderly woman had told him. 'They had all our names and came looking for us.'[1] This was the first account of the Holocaust written by an Australian journalist from the front-line. Blunden's report failed to inspire editorial comment; nor did the editors link Blunden's revelations of the Nazis' murderous campaign in the Soviet territories with similar news emerging from Axis-controlled countries.

This chapter will examine Australian coverage of the genocide of the Jews from the early reports of persecution to the liberation of the concentration camps, where over 20 Australian correspondents bore witness. It will offer several arguments about Australian media memory and the Holocaust. First, despite the belief perpetuated by the Australian press organisations that they lacked significant knowledge of the Final Solution at the time, an analysis of the coverage reveals that this is deceptive. The Jewish plight was reported frequently and with accuracy, but the revelations were treated as isolated events and quickly forgotten. The way in which the press remembers events is influenced by news values, editorial control and temporality. Second, the chapter will illustrate that while the Holocaust now overwhelms the memory of the Second World War, this was not the case in Australia at the time. It was relegated to a secondary story at best. Despite the horrifying details,

---

1   Godfrey Blunden, 'Nazis hanged, starved and looted them', Sydney *Daily Telegraph* (hereafter *DT*), 3 March 1943.

there was widespread editorial apathy and indifference. News of the liberation of German concentration camps provoked widespread attention; other news, which now dominates our collective memory, such as Auschwitz (now *the* symbol of the Nazi epoch) and the Jewish victims, were sometimes ignored or represented very differently. Third, and this continues to distinguish the coverage of subsequent genocides, media memory is selective and is determined and defined by who does the telling. The privileging of Western journalists as the only legitimate and reliable witnesses was striking.

* * *

While there have been a number of seminal accounts of the American and British press's dereliction in their reporting on the persecution and ultimate mass extermination of the Jews, the Australian reporting and press response to the Holocaust have never been subjected to the same scrutiny. Of immense importance in the international context and for this chapter is the work by Deborah Lipstadt, Peter Novick, Barbie Zelizer, Robert Shapiro and, later, Laurel Leff and Antero Holmila.[2] Paul R Bartrop provides an authoritative study of Australia's political response to the Holocaust and Suzanne Rutland considers the coverage of the Holocaust by the Australian Jewish press.[3]

Memory, also, has been considered in the US press reporting of the Holocaust. Barbie Zelizer's work most prominently explores the issue of memory and atrocity by examining the visual representation of the liberation of the concentration camps in *Remembering to Forget: Holocaust Memory through the Camera's Eye*. Her other work on the assassination of President Kennedy raises questions about the role of the media in defining our reality, and in shaping our myths and collective memories. Saul Friedländer, Raul

---

2   Deborah E Lipstadt, *Beyond Belief: The American Press and the Coming of the Holocaust* (New York: Macmillan, 1986); Peter Novick, *The Holocaust in America* (Boston: Houghton Mifflin, 1999); Barbie Zelizer, *Remembering to Forget* (Chicago: University of Chicago Press, 1998); Barbie Zelizer, ed., *Visual Culture and the Holocaust* (New Brunswick: Rutgers University Press, 2000); Robert Schapiro, ed, *Why Didn't the Press Shout: American and International Journalism During the Holocaust* (New York: KTAV Publishing House, 2003); Laurel Leff, *The Holocaust and America's Most Important Newspaper* (Cambridge University Press, 2005); Antero Holmila, *Reporting the Holocaust in the British, Swedish and Finnish Press, 1945–50* (New York: Palgrave Macmillan, 2011).

3   Paul R Bartrop, *Australia and the Holocaust 1933–1945* (Melbourne: Australian Scholarly Publishing, 1994); Suzanne D Rutland, *Pages of History: A Century of the Australian Jewish Press* (Sydney, Australian Jewish Press, 1995).

Hilberg, Lawrence Langer and Geoffrey Hartman's edited volume, amongst many others, have examined the issue of the Holocaust and memory.[4] Yet press memory as a separate phenomenon from historical memory is not usually the primary concern.

It is timely to consider the Australian reportage because it sheds light on Australian reporting practices and the press's role in shaping our collective memory of genocide. The Australian reporting and representation of the Holocaust reveal differences and priorities and provide illuminating comparative examples. It is also a reminder that memory is transitory, fluid and limited.

'Nazis are coming'

The way in which the press remembers and represents events is shaped by political and cultural assumptions and journalistic realities. These factors in Australia warrant attention because they provide compelling context for press indifference, the way the Holocaust was immediately remembered, and the distortion of memory. The journalists themselves grew up in an era when British imperialism, the notion of racial eugenics and the implementation of the Immigration Restriction Act were applauded. In 1933, the Australian journalist Selkirk Panton, who was based in Berlin for the London *Express*, wrote to friends in anticipation of Hitler's ascendancy that the 'Nazis are coming, Hurrah! Hurrah!' He remained an avowed sympathiser after Hitler gained power.[5] Marianne Hicks, Panton's biographer, argued that the concepts of race and empire, which underpinned much of the ideology surrounding nation, featured in his self-identity. For Panton, his Australian-ness complemented his 'superior' racial characteristics.[6] While Panton's colleagues did not necessarily share his overt anti-Semitism, it was a feature of society that affected even the most progressive journalists.

---

4   Barbie Zelizer, *Covering the Body: The Kennedy Assassination, the Media, and the Shaping of Collective Memory* (Chicago: University of Chicago Press, 1992); Saul Friedländer, *Memory, History, and the Extermination of the Jews of Europe* (Bloomington, Ind.: Indiana University Press, 1993; Raul Hilberg, *The Politics of Memory: The Journey of a Holocaust Historian* (Chicago: Ivan R Dee, 1996); Lawrence Langer, *Holocaust Testimonies* (New Haven, Conn.: Yale University Press, 1991); Geoffrey Hartman, ed., *Holocaust Remembrance: The Shapes of Memory* (Oxford: Basil Blackwell, 1994).

5   Marianne Hicks, 'R. Selkirk Panton, an Australian in Berlin: A foreign correspondent for the *Daily Express* in Europe, 1929–1950', PhD, University of Western Australia, 2005, 76, 104.

6   ibid., 27.

On the eve of the Second World War and as the plight of the Jews had worsened, the Australian Minister for Trade and Customs, TW White, made it clear at the Evian Conference that Australia would not accept more refugees because 'we have no real racial problems, we are not desirous of importing one'.[7] As Paul Bartrop observes, White had effectively announced that Australia was out of bounds for Jewish refugees.[8] Certain sections of the press were also ambivalent. In July 1939, the Australian Broadcasting Commission's (ABC) London correspondent EH Jackson announced:

> The writer of this broadcast is not a Jew nor has he any particular fondness for Jews, but it is surely impossible to deny that throughout the history of the Jewish race the Jews have never yet gone through such a monstrous period of injustice and cruelty in Europe.[9]

While Jackson emphasised Nazi brutality, he felt compelled to distance himself racially from his audience.

In addition, the Australian press organisations were always under-resourced and, with the exception of London, had no foreign bureaus in other countries. Thus, European stories were either syndicated or taken from wire services. As Bartrop argues, the Australian newspapers were prisoners of overseas cable networks.[10] This meant that Australian correspondents were unable to witness the Nazi assault on the Jews as a continuing, running narrative, and since press organisations privileged staff-produced copy, accounts of this persecution were buried in Australian newspapers.

The reporting was also influenced by Australia's military preoccupations and distinct form of martial nationalism. The Holocaust has now become a central narrative of the Second World War, but for Australians at the time it was just one story in a long war that offered countless, graphic accounts. Unlike for the United States, the Pacific was the principal theatre of war. In total over 300 Australian journalists covered the war, and their chief concern was the Australian Imperial Force. The Department of Information, which was responsible for the accreditation of all Australian journalists,

---

7   Bartrop, 71. See Bartrop's chapter on Australia and the Evian Conference July 1938, 61–78.

8   ibid.

9   EH Jackson broadcast, 'Palestine Problem: Government's immense difficulties, illegal immigrants and the flight from Europe', 20 July 1939, Series SP286/4 WOB 2 Barcode 12038018M, NAA.

10   Bartrop, 198.

expected them to mainly concentrate on celebratory eyewitness accounts of the Anzacs' 'fine work'.[11]

Nevertheless, Europe was an important focus for Australian press organisations. The newspaper coverage of the Nazi era can be categorised into three distinct stages: the persecution of the Jews, extermination and liberation. The press, as Phillip Knightley reminds us, has a very short institutional memory,[12] but it also has a selective historical one. The nature of the industry, particularly before the advent of investigative journalism, dictated that correspondents focused on events as singular episodes and previously published news was relegated to the bin as 'old news'. Consequently, Nazism was viewed as a new phenomenon. Yet as Saul Friedländer has pointed out, German anti-Semitism and racial eugenics existed long before 1933, as did the expulsion of the Jews and even their eradication.[13]

The Australian press did cover Hitler's brand of racial hatred: the systematic policies of segregation and expulsion; the boycotts against Jewish businesses; the Nuremberg Laws; Nazi aggression and the venomous anti-Semitism; the Berlin Olympics; the exodus of Jews and their status as refugees; the plans to find a homeland and corresponding tension in Palestine; and the expropriation decrees. The concentration camps, a reality in Nazi Germany since 1933, were a particularly popular curiosity for visiting journalists during the decade. Some reports detailed the atrocities committed and the persecution of the Jews in Dachau and Buchenwald before 1939.[14] Other dispatches portrayed the camps as almost benign, temporary camps for political opponents. The press rarely connected previous reports to show the increasingly draconian character that Nazi policy was taking.

The reporting of the pogrom on 9 and 10 November 1938 – known as Kristallnacht – was the only event that sustained extended attention. It was covered for an unprecedented nine days and given front-page coverage for three of them in five Australian broadsheets. The pogrom was undeniably shocking: 267 synagogues were destroyed, 7,500 businesses were vandalised and 91 Jews were murdered, in addition to the hundreds who committed suicide or died as a result of mistreatment.[15] It is telling, nevertheless, that Kristallnacht captured this level of interest in Australia. Like all 'news

---

11 Uncredited, 'Fine Work by Australians', *SMH*, 24 January 1941.
12 Phillip Knightley, *The First Casualty: The War Correspondent As Hero And Myth-Maker* (London: Prion, 2004), 484.
13 Friedländer, 70–1.
14 'Nazi atrocities', *West Australian*, 6 August 1938.
15 Friedländer, 276.

events', it was perceived as an event with a beginning, middle and an end, and separated from the developments that had preceded it. Kristallnacht was also photographed; images were becoming a necessary form of evidence in what would become the 'show me' syndrome.

The second significant stage of coverage occurred from 1940 as Australian newspapers began to publish fragmented but frequent accounts of 'Nazi terror': the slaughter of hostages, the mass deportations to Poland, the creation of ghettoes and the widespread executions. Information about conditions in the ghettoes had been accumulating in the press since late 1939, when reports circulated with the headlines 'new home in Poland' and the 'ghetto state that was planned in Poland'. By 1940, no Western journalists had access to the occupied territories, a deliberate Nazi policy after the Wehrmacht swept westward and subjugated the countries of Western Europe. So all the news was offered with a caveat: the information was sourced from others and in effect the memory was unreliable.

The concentration camps were treated as separate news events from the ghettoes. Reports from refugees and the White Paper issued by the British government prompted more frequent, but still muted, attention, from 1940. 'Shocking' revelations appeared in the Australian press of prison camp atrocities and Nazi brutality against Jews and Catholics in the camps.[16] The fate of the ill, blind, aged and intellectually disabled emerged in dispatches in 1941, documenting their murder in 'poisoned gas chambers'.[17] In the same year, Hitler had made public announcements of 'the extermination of the Jews' on four occasions;[18] his fanatical obsession continued to be mentioned in the Australian press.

By 1942 there was little doubt of the fate of the Jews in the ghettoes when in June the London-based Polish government-in-exile released a report which they had received from the Warsaw Bund, the Jewish socialist party, and confirmed that the persecution of the Jews had become a systematic program of murder. On 2 June, the BBC broadcast the substance of the report, but the Australian press was slow to pick up this first public announcement. The *Daily Telegraph* published an account with the sobering headline '700 000 Jews massacred' over three weeks after the BBC's broadcast, though it reiterated the methods of killing, in which victims between the age of 14 and 60 dug their own graves and 35,000 Jews were taken from the Lodz

---

16 'Cruelty of Nazis', *Sydney Morning Herald* (hereafter *SMH*), 1 November 1939.
17 'Poisoned gas chambers', *DT*, 3 May 1941.
18 Friedländer, 281.

ghetto and killed in 'vans fitted as gas chambers'.[19] The Tasmanian *Mercury* was even slower to publish the news but issued a lengthier report in October that the Jews herded into the ghettos of Warsaw, Lodz, Cracow, Lwów and Wilno were driven further east in occupied Europe and eradicated in tens of thousands.[20] The link had been established between loss of rights and liberty, deportations from the ghettoes, and eventual mass killings in named death camps.

The 11 Allied governments confirmed the 'bestial policy of cold-blooded extermination' in December 1942, and throughout the month the Australian reports reflected the confirmation with the headlines: 'Jews sent to death camps'; 'Jews herded into Polish concentration camps knowing they are to be massacred'; and 'over two million Jews had already perished in Europe since 1939'.[21] Unlike hundreds of US and UK newspapers,[22] however, no Australian mainstream newspaper published editorials to coincide with a day of mourning called by Jewish organisations. Indeed, few Australian editorials were devoted to the Jewish fate throughout the war.

It was clear in the Australian press by 1943 that the remaining European Jewry was destined for complete eradication. Yet Australian attention continued to be sporadic and inconsistent; the portrayal was detached. The delayed news of the Warsaw ghetto uprising beginning in April 1943, for example, was reported in only six newspapers and without any editorial comment.[23] While the uprising came to be later remembered as the evocation of Jewish resistance and its first anniversary was solemnised in Australian synagogues, the press had quickly moved on. On 12 November, the *Daily Telegraph* provided a 'statistical picture of the horror Hitler has perpetuated against the [Jewish] race'.[24] The report was illustrated with a comprehensive graph listing the occupied countries, the number of Jews murdered from each country and the numbers of survivors remaining. In total, it was announced five million Jews had been exterminated in Nazi Europe.[25] Under the inspired editorship of Brian Penton, the Sydney *Daily*

---

19 '7 000 000 Jews massacred', *DT*, 26 June 1942.

20 'Exterminated in thousands: Treatment of Jews', *Mercury*, 31 October 1942.

21 'Jews sent to death camps', *DT*, 11 December 1942; 'Polish Jews ask for death', *DT*, December 1942; 'Anti-pogrom broadcast', *DT*, 19 December 1942; '2 000 000 Jews Die', *DT*, 21 December 1942. All other newspapers carried the news after the Allies' confirmation.

22 Leff, 157.

23 'Warsaw Jews fight Germans 5 weeks', *DT*, 24 May 1943

24 '5,000,000 Jews exterminated in Nazi Europe', *DT*, 12 November 1943.

25 ibid.

Telegraph had gained a reputation for being progressive, liberal and with a strong focus on world events. Consequently the newspaper devoted the most consistent attention to the genocide. The *Sydney Morning Herald* was the other newspaper sympathetic to the plight of the Jews, which was 'out of step with most other daily newspapers'.[26] In a rare editorial published on 7 August 1942, its editor damned the French government for collaborating with 'the Nazis' determination to exterminate all Jews in Europe'.[27]

If readers were paying close attention, they might have become familiar with the names of the Nazi camps in Poland. In the case of the most infamous and largest, Auschwitz, the press often identified it by using the Polish name of the town, Oświęcim. It was also sometimes described as 'the notorious concentration camp at Oswiecim' or 'Auschwitz extermination camp'. In total there were 29 articles in Australia about the camp between 1942 and its liberation in January 1945 and there were some inaccuracies. The Tasmanian *Mercury*, for example, claimed in March 1944 that 'the notorious concentration camp', had become the German's latest "death factory"'. (Auschwitz II [also referred to as Birkenau] had received the first transports and had functioned as a death camp from February 1942. Auschwitz I was established in 1940.) This sort of erratic coverage was fairly typical and perhaps, inevitable; statistics were commonly underestimated or inflated, and the Jewish victims were sometimes obscured.

There has been much conjecture in the United States and the United Kingdom about press negligence in revealing the persecution and mass extermination of the Jews. As this chapter argues, the Australian press covered the genocide but intermittently. Previous reports were ignored and new revelations buried in the inner recesses of the papers. Some of the explanations for the lack of sustained attention can be attributed to the journalistic standards of the time. The demands of covering a world war, the preoccupation with the Australian Imperial Force (AIF) in Tobruk, Greece and Crete, and the struggle in Papua New Guinea cannot be underestimated. In addition, there was a widespread scepticism due to fabricated atrocity stories in the First World War, a failure to grasp that the brutal persecution had extended to a systematic policy of mass murder with a view to murdering the entire Jewish population and a confusion between concentration camps and extermination camps. Individual journalists could, of course, not be expected to anticipate the full extent of the Nazis' murderous rage, nor did they have much autonomy to determine what they reported on.

---

26   Bartrop, 193.
27   'Editorial', *SMH*, 7 August 1942.

While the massacre of Jews was an everyday occurrence, the Jewish plight was considered just another story of wartime suffering, often minimised, universalised or absorbed into other accounts of murder in Nazi-occupied countries.[28] 'Mass killings', the *Daily Telegraph* reported in 1941, was 'a stamp of Nazi occupation'.[29] Descriptions of executions, reprisals, forced labour, the slaughter of innocent women and children, pillaging, and the toll of bombing, disease and starvation in Nazi occupied territories were endemic. The reported massacre of 7,000 in the Krasnodar region, for example, concealed the Jewish identity of the victims. One dispatch reported that the Germans 'executed 7000 men, women and children in diesel trucks fitted as lethal chambers' and also 'bashed a child's head with a rifle'.[30] This pogrom was only prioritised in Australia because the Soviets had captured, tried and executed eight Russian Quislings charged with having aided the Gestapo.

The killings of a few often attracted greater attention than the destruction of thousands. The execution of four Jewish women in Crete and the murder of every adult Jewish male and some fifty-two Jewish women in Lidice in June 1942 appeared on front pages, while reports exposing 'the deaths of two million Jews' were buried in later pages. Crete had resonance for an Australian audience because 274 Australian soldiers had died defending the island and 3,079 were taken prisoner. The Lidice massacre was newsworthy because it had occurred in reprisal for the assassination of Reinhardt Heydrich, a top Nazi official, on 26 May 1942. Known as the 'butcher of Prague' and considered even then as one of the architects of the extermination policy of the Jews, Heydrich was a favourite tabloid villain.

The reporting of death contributed to the confusion. The words used – barbarity, horror, terror, slaughter, torture chambers – failed to convey the full magnitude of the situation. The phrases 'horror camps', 'poison death camps' and 'death camps' made little sense. And words such as extermination and annihilation, as the fate of the Jews was now called, were difficult to comprehend. In Nazi parlance, 'liquidation' meant killing and journalists employed the term without really analysing its implications.[31]

Another reason for the lack of engagement was that for much of the war the narrative style of the reporting of genocide was statistical rather than personal. This was partly caused by the lack of access to the occupied territories, but there was also a distinct lack of identification with the Jews;

---

28   Friedländer, 226; Lipstadt, 135.
29   'Mass killings stamp of Nazi occupation', *DT*, 21 November 1941.
30   'Nazi given orders to murder', *DT*, 20 July 1943.
31   'Polish Jews ask for death', *DT*, 15 December 1942.

in a sense they were considered less worthy victims than the British who died during the Blitz or the POWs in Japanese camps.

Godfrey Blunden was one of the few Australians who had some level of access and was able to use personal testimony in an attempt to evoke the full tragedy. The Sydney *Daily Telegraph* gave Blunden unusual latitude. In Russia, Blunden was the first Australian journalist to report accurate revelations of the genocide and challenges Peter Novick's claim that no Western journalists had firsthand experience of the Holocaust.[32] Though Blunden did not witness the killings in Kharkov, he entered the city after the Einsatzgruppen C had left. In early 1943, he reported the true horror of the genocide:

> The first thing the Germans did when entering Kharkov was to announce a 'crusade' against the Jews and the Communists. They went from house to house shooting but more often hanging all of whom they suspected of both or either ... They then rounded up all Jews they could find including women and children ... two days after being sent to the camp they were made to dig trenches. Then a company of S.S. men with submachine guns went to the camp and shot them all, making them stand in the trenches that they had dug, so that they fell into their own graves.[33]

Finally, the reports failed to provoke outrage because they came mainly from a handful of Jews who had escaped as well as from underground sources, anonymous German informants and the Soviet government, rather than from Western journalists. The editors also always ensured that the provenance of the reports was made explicit and the accuracy of the testimony was predicated on the identity of the source. Without official confirmation and extensive photographic evidence, editors greeted much of the information with cynicism, even apathy, and a belief that, at best, it was a secondary story. The annihilation of the Jews remained an inside story.

The 'horror camps'

By late April 1945, the revelations of the concentration camps were no longer deemed secondary by the Australian press organisations. Even then, the early accounts of the Allied liberation of the camps were covered erratically.

---

32   Novick, 23.
33   Godfrey Blunden, 'Nazis hanged, starved and looted them', *DT,* 3 March 1943.

Almost a year had elapsed since July 1944, when the Soviet forces reached Majdanek near Lublin, Poland. Confusion prevailed because the town was sometimes spelt incorrectly as Maidanek, and one report failed to mention that a massacre of 'Jewish men, women and children' had occurred in the camp hours before Red Army troops entered the town. Majdanek camp was instead referred to simply as Lublin and described as a 'great ghetto city'.[34] Editors never offered corrections because they continued to report the Holocaust episodically without seeing it as part of a pattern. Any new report was treated as the first 'possible confirmation'.[35] In total there were five Australian reports of the liberation of Majdanek and no editorials. Treblinka was simply referred to as another 'death factory' or 'execution camp' and its liberation inspired only two reports in Australia.

The first Australian journalist to report on the liberation of the camps was Chester Wilmot, who was accredited with the BBC. Wilmot accompanied the British 2nd Army into the relatively unknown Vught concentration camp in Holland on 27 October 1944. Only one account about the camp had been published in Australia before its liberation: in September 1943 the *Canberra Times* obtained information from the Netherlands Press Agency and reported the 'indescribable fate' of the 20,000 inmates in striped clothes.[36] So indescribable was the prisoners' plight that the newspaper left it to the reader's imagination. Wilmot's vivid but unemotional broadcast was picked up by 10 other newspapers over a three-month period, but without photographic evidence, his revelations were quickly forgotten and overtaken by other events.[37]

While the liberation of Auschwitz by the Soviets was ignored by the Western press in January 1945, it has subsequently become *the* symbol of the Holocaust. Australian press organisations showed a particular lack of interest, and most of the major newspapers failed to cover the liberation or continued to print the reports in obscure places, thus suggesting to the public that the revelations were not of central significance or even reliable.[38] In total, the liberation attracted eight, perfunctory articles at the time. Auschwitz began to assume importance during the Nuremberg trials when

---

34 'Nazis kill Jews before Red Army enters Lublin', *DT,* 29 July 1944.
35 Lipstadt, 270.
36 'Big underground army in Holland', *Canberra Times,* 21 September 1943.
37 Chester Wilmot, 'The Nazi concentration camp at Vught', 27 October 1944, Box 10, Chester Wilmot Papers, MS 8436, NLA.
38 An exception was the *Daily Telegraph,* which devoted the greatest level of sustained coverage to the Holocaust.

Australian journalists reported all the ghastly details. Until then, it was the camps in Germany that attracted the overwhelming attention.

The reasons for the neglect can be explained by the competing news: graphic stories of Australian POW experiences in German 'hell camps', grim camp conditions in Manila after Australian POW's were released, 'appalling stories of Jap atrocities', Australian losses in the Pacific and Allied progress after D-Day. It was also clear that the West paid little heed to the Soviet press. In Australia, Western correspondents were privileged. So too was the nationality of the liberators and those liberated.

News about the 'horror camps' in Germany began to emerge in April 1945 as over 20 Australian journalists advanced towards Berlin with British and American troops. The American forces first encountered the camps in Natzweiler in German-occupied Alsace; then Ohrdruf, a sub-camp of Buchenwald; and Nordhausen, Buchenwald and Dachau. The British 11th Armoured Division liberated Belsen on 15 April.

Sam White was one of the first correspondents (and the only Jewish Australian reporter) to enter a German concentration camp when he accompanied the US 3rd Army into Ohrdruf and described the 'gruesome sights' in a dispatch for the *Argus*.[39] Harold Austin wrote about 'amazing disclosures' of a Nazi 'horror house'.[40] Harry Standish described the hundreds who had died in German 'horror trains' as he encountered pits containing corpses shot after they attempted to escape the death marches.[41] Ian Bevan, the *Age*'s staff reporter, wrote about the 'starvation, torture and whippings'.[42]

For the first time news of the Holocaust was propelled onto the front pages – though the lengthier reports were published on later pages and White's piece appeared on page 16. Often the photographs were given greater precedence as every newspaper published full-page pictorials of the camps, often without context.[43] Salacious captions included: 'German barbarity revealed inside horror camps'; 'Ghastly photos confirm horror camp reports'; and 'The German horror camp that shocked the world'.[44] Such headlines

---

39   Sam White, 'Germans massacre prisoners', *Argus*, 11 April 1945.
40   Harold Austin, 'Prisoners' brutal treatment', *SMH*, 11 April 1945 and 'Nazi prison camp horrors', SMH, 19 April 1945.
41   Harry Standish, 'Lack of relief in horror camps', *SMH*, 21 April 1945.
42   Ian Bevan, 'Union Jack raised over ruins of Belsen', *SMH*, 19 April 1945, and *Age*, 22 May 1945.
43   'German horror camp which has shocked the world', *SMH*, 23 April 1945.
44   'German barbarity revealed inside horror camps', *Age*, 23 April 1945; 'Ghastly photos confirm horror camp reports', *Sun*, 22 April 1945; and 'German horror camp that shocked the world', *Argus*, 23 April 1945.

suggested that earlier accounts lacked credibility without photographic evidence and previous reports were disbelieved. The editors claimed it was the photographs that confirmed news of atrocities.[45] The photographs were particularly graphic for Australian audiences, since unlike other Western newspapers, the censorious mainstream Australian newspapers had previously published few if any images of dead soldiers. As Barbie Zelizer argues, the images became the basis of the dominant memory of the Holocaust.[46] They would also establish the paradigm for subsequent genocides. Many of the grainy, grimly familiar images of piled, emaciated cadavers, mass graves and refugees waiting at train stations during the Balkan wars in the 1990s were anachronistic reminders of Hitler's murderous regime.[47]

The journalists played a role in forming the collective memory because they followed a schematic and stylised pattern of writing. Allied witnesses, Nazi perpetrators, German bystanders and victims were assigned particular roles that allowed little ambiguity or variation. The correspondents themselves were most prominent and they mediated the experience of liberation. They did not just relate the news of the camps but promoted themselves as central narrators who had previously been unaware of the Nazis' true intent.

Already brutalised by years of covering violence, most of the journalists claimed that they found it difficult to communicate the reality of the camps, that somehow the journalistic narrative was insufficient. As Saul Friedländer writes, the events were so extreme and unusual that they were considered events at the limits, posing unique problems of interpretation and representation.[48]

There was also an overwhelming preoccupation in the reportage that the camps had to be *remembered*. The correspondents concentrated on persuading their readers of the truth of the accounts, fearing that scepticism associated in part with lingering anti-Semitism would make them believe that the news was fabricated or exaggerated. Sam White concluded his report from Ohrdruf: 'I shall never forget it. Next time anyone asks me if these atrocity stories are true I shall spit in his face.'[49] The journalistic accounts took precedence over all other interpretations, including those of the victims; it

---

45   'Ghastly photos confirm horror camp reports', *Sun*, 19 April 1945; 'Ghastly photos confirm horror camp reports: Some instances of brutality beyond description', *Army News*, Tuesday 24 April 1945.

46   Zelizer, 1.

47   Croatian offensive evokes images of Hitler', *Australian*, 9 May 1995.

48   Friedländer, x.

49   Sam White, 'Germans massacre prisoners', *Argus*, 11 April 1945.

was made clear that press memory had the greatest authority. Journalists also exhibited a self-consciousness in the coverage: their role as witnesses lent a moral clarity to the war.

At the same time, the correspondents were forced to process their own distress as they gathered information.[50] Impartiality was impossible when confronting the incomprehensible barbarity of genocide. Osmar White wrote that after seeing Buchenwald and moving 'among its living dead, I cannot now, or ever will be able to write objectively of what I have seen'.[51] The Second World War was a war of survival: the cause and the enemy were not ambiguous. The issue of objectivity was not raised in coverage of the Australian Imperial Forces, but it was a consideration during the liberation of the camps.

Despite the formulaic reportage, the Australian coverage differed from that of the United States and United Kingdom. First, the US press tended to focus on Buchenwald and Dachau because American forces liberated both camps, whereas the press in the United Kingdom concentrated on Belsen, which was liberated by their forces. Laurel Leff argues that Belsen lacked a 'hook' such as the reaction of the German civilians at Buchenwald, the fighting that was the centerpiece of Dachau and the presence of Eisenhower and his condemnation at Ohrdruf.[52] The Australian journalists who were embedded with both the British and United States covered the liberation of all the camps, including 114 reports on the liberation of Buchenwald, 42 dispatches on Dachau and 111 on Belsen, in 26 Australian newspapers. Contrary to Leff's suggestion, Belsen proved compelling for the Australians: further visual evidence of mass killing and British supremacy demonstrated by the symbolic raising of the Union Jack 'over the ruins of Belsen'.[53]

Second, unlike other Western press, the Australian correspondents who covered the liberation of the camps did not always obscure the fact that most of the victims were Jewish.[54] William I Hitchcock observes that to a contemporary reader the first striking feature of the reports is the absence of any acknowledgement of Jewish victimisation.[55] Raul Hilberg defines the tendency to obliterate the particular identity of the Jews as 'functional

---

50   Zelizer, 81.
51   Osmar White, 'Invaders rip veil from Nazi Horrors', *Sun*, 18 April 1945.
52   Leff, 304.
53   Ian Bevan, 'Union Jack raised over ruins of Belsen', *SMH*, 19 April 1945.
54   Leff, 3.
55   William I Hitchcock, *Liberation: Bitter Road to Freedom, Europe 1944–1945* (New York: Faber and Faber, 2009), 298.

blindness', resulting in a minimisation of the fate of the Jews.[56] This was not always evident in the Australian press reports, and some correspondents actually emphasised Jewish identity. An uncredited *Age* correspondent wrote that 'men, women and children, most of them with no other crime than Jewish ancestry', were in Belsen.[57] Betty Wilson similarly emphasised the Jewish survivors in Dachau.[58] Ronald Monson's dispatch from Belsen cited a Parisian female doctor who had survived Auschwitz, where, he said, 'four million Jews, men, women and children, were asphyxiated and burned'.[59]

Some accounts were more oblique; an uncredited correspondent reported on an unnamed 'prison camp for Jewish women' but failed to provide any further information.[60] Sam White described Ohrdruf as a concentration camp for Russians, Poles, Jews and German political prisoners.[61] Chester Wilmot, who was a formidable journalist and military strategist, referred to both the political prisoners and the Dutch Jews incarcerated and murdered in the Vught camp. Others concealed Jewish identity, but often they were not even reporting directly from the camps but were London- and Australian-based journalists who had taken copy from the wire services. The *Age* 'Special' London correspondent referred to the victims who perished in Buchenwald as 'opponents to Hitler' and in Belsen the prisoners were simply referred to as 'slaves' by a *Sydney Morning Herald* staff reporter.[62]

Third, some of the Australian reportage deviated from other Western press in the representation of the victims by humanising them. Hitchcock argues that the names and personal experiences of the victims were largely absent in the Western press and Leff observes that the accounts were devoid of individual Jewish stories in the dispatches. The dead, according to Hitchcock, were often reduced to an undifferentiated mass of human refuse and even the living were described as inanimate, nonhuman objects of pity and almost contempt.[63] While the Australian reportage was detached, particularly of the dead, several Australian journalists managed to communicate the survivors' perspectives and humanity. Douglas Wilkie described the children in Belsen as 'mere shreds of bones and rags – gathering

---

56 Cited by Lipstadt, 260.
57 'Brutality of Nazis', *Age*, 21 April 1945.
58 Betty Wilson, '23 000 men still in Dachau', *SMH*, 21 May 1945.
59 Ronald Monson, 'Ghastliness of Nazi prison camp', *Argus*, 21 April 1945.
60 '100,000 women killed in Nazi gas chamber', *Sun*, 12 April 1945.
61 Sam White, 'Germans massacre prisoners', *Argus*, 11 April 1945.
62 'Nazi area of death', *Age*, 17 April 1945; 'Death Toll of 60,000', *SMH*, 17 April 1945.
63 Hitchcock, 299; Leff, 314.

round me, each repeating one word in diverse languages. That one word was "bread!"[64] Sam White interviewed a Jewish prisoner from Lodz in Ohrdruf who explained the policy of the camp, the process of selection and survival.[65] Ronald Monson, who was with the first troops to enter Belsen, provided a personal dimension as he witnessed men oblivious to their liberation who had shuffled off to die.

It is difficult to speculate why these subtle differences in press treatment occurred – some of the Australian journalists were resourceful outsiders who had worked as freelancers from much of the 1930s. The quality of the reportage was also often determined by the time they spent newsgathering and their talent. Douglas Wilkie, for example, stayed for an unprecedented two days in Belsen. Barbie Zelizer argues that in effect the press lacked a frame to explain atrocity.[66] The two possible exceptions were Sam White and Ronald Monson. White had escaped the pogroms against Jews in Ukraine and migrated to Australia when he was a young boy in the 1920s. Monson too was possibly different, for he recognised the importance of interviewing and sought to reject simple stereotypes of distress and death. His experience in reporting civilian suffering and atrocity had been refined in 1937 when he covered the Spanish Civil War and the Japanese atrocities committed during the fall of Nanking. Yet even Monson failed to identify with the victims in the same way as he did with the Australian servicemen released from German POW camps. Drawing on a casual parochialism, Monson described the 'decent young' Australians, 'who naturally think everyone is a good bloke just because he is friendly'.[67] The victims in the camp remained alien to such familiarity.

The reports often minimised the historical context of the Final Solution. Indeed, many journalists denied even remembering the earlier accounts of the persecution and extermination of the Jews before their liberation. Alan Moorehead, who reported in Europe for much of the 1930's, observed in his biography: 'What we are seeing is something from the dark ages, the breaking up of a medieval slave state. And yet, in early April, we had only begun to glimpse the extent and depth of the Nazi terror system.'[68] Most correspondents failed to relate the earlier accounts of the Third Reich and the beginning of the anti-Jewish campaign from 1933 in order to understand

---

64   Douglas Wilkie, 'Nazi charnel house', *Sun*, 19 April 1945.
65   Sam White, 'Germans massacre prisoners', *Argus*, 11 April 1945.
66   Zelizer, 31.
67   Ronald Monson, '300 Australians freed from Nazi hell camp', *Argus*, 19 April 1945.
68   Tom Pocock, *Alan Moorehead* (London: Bodley Head), 199.

the transition to mass murder. Consequently they often failed to differentiate between political prisoners, slave labour and Jews, but more specifically they did not have the space or desire to document the campaign of extermination.[69]

Even if they had the motivation to do so, many journalists could not have grasped the bigger picture: they had been denied access to the camps before their liberation, they visited the camps briefly while accredited with the forces who had a military objective in Berlin, and few had the requisite historical knowledge or a complex understanding of the Nazis' ideological and racial intention to exterminate the Jews.[70] The reporting traditions, editorial agendas, the concept of time and the nature of press memory also contributed to the gaps; the journalists had to meet deadlines and there was no temporal distance.

Consequently, there were significant omissions or suppression in the coverage. Nicolas Mills and Kara Brunner have alerted readers to the 'language of slaughter', the dangers of writing about terror either melodramatically or reductively.[71] Some journalists drew upon a common vernacular that limned victims as the skeletal dead, the living dead, living skeletons, charred bodies, the emaciated.[72] Interest lay in the dead rather than the living. 'I saw Belsen today', Douglas Wilkie wrote. 'I saw the piles of dead and its aimless swarms of living dead, their great eyes like animal lights in skin-covered skulls'.[73] Particularly in some of the syndicated reports, there were tales of nightmares: gallows, crematoriums, laboratories where fiendish experiments took place, parchment, consisting of large pieces of human flesh marked with tattoos.[74] As William Hitchcock observed, it was the stuff of ghoulish fairytales.[75]

The revelations of cannibalism, which appeared in the medical records and soldiers' letters from Belsen, trial records, testimonial accounts and publications, were quickly forgotten by the Australian press after the Nuremberg Trials.[76] One unaccredited report described the 'crazed prisoners' resorting to cannibalism. 'Cannibalism was practiced. Some bodies had been picked

---

69   Leff, 310.

70   ibid.

71   Nicolaus Mills and Kira Brunner, eds, *The New Killing Fields* (New York: Basic Books, 2002), 6.

72   Hitchcock, 303.

73   Douglas Wilkie, 'Bulldozers bury dead in Nazi horror camp', *Sun*, 21 April 1945.

74   'Buchenwald camp of horrors', 19 April 1945.

75   Hitchcock, 303.

76   See the official Report on Belsen Camp by Lt-Col RIG Taylor. The revelations also appear in the several collections at the Imperial War Museum: ME Allan, 95/8/7 and G Walker, 84/2/1.

clean, livers, hearts and kidneys had been cut from others', the Australian correspondent wrote.[77] In total only 15 Australian articles mentioned cannibalism in Belsen at the time of its liberation; the revelations were then eradicated from Australian press memory after the 1940s.

Another account that appeared in only a handful of Australian newspapers was the murders of the SS guards by American soldiers from the 45th Infantry of the US Seventh Army in Dachau. Both the *Daily Telegraph* and the *Cairns Post* printed the story on their front pages, but most newspapers either ignored the reports or buried the account in later pages. The tone of the stories was of sympathy for the soldiers, describing their grief at the sight of 50 trainloads of 'horribly emaciated prisoners' and how the 'rescuers' ran 'amok' as 'they went through the camp shooting every German within sight'.[78] The journalists' own feelings of outrage were also sometimes buried. Ronald Monson was one of few to admit in 1945 that that he was so angered by the SS's brutality that while driving past he 'brushed their uniforms. How I would have liked to have swung the wheel into their ranks. But the terms of the truce had to be observed.'[79] In the early 1970s he told a Rotary audience that he punched an SS officer in Belsen and, later still, he confided to Phillip Knightly that he had not simply brushed past the SS prisoners but had driven his car directly at them, killing several. 'My God, did they scream.'[80]

The correspondents' reports were controlled by military censorship and editorial interference, and influenced by the particularities of memory. Press memory eliminated nuance. What was reprised and then remembered had to be officially acceptable, simple and conventional.[81] Cannibalism would have suggested a desperate will to survive when much of the reportage portrayed the victims as passive and indifferent to death. The soldiers' acts of reprisal

---

77   'Nazi prison camp horrors: Crazed prisoners turn cannibal', *DT,* 19 April 1945.

78   'US troops kill Dachau guards', *DT,* 1 May 1945; 'Rescuers "run amok": Camp guards shot on sight', *Cairns Post,* 2 May 1945; Dachau liberated: Horrors revealed: Soldiers enraged', *Western Australian,* 1 May 1945. For sources relating to the so-called 'Dachau-Massacre' see: Stephen Goodell, Kevin A Mahoney; Sybil Milton, *1945: The Year of Liberation* (Washington: US Holocaust Memorial Museum, 1995); Jürgen Zarusky '"That is not the American Way of Fighting": The Shooting of Captured SS-Men During the Liberation of Dachau', in *Dachau and the Nazi Terror 1933–1945,* Wolfgang Benz, Barbara Distel, eds (Brussels: Comite International de Dachau, 2002); Harold Marcuse, *Legacies of Dachau: The Uses and Abuses of a Concentration Camp, 1933–2001* (Cambridge: Cambridge University Press, 2001).

79   Ronald Monson, 'Ghastliness of Nazi prison camp', *Argus,* 21 April 1945.

80   Knightley, 346.

81   Zelizer, 7.

in Dachau allowed for a narrative about the Allies that was too complicated and, therefore, not widely covered. And in the case of Monson, if he was not self-mythologising, he could not have reported his attack on the SS officers because the journalist was not meant to assume the role of combatant. If it was purely a fabrication of memory, it suggests Monson felt the need to be an actor in the story as interest in the Holocaust was taking hold.

There was also institutional resistance to the accounts. The BBC told Chester Wilmot that they were not going to devote the whole of the *War Report* for a 'third consecutive night to horror' in deference to the British listeners who were in 'great shock' about both the concentration camps and the release of the British and American POWs. 'It seems to me that this material is of historic importance', a BBC executive informed Wilmot, 'but I cannot believe that listeners will wish to have it more or less rammed down their throats night after night'.[82] If, on the rare occasion, a correspondent dared to acknowledge press negligence and prior knowledge, as Wilmot did when he attempted to broadcast the news that the world had long been aware of the 'persecution and killing of Jews', the censor simply removed the damning passage.[83] Newspaper editors were similarly censorious, and a number refused to allocate the space to lengthier articles on the concentration camps or shortened those that were filed, thus removing context. Harry Standish's son, Dick, recalls his father's outrage that the *Sydney Morning Herald* did not publish his dispatch in its entirety on 21 April even though the London *News Chronicle* had devoted the front page to the article in its original length.[84]

If the press organisations were negligent for most of the war in their treatment of the genocide, the failure extended to the coverage of the victims after their liberation from the camps. After the initial revelations, the coverage diminished with Roosevelt's death on 13 April, the ignominious end to Mussolini, the announcement of Hitler's suicide on 1 May, the German surrender and the continuing war in the Pacific. Instead of documenting the refugee crisis, or providing stories of reunion and trauma, prominence was given to sensational accounts of the punishment of high-ranking Nazis and various commandants and SS guards, particularly Josef Kramer, known as the 'beast of Belsen', and the female SS guards. As Barbie

---

82 BBC to Chester Wilmot, 20 April 1945, folder 3a-4, box 9, Chester Wilmot Papers, MS 8436, NLA.

83 Chester Wilmot, BBC broadcast and notes, Nuremberg, series 3, folder 12, box 12, Chester Wilmot Papers, MS 8436, NLA.

84 Author's interview with Dick Standish, 2010.

Zelizer observes, remembering was important but so, too, was forgetting.[85] The press organisations simply lost interest.

Yet as the years passed, the liberation of the concentration camps became one of the defining memories of the war for the journalists themselves. Ronald Blunden, according to his son, was devastated by his experiences.[86] Ronald Monson continued to revisit Belsen in public lectures:

> Suffice to say that the first human skeletons I saw were women who seeing my uniform tried to wave to me as they squatted by a death heap about 50 yards long and 30 feet high. One woman brought tears flooding through my eyes as she produced a piece of red cardboard from somewhere, licked it, and tried to use it as lipstick.[87]

Holocaust consciousness and the journalists' pride in their role as witnesses to the calamitous events had taken hold by the 1970s. It reflected the international revival of interest in the Holocaust and possibly also the fact that the Australian Jewish community had the highest percentage of Holocaust survivors in the Diaspora outside of Europe, in relation to the country's overall Jewish population.

Conclusion

Peter George, an ABC foreign correspondent who covered the Balkans during the 1990s, recalled the conduct of the media in recording atrocities:

> It became a rat pack, as most wars do, in which the race to produce the more horrific images, and the more horrific stories, outweighed the need to tell the story and the balance of the story. There was a failure in which I would include myself.[88]

The Holocaust left a profound legacy on Australian press reporting and the coverage of genocide more specifically. Barbie Zelizer argues that the Nazi epoch defined both the memory of the Second World War and the practice of modern journalism.[89] Since the Holocaust, there has been a shift in how the media report genocide. As Peter George observes, there is now a rush to report the most salacious details, but there is also an articulated tension

---

85   Zelizer, 206.
86   Author's interview with Ronald Blunden, October 2010.
87   MSS Ronald Monson's address to Rotary, circa 1970, PR89/152, AWM.
88   Author's interview with Peter George, October 2009.
89   Zelizer, 12.

between reporting and humanitarian intervention. The personal stories are treated as credible, the idea of objectivity is regularly challenged, language is seminal and the importance of visual evidence is widely accepted. Yet in one singular way, the Holocaust did not change reporting: media memory continues to be determined by who does the seeing and more importantly by who does the telling and the political agendas of editors and owners. As the Holocaust demonstrated, if the Western press organisations refuse to privilege a story and if the journalists do not gain access to it, genocide is a secondary story at best. This condition shaped the reporting of subsequent genocides and other mass killings of ethnic groups in East Timor and Rwanda – and it continues to haunt journalists today.

Chapter 5

THE POLITICS OF DETACHMENT

Franco's Spain and the public perception
of the extermination of the Jews

Salvador Ortí Camallonga

Introduction

The attitude of Franco's Spain towards the extermination of the Jews is largely regarded as a remarkable episode within the Spanish political response to the Second World War.[1] Supposedly, the dictatorship actively helped Jews who were being persecuted by Nazis, and even Franco himself took an active part in the rescue efforts. The recent findings of the Jewish journalist Israel Garzón, however, have completely undermined this understanding of events. Garzón discovered that in 1941, Francoist authorities had produced a list of approximately 6,000 Jews living in Spain (called the *Archivo Judaico*), which presumably had been given to Heinrich Himmler. In June 2010 the Spanish newspaper *El País* published these findings, yet it neither caused public outrage nor triggered any interest in uncovering the facts.[2] Why has there been such a minimal interest towards an event that occupies a central place in Europe's recent history? This unfeeling attitude highlights that Spain's memory of the rescue of Jews during the Second World War, and of the extermination of the Jews in general, is extremely limited. At first glance, the near total absence of Jews in modern and contemporary Spain, which resulted from the Decree of

---

1   This investigation will refer to 'the extermination of the Jews' in order to avoid the religious connotations that 'Holocaust' and 'Shoah' might contain.

2   Jorge M Reverte, 'La lista de Franco para el Holocausto', *El País* 20 June 2010.

Expulsion issued by the Holy Kings in 1492, could be the reason for such generalised disinterest.[3] However, I argue that this disinterest results from Franco's politics of memory over Nazism and its crimes.

Arguably, between 1939 and 1945 the Franco dictatorship was a Fascist-like state in many regards, from power structures to aesthetics. Among many other themes, the Francoist political discourse included open hostility toward Jews – who were associated with the regime's enemies. Due to these affinities and other pragmatic interests, Franco supported the Axis during the Second World War – a position that would gradually decrease – and was aware of many of the Nazi crimes, including those against the Jews. Francoist diplomatic leadership received information from Spanish embassies and councils in Bucharest, Paris and Sophia,[4] along with the firsthand testimony of the Blue Division soldiers – a group of volunteers sent to assist Germany on the Eastern Front.[5] Additionally, the Ministry of Foreign Affairs knew about the murder of thousands of *Rotspanienkämpfer* – Republicans who had joined the Resistance and were captured by Nazis in occupied territories.[6]

The fall of the Axis powers and the end of the war forced the regime to transform its image externally and consolidate its legitimacy domestically. Ironically, however, Franco's dictatorship undertook a cosmetic democratisation using the Fascist-like 1938 Law of the Press, which entailed a brutal control of information by state censorship.[7] It was through this means that

---

3   None the less, anti-Semitism persisted in Spanish traditions and expressions. For a general view on Spanish modern and contemporary anti-Semitism see G Álvarez Chillida, *El antisemitismo en España. La imagen del judío* (Madrid: Marcial Pons, 2002).

4   B Rother, *Franco y el Holocausto* (Madrid: Marcial Pons, 2005), 158–179 and 126.

5   The testimony of the Blue Division with regard to the Jewish extermination has barely been addressed by historians. I have only found a recent work by Wayne Bowen that argues that the Blue Division treated the Jews of Suwałki and Grodno (Poland), Novgorod (Russia), and Riga and Vilnius respectfully and even defied Nazi racial policies. W Bowen, "'A great moral victory': Spanish protection of Jews on the Eastern Front, 1941–1944', in R Rohrlich, ed., *Resisting the Holocaust* (Oxford and New York: Berg, 1998) 195–213.

6   It is necessary to remark that the *Rotspanienkämpfer* suffered Nazi violence in very different circumstances from Jews, since they were not systematically murdered. There are several studies about the fate of around 15,000 Spaniards that were sent to Nazi concentration camps during WW2. The case of Mauthausen is highly relevant; thousands of Jews, mostly Dutch, were also deported to this camp between 1939 and 1945. E Le Chêne, *Mauthausen: The History of a Death Camp* (Bath: Chivers Press, 1971) 11–115. D Wingate Pike, *Spaniards in the Holocaust: Mauthausen, the Horror on the Danube* (London: Routledge, 2000).

7   Justino Sinova, *La censura de prensa durante el franquismo, 1936–1951* (Madrid: Espasa-Calpe, 1989), 39.

the dictatorship succeeded in consolidating political myths that helped to rewrite its recent and politically problematic past. Among those myths was the 'Theory of the Three Wars' and the 'Peace of Franco'. The Theory of the Three Wars differentiated between the war between the Soviet Union and the Axis, that between Japan and the United States, and that between the Axis and the Allies. This inconsistent explanation, however, helped the dictatorship to justify its support of Germany. The Peace of Franco, on the other hand, defended the position that Franco had intentionally preserved Spain by keeping it out of the war.[8]

Furthermore, the reconfiguration of the recent Spanish past came along with a depoliticisation of the masses that led to a general apathy and fear of re-enacting past traumas. In retrospect, the Francoist reiterative propaganda and re-education of the population had major consequences in the following years, moulding people's knowledge of distant elements of Spanish domestic life around the interests of the regime.

I believe that the Spanish postwar official discourse on Nazi crimes has been critical for contemporary social responses to the memory of the extermination of the Jews. A brief look at literature of other European countries shows that regardless of the involvement in the Second World War and the extermination of the Jews, national rhetoric dominated post-war European discourses. Ranging from countries that were occupied by Nazis, such as the Netherlands, to those that collaborated with them, such as France, most European countries made use of the 'anti-Fascist paradigm' in the wake of the war.[9] The annihilation of the European Jews was at odds with the themes that would prevail in the newly official discourses about the war. Even in a former Axis country such as Italy, a nationalising postwar narrative prevailed, one that obscured its Fascist past and its responsibility in the crimes perpetrated by the Nazis. As Oscar Österberg has pointed out, the anti-Fascist paradigm dominated 'Italian historiography and political debate for decades to come'.[10] However, the extermination of European Jews did become part of the official memory of the Second World War where it

---

8   Antonio Cazorla Sánchez, *Las políticas de la victoria: La consolidación del nuevo Estado franquista, 1938–1953* (Madrid: Marcial Pons, 2000), 224–5.

9   For the Netherlands see P Lagrou, *The Legacy of Nazi Occupation: Patriotic Memory and National Recovery in Western Europe, 1945–1965* (Cambridge: Cambridge University Press, 2000), 22, 35, 251 and 260. For the French case see H Rousso, *The Vichy Syndrome* (Cambridge, MA: Harvard University Press, 1991), 16–59.

10   O Österberg, 'Taming ambiguities: The representation of the Holocaust in post-war Italy', in KG Karlsson and U Zander, eds, *The Holocaust on Post-War Battlefields: Genocide as Historical Culture* (Malmö: Sekel Bokförlag, 2006), 25.

fitted conveniently with national interests. In Sweden, Folke Bernadotte's activities to save Jews were a central part of the country's interpretation of its role in the war because, as Ulf Zander argued, '[t]he image of peace-loving Sweden as a compassionate Samaritan fitted very well with the conception of "people's home" definitions and was therefore easily integrated into the post-war national Swedish identity'.[11]

In sharp contrast with these contributions, there is a clear academic gap on the reception of the extermination of the Jews in Spain, where scholars instead have largely concentrated on whether Franco truly saved as many Jews as the regime claimed[12] and whether the dictatorship's hostility to Jews stemmed from religious prejudices or evolved into racism.[13] This article will analyse some of the main features of the official narrative about the extermination of the Jews and about Nazism in Franco's Spain during the postwar years. This analysis addresses key issues around a major event that, unlike the Civil War, did not happen on Spanish soil – thus limiting the regime's ability to shape an official version of this event – and showed the world the criminal nature of Fascism. Moreover, it provides a new angle for understanding the nature of Franco's Spain in a period of extreme challenges to its very survival – in the postwar years Franco, who was an ally of the Axis powers, needed to be disassociated from Fascism and the crimes of Nazi camps.

Postwar official narrative of Nazism and the extermination of the Jews

Spain faced international isolation in the postwar years on the basis of its former collaboration with the Axis. The United Nations approved diplomatic sanctions against a country that symbolised 'a Fascist regime equal

---

11   U Zander, 'To rescue or to be rescued: The liberation of Bergen Belsen and the white buses in British and Swedish historical cultures', in KG Karlsson and U Zander, eds, *The Holocaust on Post-War Battlefields: Genocide as Historical Culture* (Malmö: Sekel Bokförlag, 2006), 359.

12   There has been a quite relevant debate on the figures of Jews that were saved. For a recent contribution see B Rother *Franco y el Holocausto* (Madrid: Marcial Pons, 2005).

13   Some historians argue that Spanish hostility towards Jews was based purely upon religious premises. See, for example, Graciela Ben-Dror, *La iglesia católica ante el Holocausto: España y América Latina, 1933–1945* (Madrid: Alianza Editorial, 2003). Others, however, believe that Spanish anti-Semitism included racial arguments. See Isabelle Rohr, *The Spanish Right and the Jews, 1898–1945: Anti-Semitism and Opportunism* (Eastbourne: Sussex Academic Press, 2007).

to Hitler's Nazi Germany and Mussolini's Fascist Italy'.[14] Facing such a compromising situation in the international sphere, the regime devoted a great deal of effort to detaching itself from Fascism and the extermination of the Jews, based on the following four strategies.

I. Silence

The dictatorship silenced the discussion on the concentration and extermination camps. The first news in Spain about the Nazi camps was generally very plain, purely descriptive, located in secondary sections of the papers and provided by news wire services. Following the last stages of the European war, the press eliminated any pro-Axis rhetoric and instead echoed in a 'telegraphic style', and without any editorialising, the reactions of Americans and Britons when they discovered the Nazi atrocities. Spanish newspapers released censored written and even visual information on what was being discovered in Bergen-Belsen, Buchenwald and Lidice, along with the fact that Nazis had made use of gas chambers to eliminate Jews.[15] And yet, such evidence triggered neither opinion by journalists nor an official response to such crimes.

Such silence, however, contrasted with fast and fierce reactions against external comparisons between Nazi and Spanish concentration camps that could have called the regime's legitimacy into question. On 18 May 1945, at the very same time as Allied commissions brought to light the atrocities in Nazi camps, the Associated Press wire service reported the terrible living conditions in the Spanish concentration camp of Nanclares de Oca. Immediately, the Falangist newspaper *Arriba* directly deplored the lack of reliability, honesty and quality of the Associated Press and pointed out that the company's desperate financial situation forced it to create sensationalist journalism. The newspaper *Arriba* also condemned the Associated Press's opportunism, since information about Nanclares de Oca was released amid public outrage toward loathsome pictures of Buchenwald, Dachau and Oranienburg. Interestingly, *Arriba* claimed that unlike in Nazi camps, the prisoners of Nanclares de Oca were a 'band of bums and tattered people, and representatives of sexual crime that are being purified by the 'good' waters of the Zadorra River'. Such 'infamous'

---

14 Quoted in J Lleonart, *España y la ONU I, 1945–1946* (Madrid: CSIC, 1978), 86. This and all subsequent translations are by the author.

15 'Lamentable estado de los internados en los campos de concentracion alemanes', *Arriba*, 28 April 1945; also 'Cinco gobiernos presentan siete acusaciones contra Himmler', *ABC*, 15 May 1945.

apparent similarities were not accidental, said *Arriba*; the newspaper believed that hidden interests aimed to disclose a 'Spanish Buchenwald' to the rest of the world.[16] The pro-monarchic newspaper *ABC* agreed with *Arriba* on the existence of ulterior motives that were intended to damage Spain's international image.[17]

In an emphatic official reaction, the Secretary General of Governance rebutted any claims of ill-treatment, defended the absence of reports of death because of violence or illness and rejected the accusation that prisoners had been held for political reasons, claiming instead that only criminals and outlaw foreigners had been sent to Nanclares de Oca. He also argued that the resemblance between prisoners of Spanish and Nazi camps was coincidental; according to him, striped uniforms and shaved heads were common in schools and military facilities for hygiene purposes.[18]

Interestingly, theories of a plot against Spain were very often used by the Franco regime when facing a crisis of legitimacy. For example, in the first few months after it came to power, the dictatorship argued that the Civil War broke out because of a plot organised by the Left. In the aftermath of the Second World War, Xavier de Echarri – journalist and chief editor of the journal *Arriba* – blamed the Republicans for distorting Franco Spain's state of affairs by providing false information to the international press, simplifying Spain's domestic affairs and identifying Franco with tyranny, despotism and 'totalitarianism'. Echarri lamented the Republicans' omission of the mass murder they committed during the Civil War.[19] In addition to Echarri's accusations, the media publicised every single piece of external support for the dictatorship.[20]

II. Catholicism vs. Nazism

Along with the 1945 *Fuero de los Españoles*, a piece of legislation that highlighted the religious nature of the regime and of Spanish society, the Parliament approved the 1947 *Ley de Sucesión*, which defined Spain as a monarchy and Franco as a lifelong regent. These manoeuvres signalled an

---

16 'Periodismo fácil y barato', *Arriba*, 18 May 1945. This and following translations are made by the author.

17 'La falsedad contumaz', *ABC*, 18 May 1945.

18 'Se desmiente oficialmente una falsa información de Associated Press sobre Nanclares de Oca', *Arriba*, 18 May 1945.

19 Xavier de Echarri, 'España en el panorama de Europa', *Arriba*, 23 May 1945.

20 See, for example, 'El régimen de Franco es defendido por la prensa del Perú', *Arriba*, 19 April 1945.

institutional mask whereby the Falangist power diminished while Monarchic and Catholic groups saw their influence increase. This significant turnabout was behind the Franco regime's exploitation of a Spanish Catholic identity and religious traditions, as opposed to any reference to National Socialism. Nazism, formerly praised in public, was now vilified as a political system based on state idolatry. In contrast, as was now argued by the Spanish media, the ideological foundations of the Franco regime, namely the ideas of Falange's founder Jose Antonio Primo de Rivera, excluded 'theocracy', 'racism' and 'cult of the State' and genuinely sought a Hispanic identity. The journalist Alfonso Junco argued in the pro-monarchic newspaper *ABC* that 'the Catholic doctrine excludes radically and inexorably (…) the Totalitarian conception of the State as the single source of Law', and that Spaniards aimed for a true democracy, in which the population felt that it was 'governed' and 'guided' by the State.[21]

The Spanish Church insisted that racial theories had no place in Franco Spain's ideology and pointed to profound differences between the Third Reich and Franco's Spain.[22] In messages about the Second World War and Nazism, emphatic distinctions were made between the world war and the Spanish Civil War, the latter being portrayed as the Communists' persecution and extermination of Catholics. Archbishop Pla i Demiel, one of the most important figures within the Spanish Church, argued that the European war illustrated the loss of Christian unity that resulted from the 16th-century Reformation, which laid the foundations for the emergence of states that 'deified strength (…) and that have ruined the peoples that implement them'. Pla i Demiel believed that the postwar world ought to be built by prioritising Christian values over 'icons of blood and race' and be based upon love and brotherhood among peoples.[23]

Accounts of Spain's involvement in the Second World War emphasised the motivations for Franco's neutral position during the conflict. They pointed out that Franco reacted to a threat from the whole of Europe; the dictator aimed to preserve peace in the continent and raise the voice of 'Christian serenity and fraternity and the European community in order to put an end

---

21 Alfonso Junco, 'La España de hoy', *Arriba*, 14 April 1945.

22 The Church became one of the most vocal allies of Franco and became very insistent in the public defence of Spain's stance during WW2. See Javier Tusell, *Franco y los Católicos. La política interior española entre 1945 y 1957* (Madrid: Alianza Editorial, 1984), 119–121.

23 'Ojalá que la paz futura se procure asentarla sobre el derecho de grandes y pequeños', *Arriba*, 9 May 1945.

to the war'.[24] Franco, as portrayed by the official narrative of the Second World War, was a messianic leader who had resisted pressure from Hitler to enter the war and protected Spain from another catastrophe. Franco became providential for Spain's fate, as he did everything in his power to avoid new crimes being committed on Spanish soil. He had managed to keep Spain safe and peaceful, a fact that was stressed as a historical exception in Spain's modern history.[25]

The postwar official memory on the Third Reich, albeit not clear-cut, became highly critical of the German spiritual chaos and of the country's desperate need for a messianic leader immediately after the end of the First World War. In clear contrast with previously praising narratives, Hitler now embodied weak leadership, mediocrity and sexual depravity; he was portrayed as an insane social agitator of the German population through a Pagan, anti-Semitic and anti-Catholic ideology that originated in Nietzsche, Spengler and Rosenberg.[26]

Among countless examples of Nazi violence and crimes, it was anti-Catholicism on which official attention focused. Nazi concentration and extermination camps symbolised Nazi persecution and murder of Catholics, as illustrated by the mysticism attached to Dachau and Buchenwald. For example, in 1953 the press publicised the beatification of the Italian Princess Mafalda of Savoy, who died in Buchenwald in 1944.[27] However, such a view was not exceptional, and it echoed the Vatican's rhetoric of victimhood over its relationship with Nazism. Pope Pius XII's speech to the cardinals in June 1945 was devoted to the martyrdom of 'millions of brave Catholics, men and women, who gathered around their Bishops, whose brave voice never stopped to resonate until the end of the war' and stated that 'the Holy See, without hesitation, extended progressively its protests to German ombudsmen'.[28]

---

24 'Ojalá que la paz futura se procure asentarla sobre el derecho de grandes y pequeños', *Arriba*, 9 May 1945.

25 'Emoción y serenidad', *Arriba*, 9 May 1945; L de Galinsoga, 'Victoria de Franco', *Arriba*, 8 May 1945; 'La validez de una política', *Arriba*, 27 April 1945.

26 JA Köpfe and M de Juan, *Nazismo contra Cristianismo. Libro Primero: El Hombre y el Mito* (Madrid: Javier Morata Editor, 1946), 46, 82, 51–5, 136 and 161–72; PA Pérez Ruiz, *Lo que el mundo debe a Alemania* (Madrid: s.n., 1946), 5–7.

27 Julián Cortés Cavanillas, 'Se ha reiterado la solicitud de beatificación de la princesa Mafalda, Mártir de Buchenwald', *ABC*, 30 September 1953; Julián Cortés Cavanillas, 'Hace doce años que la Princesa Mafalda de Saboya murió trágicamente en Buchenwald', *ABC*, 2 Oct 1956.

28 'Su Santidad expone ante los cardenales la «radical oposición entre el Estado nacional-socialista y la Iglesia»', *ABC*, 3 June 1945.

III. Anti-Communism and the 'obfuscation' of Nazi crimes

Animosity towards the Soviet Union was a core feature of the Franco dictatorship throughout its existence; the outbreak of the Cold War further enhanced this attitude. Anti-Communism was behind the regime's double standard vis-à-vis Nazism, and pro-Nazi accounts based on this premise were not uncommon. On 2 May 1945, for example, *Arriba* reported that Hitler had died in his restless struggle against Communism and was regarded as a man of 'incredible qualities', whose death, 'unblemished under the terrible German tragedy, deserves more respect, since it is Communist shrapnel that has taken his life'.[29]

The press used a plethora of arguments that distorted the nature of Nazi crimes through such fierce anti-Communist rhetoric. Firstly, the media depicted Nazism, Fascism and Communism as expressions of the un-defined term of Totalitarianism, while remarking that Fascist states arose as a reaction to Socialism and that Communism was the ultimate version of Totalitarianism.[30] Moreover, the official narrative highlighted that in the Soviet Union, anti-Semitism was rife. In May 1945, *Arriba* used a 1930 Romanian publication in order to condemn Soviet persecution of Jews 'as simple evidence that extremes always coincide, from Buchenwald to Kiev', and provided several examples of attacks against Jews, from social exclusion to mass murder.[31] Thirdly, it was stressed that Soviet expansionism used ex-terminatory means to achieve success, as the press reported 'supposed' Soviet plans for exterminating politicians and civil servants in the Balkan region in order to establish Communist systems.[32] Finally, Communist crimes became a useful means for legitimising the very existence of the Franco regime, by exploiting the analogies between the 'graves of Katyń' – referring to the mass execution of Polish soldiers by the Soviet People's Commissariat of Internal Affairs – and Republican crimes in Paracuellos, Aravaca and Torrejon.[33]

Poland epitomised the assertion that Nazi and Soviet crimes were equiv-alent. It was a very convenient scenario, since the official narrative dwelled on the issue of Catholicism against Nazism, and because Poland represen-ted Nazism and Communism as equally Totalitarian systems. In the 1945 book *Europa Liberada* (Europe Freed), José Miralles argued that the Polish

---

29   'Adolfo Hitler ha muerto en su puesto de mando', *Arriba*, 2 May 1945.
30   JM Escudero, 'La batalla de las ideas', *Arriba*, 7 May 1945.
31   'El comunismo ha conseguido recrudecer en Rusia la persecución contra los judíos', *Arriba*, 22 May 1945.
32   'El panorama en los Balcanes es inquietante', *Arriba*, 21 May 1945.
33   'Reprobación, ahora como siempre', *Arriba*, 4 May 1945.

fate under Nazis was not worse than their fate under the Communists, and that in view of crimes such as those in Katyń, Nazi murders were not extraordinary. He believed that 'while Germans just want what is theirs, Bolsheviks, however, gave their first Imperialist bites [to Poland], in order to conquer the country'.[34] Sofia Casanova and Miguel Branicki shared this view in the 1945 publication *El Martirio de Polonia* [The Martyrdom of Poland], a personal testimony in which suffering becomes the leitmotif of Polish national history. Casanova and Branicki drew an analogy between the Communist repression and the tragedy of the Spanish Civil War, and argued that Communists had imitated the Nazi system of concentration camps as a means to control the territory and to eliminate the Jews. Casanova and Branicki gave a detailed account of the Soviet exterminatory policies in Poland, namely the deportation of two million Poles to Siberia and the annihilation of Polish officers in Katyń.[35]

IV. An exceptional case study: 'I was in Mauthausen'

Amid official efforts to eliminate any hint of similarity between Spain and Germany, *Arriba* published daily, for a month, a report entitled 'I was in Mauthausen', by the *Rotspanienkämpfer* Carlos Rodriguez del Risco. This report is an invaluable document with regard to the official view on Nazism and the crimes committed in the camps, which was a very delicate issue, and it shows the extent to which Franco was interested in creating domestic awareness of the deportation of Spaniards – most of whom were Republicans – to the camps.

A careful analysis of del Risco's testimony illustrates the inconsistencies in the official Francoist view on Nazism and its crimes. Firstly, the report omitted any ideological background of the conflict or, in other words, any information about the clash between Fascism and democracy. Del Risco did refer to 'Spaniards' instead of 'Republicans', thus avoiding mentioning the circumstances behind the imprisonment of a Republican exile in a Nazi concentration camp.[36] And yet, this clear omission happened along with a direct signal of sympathy towards Nazis. Del Risco referred to Hitler as a 'great' figure who 'will acquire the greatness and splendour or tragedy that historians will decide'.[37] According to del Risco, Hitler was not to blame

---

34   J Miralles, *Europa Liberada* (s.l.: s.n., 1945), 15–19.
35   S Casanova, M Branicki, *El martirio de Polonia* (Madrid: Atlas, 1945), 85 and 195–208.
36   C Rodriguez del Risco, 'Yo he estado en Mauthausen', *Arriba*, 29 May 1946; ibid., 25 May 1946; ibid., 29 May 1946.
37   C Rodriguez del Risco, 'Yo he estado en Mauthausen', *Arriba*, 7 May 1946.

for the atrocities committed in Nazi camps or for the Wehrmacht; instead, according to del Risco, the responsibility lay specifically with the Gestapo and the SS. In fact, del Risco viewed German soldiers as 'happy, disciplined and patriotic' and unafraid of defeat.[38] Such affinity became, to some extent, ideological. In the very few references to Jews, del Risco showed an openly hostile attitude, viewing them as 'hypocrites, false and egoists' and a 'despicable race' and agreeing with Nazism's ill-treatment of them. He even understood 'the need created by the Hitlerian mind of lebensraum' because of 'the problem of Germany's overpopulation'.[39]

'I was in Mauthausen' shows that any account of the Second World War would need to first of all serve Francoist interests, to legitimise the regime itself. The report is, in fact, an example of the conversion of a Republican into a fierce anti-Republican and anti-Communist, an otherwise typical theme of Francoist propaganda, as seen in films like *Raza*.[40] Being himself a Republican, del Risco exhibited hatred of his own collective, to which he referred as 'murderers of the priests and assaulters of Catholic temples'.[41] He celebrated the imprisonment of the socialist leader Largo Caballero in a Nazi camp: 'The news was no doubt sensational. A Republican tycoon has finally been sent to a concentration camp'.[42]

Moreover, del Risco's report has an increasingly patriotic tone with clear political objectives. Spain symbolises peace 'while the world is bleeding in the war's chaos'.[43] He even highlighted the bravery of Spaniards in Mauthausen.[44] Nazi camps become a place of transformation – the transformation of a man who becomes patriotic, but also a faithful Catholic, both attributes that reach a climax in his eventual return to Spain from Mauthausen. He then declares himself to be a 'soldier of the Church' and a 'loyal servant' of his fatherland, and returns to his beloved country, governed by 'the humble and good, Christian and Spanish figure of the Generalísimo'.[45] Ultimately,

---

38   C Rodriguez del Risco, 'Yo he estado en Mauthausen', *Arriba*, 23 May 1946; ibid., 7 May 1946.
39   C Rodriguez del Risco, 'Yo he estado en Mauthausen', *Arriba*, 1 May 1946.
40   *Raza* was a film directed by José Luis Sáenz de Heredia and written by Franco himself. The film was screened in 1942 and told the story of a family that symbolised the two main ideologies in Spain in the conflict between two brothers during the Civil War. Eventually the Republican would regret of his ideas and became a fierce defender of Franco's cause.
41   C Rodriguez del Risco, 'Yo he estado en Mauthausen', *Arriba*, 30 May 1946.
42   C Rodriguez del Risco, 'Yo he estado en Mauthausen', *Arriba*, 16 May 1946.
43   C Rodriguez del Risco, 'Yo he estado en Mauthausen', *Arriba*, 27 April 1946.
44   C Rodriguez del Risco, 'Yo he estado en Mauthausen', *Arriba*, 30 April 1946.
45   C Rodriguez del Risco, 'Yo he estado en Mauthausen', *Arriba*, 1 June 1946.

this report proves that the mass media exercised a large degree of Francoist control of the remembrance of the Nazi camps.

The extermination of the Jews in the Spanish public sphere: The 1950s and 1960s

The report of Carlos del Risco portrays some of the inconsistencies and contradictions of the postwar official narrative on Nazism and its crimes. This section will focus on whether the aforementioned discourses influenced public responses to the memory of the extermination of the Jews since the late 1950s. Although the nature and length of this article prevents an in-depth analysis, it will provide a glimpse of the official attitude on relevant developments shaping the memory of the extermination of the Jews.

In the years that followed the death of Pope Pius XII in 1958, a number of voices began to question the attitude of the Vatican towards the Jews during the Second World War. The Holy See was criticised for having been too passive and silent with regard to the extermination of the Jews. Works such as Saul Friedländer's *Pius XII and the Third Reich* gave evidence of such passivity, and yet the peak of this controversial issue broke out in many countries such as the United States as a result of Rolf Hochhuth's *The Deputy*, a play about Pius XII and the annihilation of the Jews. On top of that, the 1960s were years of critical changes for the Vatican, resulting from the Second Vatican Council.

Critiques of the Vatican's attitude towards the extermination of the Jews were largely condemned in Spain, partially reflecting tensions at the core of the Spanish Church, a large sector of which was adamantly critical of the Second Vatican Council. Luciano Pereña, representing the conservative trends, deplored the 'sense of guilt' that dominated in the Council and criticised the 'progressive Christians' for blaming Pius XII because, Pereña argued, the 'progressives' were afraid of being called Nazis or enemies of France, Britain and the United States. Pereña was very sensitive to the impact of *The Deputy* and believed that the play was nothing but a plot behind which were the Protestant Church, Bolshevism and 'the interest of the Zionist Movement in relation to the reparations of war that [Zionists] claimed from Germany'.[46] P Félix García argued in *ABC* that Hochhuth was a 'resentful racist' with 'Judaic fervour', pointing out that the memory of Pius XII was being vilified in a way that called to mind the Dark Legend, and

---

46   L Pereña, 'La Operación Vicario', *Arbor* Vol. 65 n251, 48.

indicating that the play had been very well received in the Soviet Union.[47] Similar critiques would be made of Hochhuth's relationship with Nazism and later with Communism and Judaism.[48]

Spaniards generally believed that Pius XII had secretly tried to protect Jews. Manuel Alcover Valle, for example, pointed out that Pius XII had been a 'man of letters' (probably in contrast to a 'man of action') who had been informed about the crimes very late and who had then chosen prudence and silence. Far from being a sign of complicity, argued Alcover Valle, this reaction was a sensible acknowledgement that open condemnation would provoke a much more fierce persecution of Jews. He was stricken that the Vatican was being blamed for passivity when the institution had both resisted Nazism and even suffered terrible crimes at its hands. Interestingly, Alcover Valle remarked that critiques of Pius XII's role during the Second World War were highly relevant domestically, since the pope had been linked to Spain's political position during the war.[49]

In 1961 the State of Israel tried and executed the Nazi officer Adolf Eichmann for complicity in what at that time began to be known as 'the Holocaust'. The public dimension of this trial worldwide marked a turning point in the understanding and relevance of the extermination of the Jews and its remembrance. However, the perception of the Eichmann trial in Franco's Spain was far from the public debates around the nature of executioners that arose in countries like the United States. In Spain, the general opinion about the executioners highlighted that they were all mentally ill – that racism was nothing but mental illness. Luís Álvarez argued that the Nazi leadership 'had hallucinations and that their psyche was abnormal. Hitler believed in astrology (...) Heydrich (...) was dominated by his sexual appetite; the feminine features of Eichmann, who was called 'baby face', made him full of sinister complexes, many of which are still recognisable in the prisoner's reactions'.[50] Álvarez extended such an opinion to the entire German society, who, he believed, were mentally ill.[51]

---

47   Broadly, the Dark Legend was the idea forged in the early 20th century that over the Modern Age a group of intellectuals across Europe (mainly, as was argued, Protestants and Jews) aimed to cause the image of the Spanish Empire to deteriorate. P Félix García, 'De nuevo El Vicario', *ABC*, 4 Mar 1965.

48   See, for example, B Tapia de Renedo, *Pío XII: ¿Inocente o culpable?* (Madrid: Europea de Ediciones, 1972), 99.

49   M Alcover Valle, *Pío XII, el Papa de la paz* (Zalla: Ediciones Paulinas, 1965), 14–15, 36.

50   C Luis Álvarez, 'Es muy posible que Eichman sea un enfermo mental', *Blanco y Negro*, 77–80.

51   ibid.

In addition, Spanish journalists criticised Israel's efforts to unearth memories of the Nazi crimes and to judge the criminals. Such an attitude dated back to the postwar years and, for example, Carlos Sentís, Spain's correspondent for the Nuremberg trials, stated in 1945 that the picture of Dachau was so horrible that it was better to forget it.[52] In 1961, the press criticised how the State of Israel was dealing with the traumatic past of European Jewish communities. Manuel Aznar believed that 'it would be better to forget everything, to silence evocations, bury remembrances, freeze memories and not show pictures of pain that new generations are bored of'. Aznar supported a 'positive' memory that would trigger 'sentiments and love', and not the mistaken Israeli confrontation with its past.[53]

Interestingly, Aznar and other journalists argued that the Jewish religion and Old Testament morality were behind what they believed was Israel's inability to forget and its aim of revenge.[54] Carlos Luís Álvarez argued that the Eichmann trial was a 'religious case', for Jews had a 'religious hatred' that influenced their worldview.[55] Álvarez considered, in contrast, that had Eichmann been judged in a Christian country, the sentencing of the Nazi officer would have been merciful.[56]

Finally, the trial came to symbolise Germany's failed multi-ethnic coexistence and, in contrast, how successful Spain had been in its historical coexistence of Jews, Christians and Moors during the Middle Ages. For example, in response to the Eichmann trial, the journalist Martín Álvarez Chirveches invoked the legacy of Jewish culture in Spain,[57] just as the famous thinker JM Pemán argued that 'Spain has achieved and consolidated in its History, in compensation of its technical or methodological deficits, many of the master-pieces of humanism. The assimilation of the Mozarabs (Christians of the Iberian Peninsula that lived in the Arab Islamic government of Al-Andalus) are among the greatest achievements of human culture, more factual than rhetorical'.[58] According to Pemán, Spain's assimilation of

---

52 See two very important accounts of Carlos Sentís about Nazi Camps in which he is convinced that is necessary to forget the crimes: C Sentís, 'Visita al campo de prisioneros de Dachau', *ABC*, 15 May 1945; also C Sentís, *La paz vista desde Londres* (Barcelona: Tp. Salvador Rosas Bayer, 1945), 17.
53 M Aznar, 'Eichmann', *Blanco y Negro*, 22 April 1961, 28.
54 See ibid., 30.
55 C Luis Álvarez, 'La máquina que ahorcará a Eichmann', *Blanco y Negro*, 27 May 1961, 28–31.
56 C Luis Álvarez, 'Eichmann', *Blanco y Negro*, 09 June 1962, 36.
57 M Álvarez Chirveches, 'Historias de judíos', *ABC*, 05 May 1961.
58 J María Pemán, 'Todavía no', *ABC*, 15 June 1961.

ethnicities had been exceptional in Europe, and he showed great surprise that nobody was aiming to uncover the reasons behind the genocide for which Eichmann was being judged.[59] Moreover, the regime seized the opportunity to emphasise the rescue of Jews undertaken by Franco, which supposedly had caused a profound Sephardic-Jewish appreciation of Spain, and, as the Secretary of Hispanidad announced at that moment, the regime was planning to strengthen Spanish-Sephardic relations.[60]

Conclusions

This article has uncovered the main ideological driving forces behind the shaping of Franco Spain's official view on Nazism and the extermination of the Jews. A combination of official silence, the defence of Catholicism and the exploitation of anti-Communism were all key ideological motivations behind the official narrative of the annihilation of the Jews. This confusing and often contradictory approach had consequences in the following decades, as shown in the public reactions to international critiques of Pius XII or in how the Eichmann trial was received. However, future extended analysis is needed to provide a further account of the effects of Francoist politics of the memory of Nazism and the extermination of the Jews in relation to both Spanish anti-Semitism and the worldwide impact of the 'Holocaust mass media'. Ultimately, it should reflect on whether the extermination of the Jews is truly, to use Jeffrey Alexander's term, a 'moral universal'[61] and whether the Spanish case underpins scholarly arguments on the existence of a European memoryscape of the extermination of the Jews.[62]

This issue will not only provide new academic insights into the politics of memory in dictatorial regimes. Domestically, it will provide a completely new topic through which Franco's regime can be analysed, which will be free from the tiresome (and vested) politicisation of Spain's recent history and will offer a new perspective on Francoist repression that does not consist purely of Civil War memoirs.

59   J María Pemán, 'Todavía no', *ABC*, 15 June 1961.
60   'La labor de España por los Sefarditas', *ABC*, 10 Sep 1961.
61   See JC Alexander, 'On the social construction of moral universals: The "Holocaust" from war crime to trauma drama', *European Journal of Social Theory*, vol. 5, n1, 2002.
62   D Levy and N Sznaider, 'Memory unbound. The Holocaust and the formation of cosmopolitan memory', *European Journal of Social Theory*, vol. 5 n1, 2002.

Part III

Perceptions and representations: Present

Chapter 6

LOOKING OUT FROM UNDER
A LONG SHADOW

Holocaust memory in 21st century America

Laura S Levitt

Prelude

As I returned to the text of my talk following the Aftermath conference I
was struck by the radical disconnect between my presentation and the kinds
of historical work that marked the other plenary sessions. In what follows
I want to offer a kind of prelude to my paper to explain how, and in what
ways, my work is both distinct from and connected to those more historical
presentations. In fact what I want to do here is to ask readers to consider how
this very contrast is itself a part of the politics of Holocaust memory and its
future.

My scholarly work on the Holocaust is part of a long-standing American
conversation about Holocaust memory and questions of representation and
commemoration.[1] This scholarly conversation does not presuppose that 'never

---

1   This scholarship includes works by numerous scholars especially those with
     training in literature, religion and visual culture. Classic and more recent work
     in this tradition include: James Young, *Writing and Rewriting the Holocaust*
     (Bloomington: Indiana University Press, 1988); Saul Friedländer: *Probing the
     Limits of Representation: Nazism and the 'Final Solution'* (Cambridge: Harvard
     University Press, 1992); Shoshana Feldman and Dori Laub, *Testimony: Crisis
     of Witnessing in Literature, Psychoanalysis, and History* (New York: Routledge,
     1991); Marianne Hirsch, *Family Frames: Photography, Narrative, and Postmemory*
     (Cambridge: Harvard University Press, 1996); Julia Epstein and Lori Lefkovitz,
     ed. *Shaping Losses: Cultural Memory and the Holocaust* (Urbana: University of
     Illinois Press, 2001); Barbie Zelizer, ed. *Visual Culture and the Holocaust* (New
     Brunswick: Rutgers University Press, 2000); Leo Spitzer, *Hotel Bolivia: The*

forgetting' is a foregone conclusion or, better yet, that the need to remember the Holocaust is itself a self-evident proposition. Instead, in this tradition, my paper is an intervention into the question of how to keep Holocaust memory alive for generations increasingly removed from the immediacy of these historic events.

My work is about the future of Holocaust memory, arguing against certain truisms in the commemoration of the Holocaust, like 'never forget'. I ask how we might keep commemorative and historical sites like the United States Holocaust Memorial Museum (USHMM) compelling and important to visitors and viewers who are neither the children nor the grandchildren of survivors. I am interested in addressing the vast majority of those who now visit the USHMM in Washington, DC – including most Jewish visitors – who come without such intimate connections to the Holocaust. Towards this end, my work challenges what have become set ways of engaging Holocaust memory, in which other losses must pale in comparison and otherwise be deferred. I question this stance precisely because I am not convinced of its ability to bring new generations into this particular historical legacy. My concern is with the exclusivity of precisely this well-meaning stance of deferral, its lack of elasticity, and therefore its inability to speak to or compel generations further removed from this history to engage as meaningfully as possible with the legacy of the Holocaust.

What does it mean to keep Holocaust memory alive? In this brief essay I argue that such remembrance entails a risk – the risk of allowing all kinds of visitors to bring their own ghosts with them to sites of Holocaust commemoration, not to conflate these memories with the Holocaust and its victims, but rather to let these different losses touch each other. This touching offers a new possibility for keeping the legacy of the Holocaust alive. This touching is key to a kind of living memory, a form of memorialisation which is plastic, rather than static, and very much alive.

Culture of Memory in a Refuge from Nazism (New York: Hill and Wang, 1998); Ernst Van Alphen, *Caught by History: Holocaust Effects in Contemporary Art, Literature and Theory* (Stanford: Stanford University Press, 1998); Oren Stier, *Committed to Memory: Cultural Mediation of the Holocaust* (Amherst: University of Massachusetts Press, 2003); Sara Horowitz, *Voicing the Void: Muteness and Memory in Holocaust Fiction* (Albany: SUNY University Press, 1997); Michael Rothberg, *Multidirectional Memory: Remembering the Holocaust in an Age of Decolonization* (Stanford: Stanford University Press, 2009); Brett Kaplan, *Unwanted Beauty: Aesthetic Pleasure in Holocaust Representation* (Urbana: University of Illinois Press, 2007); Susan Suleiman, *Crises of Memory and the Second World War* (Durham: Duke University Press, 2008).

CHAPTER 6

Building on literary scholar Marianne Hirsch's notion of 'postmemory',[2] in what follows, I reconsider how the visual works of artists of the second and third generations, such as Art Spiegelman and Lori Novak, exemplify what this touching looks like. I use these artistic works to explain my own response to Yaffa Eliach's photographic memorial, the Tower of Faces at the USHMM, to demonstrate how this alternative form of remembrance works. These artistic works helps us see and understand how memory remains alive when it is always already intermingling with the legacies of other times and other places. It is this intermingling that stimulates a desire to want to know more, to probe more deeply, to look more closely and, in so doing, to keep the legacy of the Holocaust vivid and compelling.

the endless fields of hair
Like these, my despised ancestors
I have become a keeper of accounts.

I do not shun this legacy. I claim it as mine whenever I see the photographs of nameless people. Standing staring off the edge of the picture. People dressed in coats lined with fur. Or ragged at elbows and collar. Hats cocked on one side glancing anxiously towards the lens. A peasant cap centered and ordinary. Hair styled in the latest fashion. Or standing ashamed a coarse wig awkwardly fitted. The shabby clothes. Buttons missing. The elegant stance. Diamond rings. Gold teeth. The hair being shaved. The face of humiliation. The hand holding the child's hand. A tree. A track. A vague building in a photograph. A facility. And then the fields of hair endless fields of hair the earth growing fertile with their bodies with their souls. (Irena Klepfisz, *'Bashert'*)[3]

What does it mean to be a 'keeper of accounts'? How do we preserve memory? And which memories get to be remembered? Which memories are worth preserving? These are some of the questions posed by poet Irena Klepfisz in this the last prose section of her poem 'Bashert'. After the Holocaust how might it be possible to imagine remembering anything but this overpowering legacy of loss, 'the fields of hair the endless fields of hair'? And yet, Klepfisz's narrator does not limit the accounts she keeps

---

2   See Marianne Hirsch, *Family Frames*.
3   Irena Klepfisz, 'Bashert', *A Few Words in the Mother Tongue: Poems Selected and New (1971–1990)* (Portland, OR: Eighth Mountain Press, 1990), 200.

only to the legacy of the Holocaust. For her, Jewish memory is replete with images and stereotypes of Jews extending backward and forward in time and space. She invokes a full range of Jewish figures, wealthy and poor, fashionable and shabby, humiliated and arrogant, and sometimes just plain ordinary. By addressing the images of these Jews, especially photographs, the narrator insists on the act of remembering, of 'keeping account' of all of these ancestors all-too-often despised by others.

Like this narrator, I too, am interested in keeping account, of re-membering Jewish pasts in the aftermath of the Holocaust.[4] And, like Klepfisz, I want to question what has been remembered since the Holocaust and raise a note of caution. Lest we forget everything but the Holocaust, I want to open up the act of remembering to include other 20th and even 21st century Jewish legacies of loss. I want to insist on seeing the ordinary and the arrogant, the despised and the beloved and always 'the endless fields of hair'. I want to use photographs, ordinary photographs, family images as a way of bringing together these disparate legacies of Jewish life. I want to use these images to take seriously the everyday legacies of loss within the lives of ordinary American Jews,[5] the more quotidian losses that

---

4   By way of explanation for the form of scholarly address deployed in this chapter, which builds on much of the scholarly work cited in note 1 above but also on feminist and literary studies more broadly, it might be helpful to reiterate some of what I argue for in the introduction to Laura Levitt, *American Jewish Loss after the Holocaust* (New York: NYU Press, 2007), 1–14.

    I offer an experiment in both form and content ... What I am trying to come up with is a way to illuminate how academic work matters and a way to bring both the broader reading public and academics into this process. I also want to make clearer the intimate stakes that animate most academic work (6).

    Although I have in places polished some more colloquial phrasing, this chapter builds on these commitments to experimentation in academic voice including the use of the first person. For more on these practices, see some of the following classic texts: Susan Rubin Suleiman, *Risking Who One Is: Encounters with Contemporary Art and Literature* (Cambridge, MA: Harvard University Press, 1994); Marianna Torgovnick, ed., *Eloquent Obsessions: Writing Cultural Criticism* (Durham, NC: Duke University Press, 1994); Nancy K Miller, *Getting Personal: Feminist Occasions and Other Autobiographical Acts* (New York: Routledge, 1991); Nancy K Miller, *But Enough about Me: Why We Read Other People's Lives* (New York: Columbia University Press, 2002).

5   My efforts here to hold the legacies of ordinary and extraordinary loss together in relation to American Jews and the Holocaust have been greatly enhanced and inspired by the efforts of many queer scholars to hold together precisely these kinds of fraught and tense relationships between different kinds and different magnitudes of loss. See Ann Cvetkovich, *An Archive of Feelings: Trauma, Sexuality, and Lesbian Public Cultures* (Durham: Duke University Press, 2003); 'Public sentiments'," Ann Cvetkovich and Ann Pellegrini, ed., *The Scholar and the Feminist Online*, 2.1 (Summer 2003), www.barnard.edu/sfonline; David Eng and David

have all too often been overshadowed by the devastating destruction of European Jewish life that is the Shoah to make clear how different losses touch each other.

For American Jews like me, born well after the war, Jews with no familial ties to the Holocaust, these contradictory desires and experiences are common. Taking possession of the Holocaust is dangerous, as is looking elsewhere to these other, more familiar Jewish legacies in order to identify ourselves as Jews. To either adopt the Holocaust as one's own or to pay attention to these other Jewish images and stories remains somehow shameful or selfish. Taking on the Holocaust as if it were one's own is an appropriation and turning to these other more ordinary stories and images of Jewish life is somehow a betrayal of the Holocaust and all of those who died. This is especially so for an academic engaged in contemporary Jewish studies. After all, how can I possibly want to use my time and energy to address common stories after the Holocaust? How can I not devote my scholarship to this critical Jewish legacy? How can anything else measure up to this central task? And how can I ask others to follow me into this seemingly less urgent domain? And yet, in order to imagine a different future where memory remains alive, I believe it is necessary to risk challenging these assumptions, because part of what makes the family photographs of European Jews whose lives were destroyed by the Holocaust so compelling to so many of us in the present is that they are traces of what were precious ordinary lives. How can we allow their deaths at the hands of the Nazis to efface what these images once meant to those who held them?

Kazanjian, ed. *Loss: The Politics of Mourning*, (Berkeley: University of California Press, 2003). In part, *Loss* is both closest and most removed from my project here. On the one hand the editors attempt to displace the centrality of the Holocaust in scholarship on mourning and trauma to make room for considering all kinds of other losses; on the other hand, the Nazi Holocaust disappears. It is an absent presence in this powerful text. Although I am moved and persuaded by the editors' efforts to address other losses more fully, I also regret that in the process the text as a whole displaces the Holocaust, when *decentring* might have been a more instructive approach to shifting the focus of trauma studies away from an almost exclusive engagement with the Nazi Holocaust. As a Jewish-studies scholar writing about other less extraordinary Jewish losses, I cannot make this kind of move in my own work, nor do I find it productive. In the case of *American Jewish Loss after the Holocaust*, such a move would do violence to the ways that the Holocaust has become a part of even the most ordinary tales of Jewish loss. I thank Ann Pellegrini for recommending that I look at many of these works.

The Holocaust Memorial Museum, Washington, DC, 1994: The Tower of Faces

Like many Americans, one of the most powerful aspects of my first visit to the Holocaust Memorial Museum in Washington, DC was the Tower of Faces. It was entering and then returning to these seemingly ordinary images of Jewish life, the visual archive of a single Eastern European town, that captured my imagination.

These photographs fascinated me. I was drawn to their familiarity. I had to keep reminding myself of their poignancy, the fact that all of these people's lives as depicted in these photographs had been destroyed by the Holocaust. There was something about seeing familiar Jewish faces, postures and poses in this public space in the capital of the United States that moved me. I wanted to imagine these people as figures from my own more intimate Jewish past. I wanted these photographs to be those of my own family's albums. And in the midst of this fantasy, I caught myself. I remembered where I was and what had happened to these people. I realised that I was not at the Smithsonian or some other national museum but at the Holocaust museum. In this place these seemingly ordinary images could not be so familiar. Unlike my family's photographs, these images were the traces of a community of families, specific lives brutally destroyed by the Nazis. They offer tantalisingly familiar visions of European Jewish life before the Nazis. Yet these homes, these communal, social and cultural organisations and institutions, these everyday lives were irreparably damaged even for those few who survived.

Compared to virtually all of the other images in the museum, these photographs were a relief. The architecture and design of the permanent exhibition seem to recognise this dimension of the Tower by allowing visitors to return to this display again and again. Visitors enter and re-enter the Tower at two different levels, from two different vantage points and, although the photographs continue up beyond our gaze, we are allowed to see what is visible from more than one perspective. From each, we encounter families, friends and lovers, a whole world of intimacies populated by so many different faces. In the museum, we are invited to take another look.

And yet, even as we are able to get ever closer to more and more of these photographs, we are reminded of our distance from them. We look up and see all of those we will never encounter, images upon images materialising the extent to which the totality of the losses of even this one town remains

The Tower of Faces (the Yaffa Eliach Shtetl Collection) in the
Permanent Exhibition at the U.S. Holocaust Memorial Museum.

Reproduced courtesy of the United States Holocaust Memorial Museum.
Photograph # N03043. Photo by Edward Owen.

out of reach, outside of our comprehension. These are the impressions I have carried with me.[6]

It is difficult for me to write about this visit and these lasting impressions. It has been a number of years since I was last at the museum. Part of what interests me is that these are the impressions that have lingered. What do these impressions say about the attraction of this display for other American Jews, like me, who are not the children of survivors and have no known relatives who died or survived the Holocaust?[7]

In part, I feel as if I am saying something obvious. And yet, I want to resist the presumption that there is a normal or natural response to this place or this display, because I am increasingly convinced that the imposition of such a norm defeats the purpose of such exhibits. By owning our own memories I want to begin to challenge the assertion of such norms of appropriate reception of Holocaust materials. In other words, I hope to show you what viewers like me bring to such places. And explain why we linger each time we enter the Tower, wishing that these were our family's photographs on the walls. And why so many of us wish that the Holocaust were our story, knowing full well how horrible this story is.

American Jews and the desire to be included in Jewish history

For many American Jews, the desire to be included in the narrative of the Holocaust is expressed literally in efforts to seek out such connection.[8] I believe that the American Jews who do genealogical research in order to find European relatives who died or survived the Holocaust do so in order to feel like they and their families' histories matter. They are desperate to see themselves as a part of an acknowledged history. They do this despite

---

6   The account I present here is intentionally schematic. It is not intended to be a thorough account of the exhibition but rather the impressions that have lingered. For a more careful and systematic account, see my reading of Marianne Hirsch's account of the Tower of Faces and how it functions within the Holocaust Memorial Museum later in this piece.

7   This process is something that I have also experienced. In *Jews and Feminism: The Ambivalent Search for Home* (New York: Routledge, 1997,) I told the story of my father's uncle Shmuel as my father had told it to me, only to discover after the book was published that Shmuel had been a prisoner of war after being captured as a soldier in the Soviet army. This is what accounted for his diminished health. I am grateful to my second cousin Phil Pearl for offering me this other explanation and correcting what my father had told me.

8   This, too, is not a simple matter. See, for example, Daniel Mendelsohn, *The Lost* (New York: Harper Collins, 1996).

the emotional costs of such revelations.[9] For me, this is only part of the story. It is not so much that I want to place myself in this specific already formed and authorised narrative; rather, I want a place for my own stories of loss. By resisting the notion that compared to the Holocaust our much more ordinary stories of American Jewish loss do not measure up, I am looking at another dimension of what happens at Holocaust memorials and museums and, in so doing, I challenge the notion that these other stories of loss are somehow unworthy, not important enough to merit either my own attention or a broader and more public appraisal in their own right.

To this end, I want to let myself stay with what I have come to recognise as my own desire for my family photographs to be seen, my longing to acknowledge my family and its grief on display, and, by staying with these contradictory desires, I want to appreciate what is lost when the Holocaust overshadows these other Jewish legacies. Again, I need to stress that these are not desires that one is supposed to have. They do not conform to the set framework or cultural expectations that have come to shape how American Jews are supposed to approach the Holocaust. Those acceptable engagements do not include these longings. At this historical moment, these other desires are not normative.

Before moving on to this other way of engaging the past, I want to return to the Tower of Faces to explain more fully how these normative practices work. In the case of the Tower, viewers are supposed to identify with those depicted in the photographs.[10] We are supposed to make some connections between them and us, our families and these families, our communities and theirs. We are not, though, ultimately supposed to linger on this connection. Instead, we are supposed to see this portion of our engagement as but one

---

9   After describing my project to an acquisitions editor at a university press, he shared with me a story about his own family and their literal efforts to find their connections to the Holocaust. After extensive research they discovered a distant relative whose life had been lost in the Holocaust. This revelation was met with great joy and excitement. The family was somehow made more real. They were a part of 20th century Jewish history in a way they had never been before this discovery.

10   This logic was also at the heart of the museum's deployment of 'identity cards' to be used throughout the museum. Initially these cards were to encourage visitors to literally identify with a single individual and see what happened to them at various points in their life that correspond to the temporal logic of the permanent exhibit. See Andrea Liss, 'The identity card project and the Tower of Faces at the United States Holocaust Memorial Museum', in *Trespassing Through Shadows: Memory, Photography, and the Holocaust* (Minneapolis: University of Minnesota Press, 1998), 13–38. See also Susan Derwin's account of the plotting of the Wiesenthal Museum of Tolerance in LA, Susan Derwin, 'Sense and/or sensation: The role of the body in Holocaust pedagogy', in Shelley Hornstein, Laura Levitt and Laurence Silberstein, ed., *Impossible Images: Contemporary Art after the Holocaust* (New York: NYU Press, 2003), 245–259.

step in a linear progression. Identification is merely the first step towards a teleological end. Ultimately the exhibit is supposed to encourage us to build on this heightened sense of identification in order to begin to recognise the devastation of the Holocaust. In other words, we are supposed to experience the horror more personally through our familiarity with family photographs, but ultimately our individual encounters are supposed to be dwarfed by the grander vision of devastation and loss that is the Holocaust. Even the loss in just this one small East European town is exponentially beyond anything most of us could ever begin to imagine.

In many ways, my own reaction conformed to this agenda, but what haunts me still is not so much this sanctioned narration but something more excessive in my desire to connect to those faces. It also seems to me that this excess resonates deeply with the logic of the permanent exhibit as a whole pointing to another way of understanding our relationship to this past. Visitors to the museum are encouraged to go back to this site as a part of their journey through the museum. And, even as they linger in other places, they are never far from the Tower. Through cutouts and bridges, we keep finding ourselves near but unable to ever touch these faces. We catch glimpses of them even when we are not in the actual Tower.

Our return to the photographs again and again in terms of the actual architectural space of the Museum enacts not so much the authorised narrative of the display but the kinds of longings I have described. What did it mean that I did not find myself in this strangely definitive Jewish family photo album?

Seeing the connections, knowing the differences

And so, I return to where I began. I am left with my desire to see my ordinary Jewish family on display in Washington, DC, my longing to have these uncanny European Jews somehow be my own. On the one hand, the desire I am addressing is very much about placing myself in this very specific historical narrative, the catastrophic central narrative of 20th century Jewish history, the Holocaust,[11] but it is also about imagining something else entirely. It is about recognising and legitimating the more ordinary tales of, in my case, East European Jews who had already established themselves

---

11   In this chapter I look specifically at this mythic narrative but also want to acknowledge that there is another related narrative, the story of the State of Israel and the recreation of a Jewish homeland in Palestine. On these issues and especially the interrelationship between these stories, see Sidra Ezrahi, *Booking Passage: Exile and Homecoming in Modern Jewish Imagination* (Berkeley: University of California Press, 2000).

in America during this same historical moment.[12] What might happen if we imagine that these other narratives and images are worthy of public recognition? What might it mean to own the fact that these Jews also long to be seen? And ironically, why is it that even to broach the topic of these other images, I find myself having to begin in the Holocaust museum?

As I will argue, American Jews need to engage the Holocaust because it provides, at least at the present moment, one of the only legitimate, morally permissible route to these other legacies. At least from this starting place we may begin to recast our understanding of 20th-century Jewish history as a series of interrelated legacies. Exhibits like the Tower of Faces enable us to confront the Holocaust in such a way that we can also allow ourselves to engage these other legacies of loss and disappointment.

Marianne Hirsch: Postmemory

In the spring of 1996, many years ago now, I went to Haverford College to hear literary critic Marianne Hirsch give a talk about family pictures and Holocaust memory. When Hirsch visited the United States Holocaust Memorial Museum, she thought a great deal about the role of photographs in preserving and transmitting Holocaust memory, connecting these images to her notion of 'postmemory'. (In *Family Frames*, she writes 'Do pictures provide the second- and third-generation questioner with a more concrete, a better access to the abandoned parental world than stories can? Or, as indexical traces, do they perhaps provide too direct and material a connection to the past?'[13])

According to Hirsch, postmemory is tied to the particular cultural, historical and intellectual context of the second half of the 20th century. As she explains in *Family Frames*, her book about photography and memory, 'Art Spiegelman's *Maus* functions as a paradigmatic and generative text'.[14]

---

12   I am also interested in the various narratives, images and stories that other non-Eastern European Jews might bring to the museum, much less non-Jewish visitors. Here I would be especially curious about the kinds of Jewish family stories someone like the American Jewish artist Shimon Attie, whose family comes from Syria, might bring to this exhibit. This kind of identification across these Jewish legacies, especially in relation to the Holocaust, is not something that Attie has addressed thus far in his work, although he has done some work on American Jewish memory with his 'Between Dreams and History,, which projected writing on the walls of the Lower East Side of Manhattan in 1998. See Michelle Friedman's discussion of this work in relation to his work on Holocaust memory in her essay 'Haunted by memory: American Jewish transformations', in *Impossible Images*, 31–50.

13   Hirsch, 248.

14   ibid., 12.

Hirsch goes on to explain that Art Spiegelman's delayed, indirect, secondary memory captures best what she means by postmemory.

> *Maus* is a familial story, collaboratively constructed by father and son. The Spiegelman/Zylberberg families have lived through the massive devastation of the Holocaust, and thus the details of family interaction are inflected by a history that refuses to remain in the background or outside the text. Their story is told, drawn, by the son, who was born after the war but whose life was decisively determined by this familial and cultural memory.[15]

Postmemory works as an ambivalent practice that captures both Spiegelman's 'passionate interest and desire' in terms of his parents' history and his 'inevitable distance and lack of understanding' of this same legacy.[16] According to Hirsch, it is this deferred, mediated, secondary memory that has cast its shadow over contemporary life and helps explain the power of family photographs in the museum in Washington, DC. As she explains, these photographs help bring whole new generations of viewers into this realm: 'at their best they allow viewers with little connection to the Holocaust both Jewish and non-Jewish visitors alike to imaginatively identify with … the memory of survivor children'.[17]

'Past Lives' revisited, 2003

In the final chapter of her book *Family Frames*, Hirsch uses an image by artist Lorie Novak to frame her argument, explaining:

> I choose as my chapter title and emblem 'Past Lives', a 1987 photograph by the Jewish American artist Lorie Novak. 'Past Lives' is a photograph of a composite projection onto an interior wall. Novak populates this domestic space with a picture of the Jewish children hidden in Izieu and eventually deported by Klaus Barbie, superimposed on a picture of Ethel Rosenberg's face [accused Soviet spy and Jewish mother convicted and executed for espionage in the early 1950s by the United States], superimposed on a childhood image, from the 1950's, of Novak herself held by her mother.[18]

---

15   ibid., 12–13.
16   ibid., 13.
17   ibid., 249.
18   ibid., 246.

'Past Lives (for the children of Izieu)', Lorie Novak 1987
(Original in colour)
www.lorienovak.com
Reproduced courtesy of Lorie Novak.

For Hirsch, this layered photographic work clearly enacts the aesthetics of postmemory. It brings together 'many ghosts', connecting public and private memories as well as different temporal moments and geographic places. Here Holocaust memory and American memories are intermingled in the intimacy of the all too familiar figure of mother and child. For Hirsch, this work 'begins to define the aesthetic strategies of mourning and reconstruction of her [Novak's] generation of postmemory'.[19] Like the various images Hirsch discusses, this work is haunting. Here, 'space and time are conflated to reveal memory's material presence'.[20] This is how, according to Hirsch, art and memorial works enact postmemory. And yet, I am struck by this notion of Novak's 'own generation'.

As I see it, what happens as viewers encounter the intimate images in the Tower of Faces is not homogenous. Hirsch emphasises through her repeated use of the phrase 'at its best' that the Tower and the Museum in Washington, DC 'elicit in its visitors an imaginary identification – the desire to know and to feel, the curiosity and passion that shape the postmemory of survivor children', and that, '*At its best*, it would include all of its visitors in the generation of postmemory'.[21] I disagree with this assessment.

For those of us with no direct ties to survivors such inclusion is not possible. Instead, within the Tower, our own ghosts confront us.[22] For us, the challenge is to distinguish between the various layers of desire that both separate and connect us to these faces. In part, this means seeing more clearly what separates me from Lorie Novak and each of us from various children of survivors. It also means seeing the distances among and between those of that first generation of postmemory.[23] Here, even at its best, the generation of children of survivors does not share a single position, especially in relation to the Tower of Faces.

---

19   ibid.
20   ibid.
21   ibid., 249 (my emphasis).
22   On this question of ghosts, see Avery Gordon, *Ghostly Matters: Haunting and the Sociological Imagination* (Minneapolis: University of Minnesota Press, 1997).
23   For a clearer account of the ways Lori Lefkovitz's position differs from Hirsch's see Lori Lefkovitz, 'Inherited memory and the ethics of ventriloquism', *Shaping Losses*, 220–230. In this essay Lefkovitz offers what she describes as 'an alternative to the concept of postmemory through a reading of ambiguity in a family photograph'. As she goes on to explain in this essay her notion of inherited memory is about ambivalence. For Lefkovitz, even as a child of survivors, what she experiences is her own 'dynamic, confused, and mixed reaction to the "entitlements" of proximity to the Holocaust'. E-mail to Laura Levitt, June 2004. Again I am grateful to Lori for her help in clarifying and nuancing these distinctions even for children of survivors, something I conjecture but I appreciate having this reference back to her essay to help substantiate the claim.

The Tower lends itself to a broad range of responses. In other words, in the Tower the gap between those with personal connections to the Holocaust and each other, much less those of us without these ties, is *never* bridged.[24] If anything, at its best, the gap is made wider, creating a space where images and memories of other times and other places, other losses, can all come together. It is in this gapping space that images like those offered in Lorie Novak's 'Past Lives' find their place. It is here that postwar and even pre-war memories become visible. Although they are often shaded by the legacy of the Holocaust, as in Novak's work, they are not effaced. They seep through. If we don't turn away and instead look more closely, we see the faces of Ethel Rosenberg and Lorie Novak and her mother as they fade in and out of the faces of the deported children.

By acknowledging this layering as ongoing, I do not believe that the Tower can bring those of us without personal connections to the Shoah into the generation of children of survivors. As I see it, Hirsch's insistence on a single stance reinforces the dominant American Jewish legacy of privileging the Holocaust to the exclusion of other memories in its current norm of commemoration. This is the desire I want to challenge. By rigidly safeguarding against the Holocaust's displacement by any other legacies, a justifiable fear becomes all consuming, keeping us from seeing those other losses, those other pasts that we necessarily bring to our engagement with the Holocaust. Ironically, by not acknowledging these other memories, I believe we are kept from more fully appreciating all that the Holocaust means for us in the present. Instead, through the interplay of connections and differences between ordinary and extraordinary losses, we come to understand how all of these losses are a part of our everyday lives. This is how they remain alive and meaningful in the present. In other words, this recognition of connections and distinctions is how we keep Holocaust memory alive and vital.

Other lives, other losses, other legacies

Although the circle of those who remember may expand, this opening up is not about allowing more people to participate vicariously in any single experience of children of survivors and/or the children of exiled Jews; instead this is an expansive process. Here, remembering the Holocaust is about owning our own memories of loss and letting them help us more fully appreciate what

---

24   Hirsch, 251.

A group of students views the Tower of Faces (Yaffa Eliach Shtetl Collection) in the permanent exhibition of the U.S. Holocaust Memorial Museum.

Reproduced courtesy of the United States Holocaust Memorial Museum. Photo # N09406. Photo by Max Reid.

the Holocaust denied to so many others. In other words, we reanimate the pictures in the Tower with 'our own knowledge of daily life'.[25]

In order to do this, we need to be open to all of the other losses that we and others necessarily bring to the Tower, including the legacies of those beside us in this place. Only by recognising *all* of these layered memories can we begin to make distinctions between what is and is not our own. As I see it, we are obliged *not* to try to lose ourselves in other people's pasts, but instead to take more seriously the stuff of our own more intimate memories of loss so that we can begin to see the boundaries that distinguish ourselves from others. In this way, we can avoid the kinds of vicarious appropriations of other people's experiences that often mar even well-meaning engagements with those who suffer. The kind of engagement I am suggesting acknowledges the desires and experiences that viewers bring to the Tower to be acknowledged. By more fully bringing these often more intimate legacies of loss together with the photographs on display in the Tower of Faces we can begin to touch, in Hirsch's words, 'the death that took those lives so violently'.[26] It is the interplay between these disparate memories that animates the Holocaust for us in the present.[27]

I want to suggest that it is only possible for us to see ourselves in relation to the Holocaust through the shadows and layers of the various memories, both public and private, that we bring to these other images, not by trying to assume the position of a generation, the generation of children of survivors who themselves do not share a single stance. Instead, it is our ongoing engagement with the ghosts who haunt all of our different imaginations that continues to shape our positions in the present. This kind of engagement makes it possible for us to touch the legacy of Holocaust. This happens in much the same way that Lorie Novak's installation works. It works by including postwar and American Jewish legacies as the templates that make visible and tangible this more distant legacy.

This more mediated shaded and shadowed engagement with Holocaust images preserves the tensions between connections and differences at the heart of photography's allusive and elusive presence. Without a single ideal stance, distinctions are maintained. We can be more honest about the lack of fit between ourselves and others, our memories and theirs. By not striving to find consensus, there is less chance of misappropriation. Given this, although

---

25   ibid., 256.

26   ibid., 256.

27   For more on this notion of Holocaust effects, see Ernst van Alphen, *Caught by History*.

the generation of children of survivors has clearly helped shape and define our understanding of the displaced memories of all of us who come after, this process has not produced a single stance; nor should it. Instead, the process of identification offers an ever-expanding range of positions, bringing a much more diverse and varied range of Americans, both Jewish and not Jewish, into the realm of commemoration.[28] In this way, it is my hope and belief that we in the United States are going to be able to continue to keep the memory of the Holocaust alive and meaningful as this history becomes more distant.

Acknowledgements

The author is grateful to the artist Lorie Novak for allowing her to reproduce her work. She thanks the United States Holocaust Memorial Museum for the reproduction of images of The Tower of Faces. The views and opinions expressed in this chapter and in this book, and the context in which these images are used, do not necessarily reflect the views or policies of, nor imply approval or endorsement by, the United State Holocaust Memorial Museum.

This essay is adapted from chapter one of *American Jewish Loss After the Holocaust* with permission from New York University Press.

---

28 This helps explain the differences among and between the various French Jewish writers and artists Hirsch discusses as well as the differences between Lori Lefkovitz's stance and Hirsch's. Some of these writers and artists include Christian Boltanski, Raczymow, Finkelkraut, and the psychotherapist Nadine Fresco. For her discussion of these artists and writers see *Family Frames*, 241–246.

Chapter 7

THE PLACE OF MEMORY OR THE MEMORY OF PLACE?

The representation of Auschwitz in Holocaust memoirs

Esther Jilovsky

In 2010, 1.33 million people visited Auschwitz – nearly triple the number recorded in 2001.[1] Not only as 'Poland's major tourist attraction' and 'a site of mass tourism'[2] does the site of Auschwitz play a significant role in contemporary collective Holocaust memory, but its function as a symbol of the Holocaust as 'an icon of evil'[3] means that its significance extends far beyond that suggested by the physical site of the former Nazi death camp. Visits to Auschwitz are a form of 'dark tourism' – John Lennon and Malcolm Foley's term for visiting sites related to death and disaster[4] – which assumes an inextricable link between a place and the events that occurred there. This explicit connection between place and event is also the driving force behind visits to Holocaust sites recounted in memoirs by the second and third generations – the children and grandchildren of Holocaust survivors, respectively – many of whom visit

---

1   '2013 Report Auschwitz-Birkenau State Museum', (Oświęcim: Państwowe Muzeum, Auschwitz-Birkenau w Oświęcimiu, 2014), 20. In 2001 492,500 visitors were recorded at Auschwitz.

2   Jack Kugelmass, 'Why we go to Poland: Holocaust tourism as secular ritual', in James E Young, ed., *The Art of Memory: Holocaust Memorials in History* (New York & Munich: Prestel, 1994), 175–83, 178.; Jochen Spielmann, 'Auschwitz is debated in Oświęcim: the topography of remembrance', in Young, *The Art of Memory*, 169–73.

3   Dan Stone, 'Beyond the "Auschwitz syndrome": Holocaust historiography after the Cold War', *Patterns of Prejudice*, 44/5 (2010), 454–68, 456.

4   John Lennon and Malcolm Foley, *Dark Tourism: The Attraction of Death and Disaster* (London & New York: Continuum, 2000), 3.

these places, sometimes together with the survivors themselves. To these descendants who have no direct experience of the Holocaust, visiting the places where it happened offers a chance to become closer to it, thereby increasing their understanding of the Holocaust in the context of its effect on their lives. However, for Holocaust survivors who were interred at Auschwitz, visiting the contemporary site is a different act entirely: it is revisiting a site of trauma which occurred in the past. Narratives of return in survivor memoirs show that visiting Auschwitz exposes a rupture in the vast differences between the site during the Holocaust and afterwards.[5]

By comparing the descriptions of visiting Auschwitz recounted in survivor memoirs with those by the second and third generations, this chapter will shed light on the evolution of Auschwitz as a focal site for perpetuating Holocaust memory. The analysis of survivor memoirs will reveal how the contemporary site of Auschwitz diverges from their memories of it; however, it will also be shown that according to second- and third-generation memoirs, visits to contemporary Auschwitz inform its representation. It will argue that survivors and their descendants have different notions of Auschwitz. This chapter deploys the term 'postmemorial Auschwitz' to refer to the postwar site visited as a tourist attraction, and thus the only version of Auschwitz to be experienced by the second and third generations. Taken from Marianne Hirsch's concept of postmemory, which 'is distinguished from memory by generational distance and from history by deep personal connection', the notion of postmemorial Auschwitz particularly draws on Hirsch's observation that '[p]ostmemory is a powerful and very particular form of memory precisely because its connection to its object or source is mediated not through recollection but through an imaginative investment and creation.'[6] In other words, postmemorial Auschwitz encapsulates post-Holocaust generations' relationship to the site of Auschwitz: it is 'an imaginative investment and creation' of what occurred there rather than a 'recollection'. For survivors, however, it is a recollection and accordingly, this chapter uses 'memorial Auschwitz' to refer to the Nazi death camp experienced by survivors during the Holocaust and recalled by them when visiting Auschwitz in later years. Memorial Auschwitz also refers to the events at Auschwitz during the Holocaust in a more general sense: the use of

---

5   The differences between how survivor and second generation memoirs draw on place to bear witness to the Holocaust are explored in Esther Jilovsky, '"All a myth? Come and see for yourself": Place as Holocaust witness in survivor and second generation memoirs of return', *Australian Journal of Jewish Studies*, XXV (2011), 153–74.

6   Marianne Hirsch, *Family Frames: Photography, Narrative, and Postmemory* (Cambridge, Mass., and London: Harvard University Press, 1997), 22.

'memorial' indicates that these events only exist in memory but are intrinsically connected to the place of Auschwitz.

The shifting boundaries of memory and place which distinguish these two distinct categories, along with the vast number of visitors to Auschwitz, indicate that the memory of Auschwitz is evolving away from the Nazi death camp towards a tourist attraction – from memorial Auschwitz to postmemorial Auschwitz. As memory of the Holocaust passes from survivors to subsequent generations, sites of Holocaust memory such as Auschwitz gain importance as a connection to the Holocaust, even though, paradoxically, they show little evidence of the atrocities that occurred there.

Landscape theory is useful for analysing visits to Auschwitz in Holocaust memoirs because it distinguishes not only between place and event, but also between a place and the perception of it. It facilitates close analysis of the function of Auschwitz as a site in Holocaust memoirs, thereby illuminating the complex relationship between memory and place. As John Wylie notes, 'A landscape is thus not just the land itself, but the land as seen from a particular point of view or perspective. Landscape is both the phenomenon itself *and* our perception of it.'[7] The notion that landscape refers not only to a place but also to the way that people see it is crucial for considering the site of Auschwitz, because it is the idea of Auschwitz that consolidates the place as central in Holocaust memory. Denis Cosgrove makes a similar observation to Wylie that '[l]andscape is not merely the world we see, it is a construction, a composition of that world. Landscape is a way of seeing the world.'[8] This emphasises the duality of the concept: place is not just what is seen, but also how it is seen. The way in which this duality manifests is obviously dependent on specific cultural and temporal parameters, which will be explored throughout this chapter.

The relationship between a place and the events that occurred there is fundamental to the designation of a place as a Holocaust site. As Maoz Azaryahu and Kenneth E Foote argue, 'According to Western cultural convention, historical sites provide a tangible link to the past that they evoke. In this sense, the presentation of history on-site only makes explicit that which is implicit in the local landscape.'[9] This is because the relationship between a place and

---

7   John Wylie, *Landscape* (London and New York: Routledge, 2007), 7.

8   Denis E Cosgrove, *Social Formation and Symbolic Landscape* (London and Sydney: Croom Helm, 1984), 13.

9   Maoz Azaryahu and Kenneth E Foote, 'Historical space as narrative medium: On the configuration of spatial narratives of time at historical sites', *GeoJournal*, 73 (2008), 179–94, 179.

the events which occurred there suggests a permanent effect on the place. Thus merely the knowledge of a historical event renders a place significant and entwined with the memory of that event. However, as David Lowenthal notes, this connection is chiefly created by people rather than the place itself: 'If the character of the place is gone in reality, it remains preserved in the mind's eye of the visitor [...] The enduring streets and buildings persuade him that past is present.'[10] Thus, the visitor possesses preconceptions of a site as related to certain historical events, and in doing so, may simply confirm these. Consequently, as Lowenthal explains, '[t]he place of the past in any landscape is as much the product of present interest as of past history'.[11] Therefore, the inherent link between a place and the events which occurred there is not explicit but dependent on the contemporary cultural assumptions of visitors.

This is important when considering the volume of visitors to Auschwitz, not to mention the myriad written, oral and visual representations of this site. Auschwitz, the German name for Oświęcim, Poland, is the site of a concentration camp established by the Nazis in 1940, which became both a death camp and concentration camp in 1942. Approximately 1.3 million people were murdered at Auschwitz, the vast majority of them Jews, predominantly in purpose-built gas chambers.[12] Referred to in the secondary literature by phrases such as 'the most significant memorial site of the Shoah', 'a notorious, universal symbol of evil', 'the most renowned symbol of ethnic genocide and Nazi atrocities', and 'Auschwitz-land', the term Auschwitz has become almost synonymous with the Holocaust itself.[13] Furthermore, many researchers, including Tim Cole and Griselda Pollock, include personal reflections on visiting Auschwitz in their academic work, which further emphasises that the experience of visiting Auschwitz is diff-

---

10   David Lowenthal, 'Past time, present place: Landscape and memory', *The Geographical Review*, 65/1 (January 1975), 1–36, 7.

11   ibid., 24.

12   Statistic taken from Memorial and Museum: Auschwitz-Birkenau, http://en.auschwitz.org/h/index.php?option=com_content&task=view&id=14&Itemid =13&limit=1&limitstart=1, accessed 16 Oct 2014.

13   Debórah Dwork and Robert Jan van Pelt, 'Reclaiming Auschwitz', in Geoffrey H Hartman, ed., *Holocaust Remembrance: The Shapes of Memory* (Oxford and Cambridge, Mass.: Blackwell, 1994), 232–51, 232; William FS Miles, 'Auschwitz: Museum interpretation and darker tourism', *Annals of Tourism Research*, 29/4 (2002), 1175–78, 1175; Janet Jacobs, 'From the profane to the sacred: Ritual and mourning at sites of terror and violence', *Journal for the Scientific Study of Religion*, 43/3 (2004), 311–15, 314; Tim Cole, *Images of the Holocaust: The Myth of the 'Shoah Business'* (London: Duckworth, 1999), 110.

erent from visiting anywhere else.[14] Significantly, the date of the liberation of Auschwitz – 27 January 1945 – has been designated by the United Nations as an International Day of Commemoration for the victims of the Holocaust, and 27 January is also the date of the annual Holocaust Memorial Day in the United Kingdom. Furthermore, Auschwitz is the site of March of the Living, a program that involves walking from Auschwitz I to Auschwitz II, the death camp also known as Birkenau, on Yom HaShoah – the day of Holocaust remembrance in the Jewish calendar.[15] Such uses of the site not only ascribe it monumental significance, but also assume a straightforward link between memorial Auschwitz and the contemporary site, postmemorial Auschwitz. However, when postmemorial Auschwitz is closely scrutinised, it becomes clear that this link is more constructed than it is intrinsic.

The vast differences between memorial Auschwitz and postmemorial Auschwitz can be seen through two aspects: the muteness of landscape and the layout of the site, including what is marked and unmarked. As Andrew Charlesworth and Wylie both argue, landscape itself is mute.[16] James E Young writes that '[w]hen the killing stopped, only the sites remained, blood-soaked but otherwise mute.'[17] Consequently, the meaning found in a particular place is not created by the site, but by its representation and perception in a particular cultural narrative framework. Indeed, Foote argues that '[t]he sites have been inscribed with messages that speak to the way individuals, groups, and entire societies wish to interpret their past'.[18] Thus, it is not the site itself that is meaningful but the aspects of presentation and perception. This is particularly important at Auschwitz, where museum exhibitions and other labels, such as memorials, define its

---

14   See, for example: Cole, *Images of the Holocaust*; and Griselda Pollock, 'Holocaust tourism: Being there, looking back and the ethics of spatial memory', in David Crouch and Nina Lübbren, eds, *Visual Culture and Tourism* (Oxford and New York: Berg, 2003), 175–89.

15   The official website states that '[t]he goal of the March of the Living is for these young people to learn the lessons of the Holocaust and to lead the Jewish people into the future vowing Never Again', thereby illustrating the centrality of Auschwitz to Holocaust memory. 'March of the Living International', http://www.motl.org/, accessed 4 Feb 2010.

16   Andrew Charlesworth, 'The topography of genocide', in Dan Stone, ed., *The Historiography of the Holocaust* (Basingstoke, Hampshire: Palgrave Macmillan, 2004), 217; Wylie, *Landscape*, 99.

17   James E Young, *The Texture of Memory: Holocaust Memorials and Meaning* (New Haven, Conn. and London: Yale University Press, 1993), 119.

18   Kenneth E Foote, *Shadowed Ground: America's Landscapes of Violence and Tragedy* (Revised edn.; Austin, Tex.: University of Texas Press, 2003), 5.

significance. In other words, the landscape of postmemorial Auschwitz – the red-brick buildings, barbed wire fences and neat paths and trees at Auschwitz I, and the train lines, barrack ruins, chimneys and crematoria at Auschwitz II – does not in itself tell visitors what happened nor explain the significance of the site. It is the narratives created, for example, by the exhibitions in the barracks at Auschwitz I, provided by tour-guides showing groups around the site, and portrayed by the black-and-white footage shown to visitors in the cinema at Auschwitz which explain the context and history of the site and therefore give it significance. This categorisation of place as not only marked because it is where events of the Holocaust took place, but somehow also embodying the events themselves, is central to the role assumed by the site of Auschwitz. Young observes that '[i]n the rhetoric of their ruins, these memorial sites seem not merely to gesture toward past events but to suggest themselves as fragments of events, inviting us to mistake the debris of history for history itself.'[19] Thus pieces of the past – or of locations of the past – are regarded as the past as a whole, thereby encapsulating why Auschwitz has become such a significant site to visit.

Thus, despite the muteness of landscape, the site of Auschwitz is marked as significant. While this does not seem problematic, the issues are evident in how this occurs and what is marked: the layout of postmemorial Auschwitz differs significantly from memorial Auschwitz. The sites visited by tourists are Auschwitz I and Auschwitz II.[20] While there are several more sites that were part of the Nazi camp, including Auschwitz III (Monowitz), they are not generally visited, and not even labelled as part of Auschwitz.[21] The presentation of a site indicates choices of remembrance, rather than a straightforward representation of events. Although Auschwitz I has visitor amenities, it is not only these modern facilities which render its current format misleading. Not only is the carpark situated on ground that is part of memorial Auschwitz, but, contrary to popular belief, the iconic gate inscribed with *Arbeit Macht Frei* was never the entrance. Nonetheless, as Charlesworth et al have observed, this informs visitors' perceptions of Auschwitz and therefore their behaviour:

---

19   Young, *The Texture of Memory*, 120–21.
20   The official Auschwitz website recommends '[i]t is essential to visit both parts of the camp, Auschwitz I and Auschwitz II-Birkenau, in order to acquire a proper sense of the place that has become the symbol of the Holocaust.' 'Memorial and Museum Auschwitz-Birkenau', http://en.auschwitz.org.pl/, accessed 4 Feb 2010.
21   Dwork and Pelt, 'Reclaiming Auschwitz', 232.

The Museum authorities have [...] disguised the fact that the reception area with its cinema, coffee shop, restaurant, toilets, bookshop, post office and currency exchange was once the prisoner reception building. [...] In summer anyone passing sees a jamboree of people, behaving in many different ways. This is because the vast majority don't know where they are until their guide starts the tour proper at the Arbeit Macht Frei gate. At that point, the guide explains the geography of the site and asks all visitors to behave appropriately; the gate becomes the moral boundary where behaviour must change.[22]

Thus, even though the role of the *Arbeit Macht Frei* gate was of limited significance in memorial Auschwitz, it plays an important role in post-memorial Auschwitz. Not only are many tour groups photographed in front of it, confirming its status as a symbol of Auschwitz, but its function as 'the moral boundary where behaviour must change' means that this symbolic status is perpetuated. Debórah Dwork and Robert Jan van Pelt argue that '[f]or the post-Auschwitz generation, that gate symbolises the threshold that separates the *oikomene* (the human community) from the planet Auschwitz. It is a fixed point in our collective memory, and therefore the canonical beginning of the tour through the camp.'[23] For visitors, therefore, the *Arbeit Macht Frei* gate symbolises where the outside world ends and the otherworldliness of Auschwitz begins. This physical boundary also acts as a metaphorical one. It is therefore problematic that while the layout of postmemorial Auschwitz is an approximation of memorial Auschwitz, it is not explicitly marked as such. Maoz Azaryahu and Foote note that '[t]his element of selectivity is not always clearly apparent in the contemporary landscape because we see only what *has been* marked, rather than what *has not been*.'[24] Thus, because the *Arbeit Macht Frei* gate is positioned as the entrance to Auschwitz, visitors assume that it was. Other consequences of not marking are evident in that the carpark lies within memorial Auschwitz, but this is not explicitly marked either. As a consequence, although the layout of postmemorial Auschwitz is

---

22   Andrew Charlesworth et al., '"Out of place" in Auschwitz? Contested development in post-war and post-Socialist Oświęcim', *Ethics, Place & Environment*, 9/2 (June 2006), 149–72, 164.

23   Dwork and Pelt, 'Reclaiming Auschwitz', 236–37.

24   Kenneth E Foote and Maoz Azaryahu, 'Toward a geography of memory: Geographical dimensions of public memory and commemoration', *Journal of Political and Military Sociology*, 35/1 (Summer 2007), 125–44, 129.

constructed by postwar decisions, it is still interpreted as congruent with memorial Auschwitz.

Revisiting Auschwitz in survivor memoirs

It is clear that postmemorial Auschwitz, the tourist attraction with a car-park, bookshop and café, is vastly different to the Auschwitz concentration and death camp run by the Nazis to systematically murder millions of people. However, postmemorial Auschwitz is still expected to represent the horrific events which occurred there. Writing by Holocaust survivors imprisoned in Auschwitz demonstrates that the contemporary site bears little resemblance to the place they remember as a prisoner. This section considers two survivor narratives of revisiting Auschwitz, *Seed of Sarah* by Judith Magyar Isaacson[25] and *Return to Auschwitz* by Kitty Hart-Moxon,[26] which both demonstrate the inability to reconcile postmemorial Auschwitz with their memories of the site. These examples show a conflict between the two aspects of Auschwitz as conceptualised in landscape theory: the *site* of Auschwitz diverges from the *idea* of Auschwitz.

While Holocaust testimonies detailing survivors' experiences have been published since the late 1940s, those that describe the survivor returning to their birthplaces, hometowns or places of imprisonment in a later decade are a minority. Many testimonies conclude with the survivor travelling back to their hometown after liberation, only to find that they are among the few, if any, Jewish survivors. Such negative experiences of survivors' hometowns, coupled with other traumatic experiences during the Holocaust, mean that many never returned to these places again. Yet some survivors do describe revisiting the places where they experienced the Holocaust.[27] However, the places visited – and the decision about whether to write about these visits – vary from survivor to survivor. Vienna-born child survivor Ruth Kluger, for example, writes in her memoir *Landscapes of Memory: a Holocaust*

---

25   Judith Magyar Isaacson, *Seed of Sarah: Memoirs of a Survivor* (Urbana & Chicago: University of Illinois Press, 1991).

26   Kitty Hart, *Return to Auschwitz* (London: Granada, 1981); Kitty Hart-Moxon, *Return to Auschwitz* (Laxton, Newark, Nottinghamshire: Beth Shalom Limited, 1997). *Return to Auschwitz* was first published in 1981 and a revised, updated edition was published in 1997. This chapter refers to both editions of this book.

27   Other survivor texts that describe returning to Holocaust sites include Livia Bitton-Jackson, *Saving What Remains: A Holocaust Survivor's Journey Home to Reclaim her Ancestry* (Guilford, Conn.: The Lyons Press, 2009); and Elie Wiesel, *All Rivers Run to the Sea: Memoirs, Volume One 1928–1969*, trans. Alfred A Knopf Inc. (London: HarperCollins, 1996).

Girlhood Remembered of spending time in Vienna and visiting Theresienstadt (Terezin), to which she was deported at age 11, but strongly refuses to visit Auschwitz. She writes that 'I never went back to Auschwitz as a tourist and never will. Not in this life. To me it is no place for a pilgrimage.'[28] It is of course a rather different act to return to one's hometown than it is to return to a place of trauma such as a concentration camp. Those survivors who do venture back to Auschwitz generally do so out of choice and are in a minority. Elie Wiesel visited Auschwitz with talk show host Oprah Winfrey in 2006,[29] and, having featured his memoir *Night* as a selection for Oprah's Book Club that same year, an episode of *The Oprah Winfrey Show* chronicled Wiesel showing Winfrey around Auschwitz in the bitter, winter cold.[30] This role of Holocaust survivors as guides to Auschwitz emphasises their importance in communicating the meaning of the site. Moreover, the choice of where to visit demonstrates the linking of memory with place, showing that even, or perhaps especially, for survivors, places become meaningful by association with experience and memories. While both Isaacson and Hart-Moxon describe quite different experiences and reactions to being back where they were imprisoned, what is evident in both texts is how little post-memorial Auschwitz intrinsically represents their experiences there.

Seed of Sarah, first published in 1990, describes Isaacson's life as a carefree teenager in Kaposvár, Hungary, before deportation to the town's ghetto in 1944 and later that year to Auschwitz. Along with her mother and aunt, Isaacson was incarcerated in Auschwitz for three weeks before they were transferred to the prison camp Hessisch Lichtenau, where they were liberated in early 1945. Isaacson's return to Auschwitz is only mentioned in the 'Sources and Acknowledgments' section toward the end of the book, and is thus excluded from the main narrative. This categorisation of Auschwitz as a place merely to undertake research for her memoir contrasts with the entire chapters the text devotes to revisiting Hungary and Germany and suggests that for Isaacson, Auschwitz is not an important place for revisiting. Moreover, perhaps the inclusion of visiting Auschwitz attests to its categorisation as a pivotal site of Holocaust memory, rather than Isaacson's memory of it. The few lines devoted to this visit, however, do contain important insights.

28   Ruth Kluger, *Landscapes of Memory: A Holocaust Girlhood Remembered* (London: Bloomsbury, 2004), 131.

29   'Inside Auschwitz – Oprah.com', http://www.oprah.com/world/Inside-Auschwitz/, accessed 4 Feb 2010.

30   'Your Guide to Night and Elie Wiesel – Oprah.com', http://www.oprah.com/oprahsbookclub/Your-Guide-to-Night-and-Elie-Wiesel/, accessed 4 Feb 2010.

That Auschwitz today is not as it was during the Holocaust is implicit rather than explicit, but the text does acknowledge the incongruity between the contemporary site and Isaacson's experience of Auschwitz:

> In Auschwitz, I had a chance to relive some of my memories. We found the puddle near the foundation of our former barrack […] The wooden barrack had been burned down, and the electric wire fence was gone, but we located its torn remnants some fifty feet from the kidney-shaped puddle.[31]

While Isaacson acknowledges the incongruence of the contemporary site with memorial Auschwitz, the matter-of-fact tone suggests that she had not expected to find otherwise.

Yet the text also references the museum exhibitions found at contemporary Auschwitz which inform visitors of what happened. Isaacson writes:

> I made the mistake of trying to identify my family and friends on too many gruesome films and photographs. Halfway through, I gasped, suddenly faint: 'I must get some fresh air!'[32]

Although it is clear that this museum did not exist when Isaacson was imprisoned in Auschwitz, it still plays an important role in her experience of revisiting. Isaacson's connection to the site is evident in her attempt to identify family and friends in the photographic display, something that descendants of survivors often also do. That Isaacson had this reaction when viewing photographs on display in a museum at Auschwitz, rather than when visiting her former barrack, demonstrates the interaction of memory and labels in creating meaning for this place. While measures such as museum exhibitions play a different role for survivors of Auschwitz than they do for other visitors, and even though they are unnecessary for survivors such as Isaacson, they may still evoke a powerful reaction.

In sharp contrast to *Seed of Sarah*'s focus on sites other than Auschwitz, *Return to Auschwitz*, focuses on only one site for revisiting. This memoir strongly emphasises the gaping chasm between the Auschwitz she revisited in 1978 and the one in which she was imprisoned during the Holocaust. Written after she went back to Auschwitz for the 1979 documentary *Kitty – Return to Auschwitz*,[33] Hart-Moxon's memoir depicts her pre-war life in

---

31   ibid., 183.
32   ibid.
33   *Kitty – Return to Auschwitz* (Yorkshire Television, 1979), Peter Morley (dir.)

Bielsko, Poland, before her family went into hiding and she and her mother were eventually caught and incarcerated in Auschwitz, arriving in 1943 and liberated approximately two years later. The final chapter of the book, entitled 'Return to Auschwitz', is written as direct speech and reads like a transcript of the documentary film. The visit to Auschwitz undertaken for the film provided the catalyst for Hart-Moxon to write a more detailed memoir, thus demonstrating the entwinement of memory and place: 'I always felt that the story ought to be told at greater length and set in the proper context. [...] The return trip to Auschwitz set the seal on it.'[34] So, like Isaacson, Hart-Moxon's return trip to Auschwitz was connected with writing her testimony of the Holocaust.

The divergence of the two aspects of landscape emerges strongly in this text. Upon arriving at Auschwitz in 1978, Hart-Moxon writes:

> You see grass. But I don't see any grass. I see mud, just a sea of mud. And you think it's cold? With your four or five layers of clothing on a bright crisp day like this, you feel the cold? Well, imagine people here or out beyond that fence working when it snowed, when it rained, when it was hot or cold, with one layer of clothing.[35]

Written in the second person and thus directly addressing anyone who was not imprisoned in Auschwitz – in the documentary Hart-Moxon is talking to her son – this excerpt emphasises the vast differences between the Auschwitz visited in 1978 and the Auschwitz remembered as a prisoner from 1943 to 1945. Encapsulating the gulf between survivor memory and sites of memory, it shows that the site of Auschwitz does not represent Hart-Moxon's memory of Auschwitz: mud has become grass; extreme weather has become 'a bright crisp day'. It seems that the idea of Auschwitz is not evident from the site. Hart-Moxon continues: 'The past I see is more real than the tidy pretence they have put in its place. The noises are as loud as they ever were: the screams, the shouts, the curses, the lash of whips and thud of truncheons, the ravening dogs.'[36] By contrasting Hart-Moxon's memories of Auschwitz with her impressions of revisiting, this passage differentiates what is visible to any visitor from Hart-Moxon's memories. It illustrates the divergence of the *idea* of Auschwitz and the *site* of Auschwitz. To survivor Hart-Moxon, the idea of Auschwitz recalls horrific memories such as 'the

---

34 Hart, *Return to Auschwitz*, 218–19.
35 Hart-Moxon, *Return to Auschwitz*, 199.
36 ibid.

screams, the shouts, the curses, the lash of whips'. However, the site exhibits only a 'tidy pretence', excluding these elements.

Visits to Auschwitz in second- and third-generation memoirs

This divergence of the dual aspects of landscape – the perception and place of Auschwitz – forms differently in second- and third-generation Holocaust memoirs. The key difference between survivor memoirs and those written by their children and grandchildren is that the second and third generations' perception of Auschwitz – postmemorial Auschwitz – comes from inherited memory rather than personal experience. As a result, in these texts the *idea* of Auschwitz is merging with the *site* of Auschwitz. Thus, rather than being informed by memory, the perception of Auschwitz is informed by the site of Auschwitz. This section explores this idea by looking at visits to Auschwitz in three second- and one third-generation Holocaust memoir.

Second-generation memoirs – those by children of Holocaust survivors – explore the protagonists' connection to the Holocaust and frequently include visits to sites of Holocaust memory. The horrific experiences of many Holocaust survivors continued to affect not only their lives, but also the next generation, born after the Holocaust, who grew up with traumatised parents and little or no extended family.[37] Moreover, transgenerational trauma[38] was not the only consequence for the second generation; a frequent characteristic of much second-generation writing is a void caused by exclusion from the experience – the Holocaust – that indelibly shapes their lives. This is theorised by various notions of 'inherited memory', most significantly as 'postmemory'[39] by Hirsch and 'absent memory' by Ellen S Fine.[40] It is precisely the deficiencies of inherited memory which characterise the second generation's relationship to the Holocaust. Thus, for the second generation, whose connection to the Holocaust is based on their non-experience of it,

---

37   For further information on the psychological effects on the second generation, see: Aaron Hass, *In the Shadow of the Holocaust: The Second Generation* (London: IB Tauris & Co Ltd, 1991).

38   For further information on transgenerational trauma, see: Dani Rowland-Klein and Rosemary Dunlop, 'The transmission of trauma across generations: Identification with parental trauma in children of Holocaust survivors', *Australian and New Zealand Journal of Psychiatry*, 31 (1997), 358–69.

39   Hirsch, *Family Frames*.

40   Ellen S Fine, 'Transmission of memory: The post-Holocaust generation in the Diaspora', in Efraim Sicher, ed., *Breaking Crystal: Writing and Memory after Auschwitz* (Urbana, Ill. and Chicago: University of Illinois Press, 1998), 185–200.

CHAPTER 7

visiting sites of Holocaust memory is an attempt to resolve this paradoxical situation.

Third-generation Holocaust memoirs share some characteristics with second-generation memoirs, but the third generation has the important distinction of being one generation further removed from Holocaust survivors, and therefore from the Holocaust itself. While the second generation's relationship to the Holocaust may be characterised by closeness, for the third generation, it is often the distance which is more significant. Nevertheless, third-generation memoirs tend to share a similar sense of purpose when describing visits to sites of Holocaust memory. Andrea Simon's 2002 memoir *Bashert: A Granddaughter's Holocaust Quest* tells of the narrator's trip to Poland, Belarus and St. Petersburg as part of an American Jewish tour group, in the search for information on her grandmother Masha's life.[41] Simon visits Auschwitz because it is on the group's itinerary, not because she has a family connection (Masha emigrated to the United States in 1923, and the relatives Simon is tracing were mostly murdered at a massacre site she gives as Brona Gora).[42] The description of this visit is rather brief and, similar to Isaacson, perhaps the only reason Simon included an otherwise seemingly insignificant visit is because of the symbolic status of Auschwitz. Simon's description of visiting Auschwitz notes the incongruity of the site with what it is supposed to represent:

> Rows of redbrick barracks flank a narrow street and, if I forget the barbed-wire fences, I almost believe I'm at a normal military base – until I go inside. A white plastic model of the line 'to the left' shows people descending into the underground changing area, where they strip and enter the gas chamber.[43]

This quotation illustrates that there is very little evidence intrinsic to the site of Auschwitz – Simon writes 'I almost believe I'm at a normal military base' – but what is interesting in this excerpt is what alters this perception. It is not confrontation with any evidence of the horror of mass murder; rather it is a 'white plastic model' of something approximating this. It is not an element of the site itself which confirms Simon's preconception of

---

41 Andrea Simon, *Bashert: A Granddaughter's Holocaust Quest* (Jackson, Miss.: University Press of Mississippi, 2002).
42 ibid., 6, 266. Thousands of Jewish victims were murdered by the Nazis in 1942 at Bronnaja Gora, Belarus.
43 ibid., 16.

Auschwitz, but a museological artefact added specifically to illustrate what the site itself cannot.

The effects of this are even more marked in Simon's description of Birkenau. She enters a former barrack: 'I can make out a dark shape below the window and another on the floor. They look like the silhouettes of human beings begging to escape. I feel their desperation; I absorb the stench, the acrid, animal odor.'[44] This multi-sensual description demonstrates how Simon's preconception of Auschwitz has informed her experience of it. The sighting of 'dark shape[s]' in an otherwise empty and abandoned barrack shows that Simon has found at Auschwitz what she expected to. Thus, if considered in relation to landscape theory, the dual aspects are merging: the perception of the site can be found at the actual site. Rather than maintaining the actual site as separate from the events that occurred there, this text simply maps preconceptions about the historical events of Auschwitz onto the contemporary site.

Such preconceptions are also evident in some memoirs' descriptions of the journey to Auschwitz. In German-born, second-generation author Helena Janeczek's memoir *Lektionen des Verborgenen* [Lessons of Darkness], published in the late 1990s, the description of the journey from Kraków to Auschwitz with a tour group of survivors and their descendants emphasises the sense of dread about the forthcoming experience facing the group.

> Eine israelische Frau um die vierzig, die ihren Vater begleitete, fragte mich, ob ich meiner Mutter Valium gegeben hätte, und ich sagte nein, sie will es nicht. Auch Natek kündigte vor der Abreise, neben dem Fahrer stehend, über Mikrophon an, daß man kurz vor der Abfahrt nach Auschwitz stehe, daß, wer ein Beruhigungsmittel nehmen wolle, es jetzt tun müsse, wer keines habe, sich eine Tablette geben lassen könne, und wer sich nicht danach fühle mitzukommen, noch Zeit habe auszusteigen.[45]

> [An Israeli woman of around forty, who was accompanying her father, asked me if I'd given my mother Valium. I said no, she doesn't want it. Before our departure Natek announced over the microphone, standing next to the driver, that we were shortly to leave for Auschwitz and that whoever wanted to take a sedative must do it now. And that whoever

---

44   ibid.

45   Helena Janeczek, *Lektionen des Verborgenen*, trans. Moshe Kahn (München: Deutscher Taschenbuch Verlag GmbH & Co. KG, 2001), 136.

didn't have any with them could avail themselves of a tablet, and whoever after that felt they didn't want to come still had time to opt out.]

This quotation illustrates the mindset and expectations not only already possessed by the group, but also imposed upon them by the tour guide, about visiting Auschwitz. It emphasises that visiting Auschwitz must be a traumatic experience, something that people, especially survivors and their descendants, may not be able to endure without sedatives. Such preconceptions formed even during the journey to the site also perhaps suggest that they are necessary in order to recognise memorial Auschwitz in postmemorial Auschwitz.

Consequently, Janeczek grapples with the concept of visiting Auschwitz:

Im Kopf wiederholte ich zum soundsovielten Mal [...] die Fragen, wie man so ein verdammtes Konzentrationslager besucht, in dem man deine Verwandten umgebracht hat, ein Konzentrationslager, das keines mehr ist, wo es nichts und niemanden mehr gibt, und diese Gedanken schienen absurd, oder wenigstens war es klar, daß sie zu nichts führten, daß sie zu nichts nütze waren.[46]

[In my head I repeated many times [...] the questions, how one visits such an infernal concentration camp, where your relatives were killed, a concentration camp, which doesn't exist anymore, where there is nothing and no one anymore, and these thoughts seemed absurd, or at least it was clear that they led nowhere, that they were of no use.]

In this passage, Janeczek attests to the absence of a framework for dealing with visiting Auschwitz, no doubt exacerbated by her experience on the bus. She regards visiting Auschwitz as unlike visiting anywhere else and cannot reconcile that her relatives were killed there with its status as a universal symbol of evil. This quotation shows clear preconceptions and a desired meaning for contemporary Auschwitz. In particular, the phrase 'wo es nichts und niemanden mehr gibt' [where there is nothing and no one anymore] suggests that Janeczek has already decided what she will find at Auschwitz before she even gets there. Thus, once again, the perception of Auschwitz merges with the site of Auschwitz.

The sense of prior expectations is also evident in Arnold Zable's 1991 second-generation memoir *Jewels and Ashes*. Born in New Zealand, Zable

---

46   ibid., 137.

grew up in Melbourne – a city with a high population of Holocaust survivors, and thus also of second- and third-generation descendants. Like the passage in Simon's *Bashert*, this section is written in present tense and weaves Zable's impressions of Auschwitz with his prior expectations: 'Like a shadow, I move through the camp entrance under the infamous words, *"Arbeit Macht Frei"*. The sign is smaller than I had expected, partly obscured by a background of trees.'[47] Zable's observation that the size of the *Arbeit Macht Frei* sign is 'smaller than [...] expected' cannot come from memory or personal experience of Auschwitz, because he was not there. Whether this preconceived notion of the sign comes from viewing photographs or reading descriptions, this quotation illustrates the combination of the two facets of landscape. In contrast to the survivor memoirs analysed earlier, where memory pertains to memorial Auschwitz and contemporary Auschwitz is the scarcely recognisable remnant, in this text, the prior notion of Auschwitz is deemed false, and the contemporary, postmemorial site is Auschwitz. Moreover, citing the *Arbeit Macht Frei* gate as significant recalls Cole's observation that 'the gate becomes the moral boundary where behaviour must change.'[48] Thus, rather than the divergence of the idea of Auschwitz from the site, as evident in survivor memoirs, this example shows that the idea of Auschwitz is dependent on the site.

Like Simon, Zable writes about Auschwitz as if its horrific past is starkly evident. Yet *Jewels and Ashes* also acknowledges the inability of the site to represent what happened: '[T]he vocabulary of silence reaches beyond its own limits. It overwhelms with the sheer force of numbers: and the fact that there, lived and worked a company of technicians and bureaucrats who went about the task of efficiently and quickly annihilating over a million human beings.'[49] This passage suggests that it is the silence of the 'sheer force of numbers' which makes the place meaningful. It implies that perhaps both the site and the events are incomprehensible, and that therefore the site is incapable of representing what occurred there. However, this incomprehensible knowledge forms Zable's preconception of the site and is confirmed by his visit there. Considered from the perspective of landscape theory, the site itself and the perception of it are combined in Zable's description of visiting Auschwitz.

---

47   Arnold Zable, *Jewels and Ashes* (Newham, Victoria, Australia: Scribe Publications, 1991), 180.
48   Charlesworth et al., '"Out of place" in Auschwitz?' 164.
49   Zable, *Jewels and Ashes*, 180.

The visit to Auschwitz described in English journalist Anne Karpf's second-generation memoir *The War After: Living with the Holocaust*, published in 1997, takes a rather different form to the other examples discussed so far by acknowledging the temporal distance between the site and the Holocaust. Karpf, a well-known newspaper columnist who is credited with bringing the second generation to mainstream attention in the United Kingdom,[50] writes: 'As the others photograph each other under "Arbeit Macht Frei" and in front of pictures of camp inmates, I regret my decision to come and dread the tour.'[51] Once again, the *Arbeit Macht Frei* gate is featured, but this time it plays a different role. In this excerpt, Karpf notes the significant role of this gate but distances herself from the behaviour of other visitors around it. Karpf continues: 'But soon I calm down, and in Auschwitz I [...] I'm relatively unmoved: the place looks like a film set, small and full of billowing poplars, and I know that much of what we see is a postwar addition'.[52] Thus, unlike the other texts discussed, *The War After* explicitly acknowledges the touristic aspects of contemporary Auschwitz, and therefore shies away from the assumption that this site unequivocally represents memorial Auschwitz.

Importantly, Karpf makes the explicit observation that 'it's time which has enfolded and buried those events, not place, and it was [survivors'] contemporaries on different continents who had the possibility of intervening, not those of us standing here now.'[53] This perspective, unusual in second-generation Holocaust memoirs, shows an innate understanding of the limitations of the connection between place and event. Karpf continues:

> [I]n Auschwitz I, I get a sense not so much of having come to a place where over a million of the doomed were brought fifty years ago, as one where millions of tourists have visited subsequently, and it's only in the relatively neglected and decayed Birkenau that the effects of time more aptly give off ravage and abandonment.[54]

This example shows how Holocaust tourism can transform a place away from its Holocaust roots. However, in contrast to the other examples discussed, in this memoir Karpf acknowledges the contemporary reality of Auschwitz, recognising that the site has evolved significantly since the Holocaust. As a result, the perception of Auschwitz practically merges with the site of

---

50   Jilovsky, 'All a myth? Come and see for yourself', 170.
51   Anne Karpf, *The War After: Living with the Holocaust* (London: Minerva, 1997), 298.
52   ibid., 299.
53   ibid., 300.
54   ibid.

Auschwitz, both relatively far removed from memorial Auschwitz. In this text, the idea of Auschwitz correlates neatly with the site of Auschwitz and the quintessential aspects of memorial Auschwitz are scarcely mentioned.

These second- and third-generation examples show that the site of Auschwitz itself plays less of a role than expectations of what postmemorial Auschwitz is supposed to be. This means that the two main aspects of landscape – the site itself and the perception of it, or in other words the idea of Auschwitz and the site of Auschwitz – are merging in postmemorial Auschwitz. This is in stark contrast to survivor memoirs, which convincingly show how different contemporary Auschwitz is from memorial Auschwitz and therefore that the idea of Auschwitz diverges from the site of Auschwitz.

The landscape of Auschwitz

To illustrate this situation further, the chapter will now briefly turn to the issues of ecological preservation at Auschwitz. An intriguing fact about Auschwitz is that '[t]he first systematic mowing of the extensive coarse grassland areas in the barrack areas appears not to have taken place until 1979, in advance of Pope John Paul II's visit to Auschwitz.'[55] This statement raises many issues about memory and place, not least the role of different collective memories, particularly Polish Catholic and Jewish, in shaping how the site is marked and memorialised.[56] That the grass was mowed for the Pope's visit portrays Auschwitz as a site of Polish Catholic memory rather than Jewish memory. The issue of grass at Auschwitz is an apt metaphor for the site's preservation in general. Analysis of the natural landscape at Auschwitz emphasises that it is impossible to retain a site forever frozen at one moment in time. As soon as the event is over, the relationship between the place and the event irrevocably changes.

Consequently, Young notes:

> While in operation, the death camps and the destruction of people wrought in them were one and the same: sites and events were bound to each other in their contemporaneity. But with the passage of time,

---

55 Andrew Charlesworth and Michael Addis, 'Memorialization and the ecological landscapes of Holocaust sites: The cases of Płaszow and Auschwitz-Birkenau', *Landscape Research,* 27/3 (2002), 229–51, 239.

56 One of the main controversies surrounding the use of the Auschwitz site in the 1980s and 1990s was the 1984 establishment of a Carmelite convent next to Auschwitz I. For a detailed discussion of this as well as a later supermarket development, see: Charlesworth et al, '"Out of Place" in Auschwitz?'

sites and events were gradually estranged. [...] Only a deliberate act of memory could reconnect them, reinfuse the sites with a sense of their historical past.[57]

Thus attempting to shape the natural environment at Auschwitz so that it resembles the site in 1943–44 is 'a deliberate act of memory': an act that reunites the site with evidence of what happened there. While the plan to replace trees was deemed feasible, 'the landscape of mud that covered the vast majority of the outdoor landscapes of the camp in 1943/44 [as described by Hart-Moxon] could not be re-created'; even though 'the grassland and meadowland areas that had developed since 1944 were declared inauthentic.'[58] Similar to memorials, ecological preservation follows the principle of transforming misleading evidence into a more accurate portrayal of what occurred at a site. However, even such meticulous plans are incapable of emulating the past. Thus, Charlesworth and Addis point out that '[t]he more Birkenau is managed as an ordered, tidy landscape of metalled roads and paths and maintained grassland, the more its appearance is going to resemble a park.'[59] No matter how Auschwitz is moulded to become meaningful as a site of Holocaust memory, its meaning for those who visit is created by these visitors themselves, who simply interpret the results of those who create the landscape.

In conclusion, rather than suggesting that Auschwitz needs to more adequately represent the Holocaust, this chapter emphasises the imperative to remember that postmemorial Auschwitz, in other words the Auschwitz visited today – and the Auschwitz written about in second- and third-generation Holocaust memoirs – is *not* the Auschwitz of the Holocaust, but a postwar creation that continues to evolve. The exploration of the intricacies of the relationship between place and memory of Auschwitz has shown that the link between place and event is constantly changing. Using landscape theory to illuminate the different aspects of Auschwitz has given a framework to the changes taking place in the role of Auschwitz as a tourist attraction and site of memory. The observation that survivor memoirs exhibit a divergence between the dual aspects of landscape – between the idea of Auschwitz and the site of Auschwitz – shows the inadequacy of place in transmitting memory. Furthermore, the analysis of second- and third-

---

57   Young, *The Texture of Memory*, 119.
58   Charlesworth and Addis, 'Memorialization and the ecological landscapes of Holocaust sites', 240.
59   ibid., 247.

generation memoirs showing that in these texts, the idea of Auschwitz begins to merge with the site of Auschwitz, has illustrated the evolution of place and memory. It suggests that in time, the contemporary site of Auschwitz encapsulated by postmemorial Auschwitz may potentially dominate the idea of Auschwitz, and in this process, the tension between these two aspects of landscape evident in survivor narratives is in danger of being forgotten.

Chapter 8

'RETURNING TO A GRAVEYARD'

The Australian debates about March of the Living to Poland

Suzanne D Rutland

> For many in our community, Poland is a painful memory, a country
> which in the end, became a graveyard for millions of European Jews
> during the Holocaust.
>
> Sam Lipski, editor, *Australian Jewish News*, 2 February 1989.

Introduction[1]

In 1988, and for the subsequent 13 years, Australia was the only major world
Jewish community to refuse to participate on an official level in March
of the Living (MOTL). It was only in 2001 that Australian Jewry joined
other Israeli and Diaspora groups in Poland. The purpose of this article is to
capture the mood of the Jewish survivors in Australia, especially those from
Poland, and the nature of the arguments they used in opposition to participation in MOTL. It is not to respond to the many assertions they made at the
time, a number of which are contested by contemporary historians. Rather,
it is to recreate the atmosphere at the time and the strength of survivor
opposition due to their pain and sense of trauma, a largely forgotten chapter
in Australian Jewish history.

---

1   Suzanne Rutland would like to acknowledge the assistance of Isi Leibler, who granted
    her access in Jerusalem to his unique personal archive relating to the Australian
    Jewish community.

In order to understand the context of the debates about MOTL during the late 1980s, this article will analyse the background to Holocaust memory in Australia. In particular, it will discuss the impact of pre- and post-Holocaust Jewish migration on Australian Jewry, the high percentage of Holocaust survivors, mainly from Poland, who settled in Melbourne, and the reasons for the general reluctance of Jewish survivors in Australia to talk about their experiences as they sought to create a new life in Australia. This reluctance was not just an Australian phenomenon and has been referred to as 'the silence' by Ruth Wajnryb in the title of her book dealing with the subject. In addition, visits to the killing sites were limited by the on-going Communist obfuscation and denial of specific Jewish victimhood by Communist authorities in Eastern Europe. It was only in the late 1970s and particularly the 1980s that, for a combination of reasons, Jewish survivors started to talk about their Holocaust experiences, leading to much greater attention to Holocaust history. In the same period, Communist regimes were being challenged by protest movements demanding greater freedom, resulting in a more open attitude to Jewish memorialisation and the sponsorship of Jewish visits to the death camps in Poland. Thus, Holocaust memory and memorialisation in the two largest Jewish communities in Melbourne and Sydney were a fairly recent phenomenon. This background is necessary to enable a better understanding of the survivors' initially strong reactions to MOTL and their opposition to returning to Poland, expressed so emphatically within the Melbourne Jewish community.

The Holocaust and Australian Jewry

When Hitler assumed power in 1933, the Australian Jewish community numbered only 23,000. This small, entrenched, well-respected Anglo-Jewish minority was mainly concentrated in the urban centres of Sydney and Melbourne. The community was largely Australian born and strove for full acceptance within the majority non-Jewish population. They wanted to be 'more British than the British'.[2]

Between 1933 and 1939, about 9,000 European Jewish refugees arrived, the majority of them in 1939. There was a clear geographic divide in terms of migration choices: most of the refugees from Central Europe settled in Sydney, whilst the Eastern European Jews took residence in Melbourne. Reinforced by 25,000 Holocaust survivors after the war, by 1960 Australia's

---

2   Suzanne D Rutland, *Edge of the Diaspora: Two Centuries of Jewish Settlement in Australia* (Sydney: Brandl & Schlesinger, 2001), 6.

small Jewish community had almost tripled in size, numbering 61,000. The same national migration patterns were maintained, with most Polish Jews settling in Melbourne, based on patterns of chain migration fostered through the various Melbourne *landsmannschaften* [immigrant benevolent associations relating to specific East European towns], which did not exist in Sydney. As a result of this migration, on a pro-rata population basis Australia has more Holocaust survivors than any other English-speaking country.

The pre- and postwar Jewish refugees changed the character of Australian Jewry in terms of its religious, educational and cultural life, its representational structures and the nature of its Jewish identification. One of the major features of this transformation was the growth of the Jewish day school movement. As a result of the arrival of survivors, as well as the impact of the Holocaust itself on the established community, the desire to nurture and protect the community's Jewish identity became imperative. The prevailing, conservative Anglo-Jewish approach that had fostered non-distinctiveness and complete acculturation was discarded in favour of religious and cultural pluralism to ensure group survival.[3] The development of Holocaust memory, however, took much longer to emerge.

Whilst Jewish schools became a feature of Australian Jewish life from the 1950s onwards, Holocaust commemoration and the emergence of museums to document the tragedy took time to emerge. In the 1950s and 1960s, the Jewish school curricula in both Melbourne and Sydney contained nothing about the Holocaust. Rather, they focused on traditional Jewish studies, including Judaism and Biblical Studies. The teaching of Jewish history ended with the destruction of the Second Temple, and almost nothing was taught about post-Second Temple history, which spans almost two millennia. In addition, the annual community commemorations held each year in this period marked the Warsaw ghetto uprising and were known as such. This emphasis on Jewish heroism during the war mirrored what was happening in other parts of the Jewish world in the 1950s and 1960s: when Yad Vashem[4] opened its main memorial in 1964, its major sculptural piece marked the heroism of the Warsaw ghetto uprising.

---

3   See Peter Y Medding, *From Assimilation to Group Survival: A Political and Sociological Study of an Australian Jewish Community* (Melbourne: Cheshire, 1968).

4   Israel's official memorial for Jewish victims of the Holocaust as well as a centre for Holocaust research and documentation.

The long code of silence

For many survivors the past was too painful to talk about. Jacob Rosenberg, a Melbourne Jewish survivor of the Lodz ghetto, Auschwitz and other concentration camps and an award-winning writer and poet, expressed this anguish in one of his poems, titled 'No Exit':

> How do you describe it?
> What alphabet do you employ?
> What words?
> What language?
> What silence, what scream?

Recently, however, there has been significant historical debate about the issue of 'the silence'. In the immediate aftermath of the Holocaust, survivors did relate their stories, many of which were recorded and published. Already in 1943 Isaac Schneersohn had established the Contemporary Jewish Documentation Centre (Centre de Documentation Juive Contemporaine, CDJC) in Grenoble as a clandestine organisation with the aim of documenting the Holocaust by pooling the information of Jewish organisations and scholars and by collecting documentary evidence. After the liberation of France in 1944, Schneersohn, with Léon Poliakov, moved the CDJC to Paris.[5] Similarly, in 1944 Philip Friedman and others in Poland established the Jewish Historical Commission in Lublin. Like Schneersohn he realised the importance of documenting the Holocaust. He sought to cooperate with state authorities in this enterprise and in February 1945 he became a member of the Central Committee of Jews in Poland and networked with other cities. In all, 25 branches were established, manned by a staff of around a hundred people. Numerous questionnaires were sent out in Poland alone and 5,000 interviews were conducted. There were similar developments in the displaced persons camps, beginning in Bergen-Belsen and then Munich. A total of 47 historical commissions were set up in both the British and American zones with about 67 people working on this, providing 2,250 testimonies. Some of these materials were published in Yiddish and circulated throughout the Yiddish-speaking world and then later translated.[6]

---

5 Archival Records: Contemporary Jewish Documentation Centre (CDJC), http://www.lootedart.com/MFEU4B37218_print accessed 18 July 2011.

6 David Cesarani, 'Challenging the "myth of silence": Postwar responses to the destruction of European Jewry', in David Cesarani, ed., *After the Holocaust: Challenging the Myth of Silence* (London and New York: Routledge, 2012), 16–17.

In July 1947 a conference was held with this founding group at Yad Vashem in order to promote collaboration between the various projects for recording testimony that were underway. Inspired by this, later in 1947 Isaac Schneersohn decided to convene a conference in Paris of all the researchers in the field. This gathering was a crucial moment in the postwar research effort. The gathering was unanimous that resistance should be the focus, but they could not find other common ground, including the issue of which language to speak, and these efforts proved to be transitory. Following the efforts to resettle the Displaced Persons (DPs) and the establishment of the state of Israel, many of the survivor historians emigrated to Israel and America, and many archives that had been collected were sent to Jerusalem to the nascent Yad Vashem, whilst others moved to the United States.[7] Thus, the Paris conference could be seen as both the high point of the gathering of testimonies and the document- ation of the Holocaust in the immediate aftermath of the Holocaust, and also its denouement. Those survivors who raised their voices after liberation felt that their words fell on deaf ears, on a 'wall' of silence by society, so that they ceased to pursue the collection of testimonies. It was to be over 30 years before similar activities began in the 1980s.

In Australia, the early postwar years were marked by the code of silence. Mark Baker, author of the *Fiftieth Gate* (1997), described the 'code of silence' as follows:

> I grew up in a household where there was silence – silence about my parents' stories. I didn't ask, so my parents never answered me. We didn't talk 'about that'. My parents never spoke, but their dreams – their nightmares – are my dreams. These dreams were inarticulate, they were communicated in silence. I carried their dreams, their pain … With my book I wanted to know. I wanted us to talk about those dreams. I wanted to break the silence.[8]

Most survivors did not talk of their traumatic experiences of suffering and survival. Many believed that the best way to secure continuity of Jewish life was by having children to replace those who had died.[9] They wished to shelter their children from the horrors they had experienced.

---

7   Cesarani, *Challenging the Myth of Silence*, 18.
8   Address by Dr Mark Baker to the descendants' group. Sydney Jewish Museum, following the publication of his book, *The Fiftieth Gate*, as quoted in Suzanne D Rutland and Sophie S Caplan, *With One Voice: The History of the NSW Jewish Board of Deputies* (Sydney: Australian Jewish Historical Society, 1998), 318.
9   ibid.

In her book *The Silence: How Tragedy Shapes Talk* Ruth Wajnryb described her experience of growing up in Campbelltown, a Sydney suburb distant from the Jewish centre in the eastern suburbs:

It was as if we'd arrived from another planet, with no records or re-collections, no memory. We lived in the present and for the future. We were busy. We had plans. We had ambitions. We had this space in time that was now. And we were working hard toward what we could imagine ahead of us. But there was no past. The past was cordoned off, sealed out. There was a complete severance with what went before.[10]

She went on to describe the reluctance of her parents to talk about their experiences:

The temptation to seal off the past so as not to allow its horrors to intrude into the present must have been overwhelming. I don't know if they made a pact not to talk about where they came from, what they'd seen and experienced, what they'd lost. But it was as if they had. I am aware now of the enormous energy invested daily, yearly and across decades, in keeping the past to the past, preventing it from engulfing us.[11]

Baker highlighted this sense of disconnection with the past to trace his parents' stories during the Holocaust, contrasting it with his experiences of growing up in Melbourne and attending Mount Scopus College, the largest Jewish day school there. Whilst he was not permitted to speak about the Holocaust at home, his father's regular nightmares were a constant reminder of a secret but threatening past.[12] He wrote: '[L]ooking back over those days now, I am more aware of how Auschwitz cast its shadow on day-to-day life. Who can dissect why this one was depressed, or how deep was the lament that ran through a thousand sighs.'[13] He referred to the way his mother fed him as though this was 'the last morsel', became worried that a common cold would prove to be tuberculosis, and 'in the way they dreamed through you and devoured the dividends of every achievement'.[14]

---

10   Ruth Wajnryb, *The Silence: How Tragedy Shapes Talk*, (Sydney: Allen & Unwin, 2001), 6.
11   ibid., 13.
12   Mark Raphael Baker, *A Journey Through Memory: The Fiftieth Gate* (Sydney: HarperCollins, 1997).
13   Mark Baker, 'As If: Born Under the Sign of the Holocaust', in Michael Fagenblat, Melanie Landau and Nathan Wolski, eds, *New Under the Sun: Jewish Australians on Religion, Politics and Culture* (Melbourne: Black Inc, 2006), 250.
14   Baker, 'As if', *New Under the Sun*, 250.

In analysing Wajnryb's book, Sophie Gelski and Jenny Wajsenberg discussed three factors that account for survivors' inability to discuss their trauma with their children: linguistic, due to inadequate English skills to explain their trauma; the internal psychological problems, inhibiting 'the survivors' ability to communicate their personal versions of hell – the pain, deprivation, abuse, humiliation, loss, and guilt of having survived – to ... the outsider, the one who was not there';[15] and the external factors, because many members of the outside community were not interested in listening to survivors tell their stories.[16] The reluctance of survivors to speak of their experiences to outsiders in general and often to their children in particular was by no means unique to Australia. Many found it difficult to find the language to 'express a trauma of such magnitude'.[17]

The code of silence about the Holocaust was seen in every aspect of Jewish life in Australia. In 1988, Jenny Wajsenberg, one of the founding figures in Melbourne's Jewish Holocaust Centre, noted that:

> The Holocaust is still a troubling subject for many of us, difficult to accept, hard to confront and easily relegated to the recess of the sub-conscience, nevertheless has a unique place in the Melbourne Jewish community due to the high proportion of Holocaust survivors ... The postwar Australian born generation has by and large attempted to sweep under the carpet any links to this seminal topic, an overwhelming Jewish experience. In our quest for stability, we have tended to ignore our past.[18]

Impact of the Cold War

A major factor in the maintenance of the silence was the Communist con-quest of Eastern Europe and the effects of the 'Iron Curtain'. Jewish efforts in Eastern Europe to collect testimonies were suffocated by the Soviet-dominated leadership. Whilst there was a trial of those who participated in the 1941 massacre of Jews in Jedwabne in 1946, half of the accused were

15 Sophie Gelski and Jenny Wajsenberg, 'Teaching the Holocaust Today', in Konrad Kwiet and *Jürgen Matthäus*, eds, *Contemporary Responses to the Holocaust* (Westport, London: Praeger, 2005), 225.
16 ibid., 225.
17 ibid., 224.
18 Jenny Wajsenberg, 'Teaching a lesson of memory: Melbourne's Holocaust Centre', *Australian Jewish News* (*AJN*), 30 June 1988, 20.

acquitted and the other half received minimal sentences.[19] For over 40 years there was ongoing Communist obfuscation with denial of specific Jewish victimhood. In 1961, the Russian poet, Yevgeny Yevtushenko, wrote a poem on Babi Yar, highlighting the denial of Jewish suffering and victimhood and the extent of Soviet anti-Semitism. This poem developed 'incredible resonance',[20] but the Communists continued with their obfuscation. They held official ceremonies, for example in the Bikernieki woods outside Riga, but referred to the murdered as 'victims of Fascism', even though the majority of those shot were Jews.[21] In the museum at Auschwitz, specific reference to Jewish suffering was severely minimised. In Warsaw there was the Rapoport monument at the site of the Warsaw ghetto, and in Auschwitz-Birkenau block number 27 referred to 'Jewish martyrdom'. However, this was evidence of Communist tokenism.

During his visit to Poland in April 1988, Australian Yiddish writer Abraham Cykiert highlighted the labelling of Auschwitz victims as 'Polish citizens and citizens of other nations', without even a mention of the Jews who represented 90 per cent of the victims.[22] The main monument constructed in Auschwitz in 1967 included 19 languages, of which Hebrew and Yiddish were two. In Poland during the Communist era, there was a dual form of the politicisation of memory: on the one hand, specific Jewish suffering in the main was denied; and on the other hand Polish nationalists denied the extent to which some Poles had collaborated with the Nazis in the Jewish genocide and only referred to instances where assistance was offered. In her recent article discussing Holocaust memory in Polish scholarship, Karen Auerbach quotes historian Gunnar S Paulsson that 'with the end of Communism … has also come the end of the distorted rhetoric, both Communist and anti-Communist, that disfigured the debate over Polish-Jewish relations for so many years'.[23] Coming to terms with its past anti-Semitism before, during and after the Second World War is part of present debate in recent Polish Holocaust scholarship.[24]

---

19   Jan Tomasz Gross, *Neighbours: The Destruction of the Jewish Community in Jedwabne, Poland* (Princeton, NJ: Princeton University Press, 2001).
20   Gal Beckerman, *When they come for us, we'll be gone: the Epic Struggle to Save Soviet Jewry* (Boston and New York: Houghton Mifflin Harcourt, 2010), 30.
21   ibid., 31.
22   Abraham Cykiert, 'The Polish-Jewish Paradox revisited', Outlook, *AJN*, 5 August 1988, 21.
23   Karen Auerbach, 'Holocaust memory in Polish scholarship', *AJS Review*, April 2011, 139.
24   ibid., 140.

Monuments were built to commemorate the suffering of Polish citizens under Nazism without any specific references to Jews. The Płaszów forced-labour camp has become well known across the globe through the movie *Schindler's List*. It was built in 1942 on the site of a large Jewish cemetery, known as the New Cemetery for Cracow, and its satellite town, Podgorze. In 1942–1943, the cemetery was completely destroyed, with the gravestones used to pave the roads and provide foundations for the barracks. Under SS Commandant Amon Goeth, conditions were appalling. Starvation and terror left its toll on the number of inmates. It was in this camp that my grandfather, Solomon Perlman, perished, and cousins of mine were selected and taken away for an unknown death. After liberation, Goeth was arrested and executed by the Poles.

By 1946, almost all the buildings in Płaszów were demolished. The terrain was overgrown, only attracting locals to walk their dogs. In 1964, the Polish Communist regime erected an imposing monument at the top of a hill overlooking the camp area. Designed by Witold Ceckiewicz, the inscription reads: 'In memory of the martyrs murdered in the Nazi genocide, 1939–1945'.[25] There was no mention that the majority were Jews. A much smaller monument, a single gravestone, was erected by the Jews of Cracow in memoriam of the thousands of Jews who perished there. Yet this Jewish memorial is still overshadowed by the Communist-built structure. Overall, despite all the publicity of *Schindler's List*, the terrain has not been maintained. In 2003, a guidebook described the camp as follows: 'The area of the camp is now derelict and neglected and there is not a single signpost that would make it easier to get around.'[26] Other monuments erected in the 1960s at the killing sites of Bełzec (1963), Treblinka (1964) and Sobibor (1965), where the vast majority of people murdered were Jews, manifested the same denial of specific Jewish suffering. The original monument planned for Treblinka had more of a Jewish theme, but this was replaced by a more universal monument, even though it was partly funded by a Claims Conference grant,[27] which was not publicly acknowledged.[28] At its unveiling

---

25 Eugeniusz Duda, *Jewish Cracow: A Guide to the Jewish Historical buildings and monuments of Cracow* (Cracow: Vis-à-vis Etiuda, 2003), 123.

26 ibid., 119–120.

27 Grants allocated to organisations that support Nazi victims or promote Holocaust education and research.

28 Audrey Kichelewski, 'A community under pressure: Jews in Poland, 1957–1967', in Leszek W Gluchowski and Antony Polonsky, *Polin, Studies in Polish Jewry: 1968 Forty Years After*, vol. 21 (Oxford, Portland, Oregon: Littman Library of Jewish Civilisation, 2009), 179.

ceremony, Prime Minister Józef Cyrankiewicz, himself a non-Jewish survivor of Auschwitz concentration camp, 'referred nonetheless to the victims
as "800,000 citizens of European nations"'.[29] The classic justification
by Poland's Communist authorities for their failure to make any specific
references to Jewish suffering was that they were not fascists and did not
make any distinction between different ethnic groups, as they all suffered,
all human beings were equal, and the Nazi murders were a crime against
humanity.

Thus, for over 40 years the areas behind the 'Iron Curtain', containing
most of the gravesites of the murdered Jews, remained unmarked and un-
disturbed. Visiting Poland for the first time in 1988, on a personal visit,
Australian Jewish writer Arnold Zable described the prevailing silence:

> During this journey through Poland I have come to know that silence
> has many levels, many possibilities. It is a language with infinite
> vocabulary. I have listened to the silence in which reverberates the
> echoes of ancestral presences, and I've witnessed the silence in which it is
> possible to focus on every slight shift in the breeze, to see the movement
> of a speck of dust, an insect or a pod floating from a dandelion with the
> faintest promise of re-birth.[30]

He referred to the silence of the cemeteries, of the mass graves in the forests,
and above all in the three death camps he visited – Treblinka, Majdanek
and Auschwitz. If the silence in Israel and the free world was largely self-
imposed, under Communism in the East it was a policy influenced by the
Soviets, who fostered anti-Semitism for their own political ends and did not
wish to acknowledge Jewish victimhood.

Breaking the silence

The awakening of a realisation of the need to speak and talk about the
Holocaust emerged in Australia in the late 1970s. Australian Jewry was
affected by worldwide trends, which created a greater sense of Holocaust
awareness, starting with the Eichmann trial of 1961. These developments
have been traced by a number of scholars and the motivation for the emergence of greater Holocaust awareness continues to be a subject of significant academic debate. Scholars such as Peter Novick have argued that

---

29   ibid., 180.
30   Second part of Arnold Zable's account of his visit to Poland, *AJN*, 15 April 1988, 28.

these changes were driven by American 'political concerns'.[31] In contrast, Wajnryb has stressed the impact of trauma in terms of the shaping of the Holocaust narrative. The Australian survivor experience reinforces this latter explanation. My own family did not speak of their Holocaust experiences and I only learned how Oscar Schindler saved members of my father's Cracow-based Perlman family in the late 1990s.

A natural progression towards greater Holocaust awareness occurred due to the convergence of a number of different events. In Australia, as discussed in detail by Judith Berman, major changes began in the 1980s.[32] In Sydney in November 1979 the New South Wales Jewish Board of Deputies formed a Holocaust Committee, which was responsible for organising the annual Holocaust commemorations. In 1981, the first World Gathering of Holocaust Survivors was held at Yad Vashem with an Australian delegation participating and a B'nai B'rith exhibition was launched in the same year in Sydney and Melbourne. Then in 1982 the Australian Association of Jewish Holocaust Survivors and Descendants was formed, holding its first function in 1983. A major initiative and key turning point in Holocaust memory in Australia occurred in 1985 when the International Gathering of Jewish Holocaust Survivors was held at the University of New South Wales in Sydney.

The staging of exhibitions was a significant part of these developments and led to the realisation of the need for more permanent museums. In 1984 the Melbourne Jewish Holocaust Centre was opened. In Sydney it took more time, due to two competing projects emerging, but the Sydney Jewish Museum was finally opened in 1992. Due to the vision of its founder, Holocaust survivor John Saunders, it was dedicated to both recording and memorialising the Holocaust and also documenting Australian Jewish history and the contributions of Jews to Australian society. Thus, in the 1980s, active participation in Holocaust memory had intensified. However, whilst Australian Jewry came to the forefront in terms of Holocaust memory, there was a very different response to the issue of participating in March of the Living.

---

31   Hasia Diner has recently written a strong response to Novick's arguments, claiming that there is an overall silence in American history and therefore that Holocaust silence was not used for political reasons. See Hasia R Diner, *We Remember with Reverence and Love: American Jews and the Myth of Silence after the Holocaust, 1945–1962* (New York: New York University Press, 2009).

32   Judith E Berman, *Holocaust Remembrance in Australian Jewish Communities, 1945–2000* (Perth: University of Western Australia Press, 2001).

The beginnings of 'March of the Living'

In 1980, the 'Solidarity' movement led by Lech Wałęsa emerged in Poland, demanding radical changes, and this led to the imposition of martial law by the Polish Communist government. In an effort to attract Western support, the Polish government organised the 40th anniversary of the Warsaw ghetto uprising and invited representatives from throughout the Jewish world to attend a commemoration to be held under their auspices. Initially the government promised not to exploit the occasion for political purposes, but they then reneged on this promise.[33] As a result, Australian Jewry refused to participate. Victor Kleerekoper, the then editor of the *Australian Jewish Times*, wrote a strong editorial stating that the commemoration was 'nothing more than a sham'.[34] However, Sydney Holocaust survivor Sophie Caplan attended in her private capacity. At the time her husband, Leslie Caplan, was president of the NSW Jewish Board of Deputies. In 1984, a conference held at Oxford formed the Institute of Polish Jewish Studies and initiated the publications of the annual yearbook, *Polin*, by Littman Library. Subsequently, a greater openness for Jewish visits to Poland developed in the Jewish world. In 1986 an international conference was held in Cracow with 250 academics attending.

In February 1988, the Polish government again issued a call to Jews and others to attend the 45th anniversary of the Warsaw ghetto uprising. It was at this time that the first March of the Living was organised, with Israeli politician Avraham Hirchson as one of its founders, together with Dr. Shmuel Rosenman. The Jewish community in Miami was the first American Jewish community to be involved and continues to produce readings for the event, although the coordination of MOTL moved to New York.[35] During this initial holding of MOTL, 1,500 Jewish teenagers participated, with 1,000 from Israel and the remainder from the Diaspora, including a contingent from Great Britain. Israeli Deputy Prime Minister Yitzhak Navon led the group as they 'retraced the infamous two-mile route from the Auschwitz to the Birkenau death camps', as a journalist described the march at the time.[36]

---

33   *Australian Jewish News*, 15 April 1983.
34   *Australian Jewish Times*, 21 April 1983.
35   Oren Baruch Stier, 'Performing memory: Tourism, pilgrimage and the ritual appropriation of the past', in *Committed to Memory: Cultural Mediations of the Holocaust* (Amherst, Mass., and Boston: University of Massachusetts Press, 2003), 154.
36   'Poland: March of the Living', *Time Magazine*, 25 April 1988, http://www.time. com/time/magazine/article/0,9171,967255,00.html accessed 7 July 2011. During the March on Yom HaShoah, Holocaust Memorial Day, the entire delegation 'followed a

During the first ceremony, Navon stressed: 'Every Jew in the world should have two definite stations in life. The first is to come to Poland and walk at least one of the paths of the Holocaust. The second is to make aliyah'.[37] Thus, the concept developed that young Jews from Israel and the Diaspora would first visit Poland, where they would visit key sites relating to Polish Jewry, such as Yeshivat Chochmei Lublin, founded by Rabbi Meir Shapiro in the 1930s and later transformed after the war into a medical college, as well as the death camps, and then follow this experience with a week in Israel, with tree planting and constant waving of Israeli flags. In this way, participants would relive the destruction and redemption of the Jewish people through a personal pilgrimage.

Oren Baruch Stier, who participated in MOTL in 1994, described the march as 'an annual silent walk from Auschwitz I to Auschwitz II-Birkenau on Holocaust Memorial Day'.[38] From its inception it has been international in nature and has involved Jewish upper high school students, accompanied by their teachers, survivors, medical personnel and community leaders. Its aim is to create a strong sense of the past and, through its Zionist ideology and the centrality of Israel in the program, to reinforce the Zionist narrative of history from Holocaust to *Tekuma* [from destruction to rebirth],[39] and build a stronger Jewish identity and commitment to the Jewish future. As such, it draws more from mythology than historical reality, even with the actual re-enactment of the 'march'.

Whilst the majority of the participants are secular, the program draws on Jewish ritual, with the reciting of the traditional Jewish memorial prayers, the *kaddish* and *el-Male Rahamin* (God full of compassion). Other key Jewish songs are included, such as singing *Ani Ma'amim* ('I believe in perfect faith', based on one of Maimonides' 13 Principles) and the Israeli national anthem, *HaTikvah*. Anthropologist Jack Kugelmass has stressed: 'For Jews visiting Poland and the death camps has become obligatory: it is ritualistic rather than ludic – a form of religious service rather than leisure'.[40] This is followed

---

two-mile path that traversed the Polish town of Oswiecim ... to the crematoria in the massive Auschwitz-Birkenau extermination complex'. See Adam Ferziger, 'Holocaust, *Hurban* and Hareization Pilgrimages', *Contemporary Jewry* (2011), 31, 27.

37　Abraham Cykiert, 'The Polish-Jewish paradox revisited', Outlook, *Australian Jewish News*, 5 August 1988, 21. Cykiert quoted this part of Navon's speech. To 'make aliyah' means to return to Israel.

38　Stier, *Committed to Memory*, 150–190.

39　Sue Hampel, 'March of the Living', unpublished paper presented at the Australian Association of Jewish Studies Conference, Monash University (February 2008).

40　As quoted in Stier, *Committed to Memory*, 155.

by events in Israel, with the students graduating as the next generation of survivors and witnesses.

In his study of MOTL, Stier argued that MOTL was successful in its aims, especially for American Jews, due to a variety of reasons. The program creates a sense of religious obligation, even though the majority of students come from secular backgrounds. Thus, the various ceremonies are based on Jewish symbols. During the March, the students keep kosher, the morning prayers of *shacharit* are recited and Shabbat is observed. The linkage of Yom HaShoah (Holocaust Remembrance Day) and Yom Ha'Atzmaut (Israeli Independence Day) has a powerful impact on the participants. The concept of pilgrimage is central to Judaism, with the annual pilgrimage festivals to the Temple in biblical days, and subsequently visits to the graves of revered Jewish religious leaders. This ritual observance and drawing on Jewish traditions create a 'sacred space' so that MOTL becomes a memorial pilgrimage. The pilgrimage aspect of MOTL is reinforced by the sense of community, with shared aspects of ritual engagement and memory developed amongst the participants.[41] Overall, the experience can have a transformative effect and galvanise graduates to rethink their Jewish identity. Stier quotes an unpublished study that after the trip participants indicated that MOTL has 'profound, long-term positive effects on marchers' Jewish identification, attitudes towards Israel and social responsibility'.[42]

Australian Jewry and opposition of Jewish Holocaust survivors

As with all Jewish communities, Australian Jewry was invited to participate in 1988. The invitation was launched by the United Israel Appeal (UIA) since MOTL linked the commemoration of the killing sites in Poland with the rebuilding of the State of Israel. This led to a heated community debate. Sam Lipski, the editor of the *Australian Jewish News* in Melbourne, raised the question of whether Jews should visit Poland, presenting the arguments for and against. He stressed that for the large proportion of Holocaust survivors in the Melbourne Jewish community, 'the issue is particularly poignant'. Many only had bitter memories of Poland and Polish anti-Semitism before and after the Second World War, he wrote, and some 'are making it emphatically clear that as a matter of Jewish pride and honour they should boycott any visits to Poland'.[43]

---

41 ibid., 175.
42 ibid., 177.
43 'Poland the House of the Living', Editorial, *AJN*, 19 February 1988, 10.

Lipski, however, took a different line and argued in favour of visiting Poland. In an editorial, he noted that even though it was a 'killing ground', Poland was also a cemetery, which is also known in Jewish tradition as 'Beit Hahayim, House of the Living'. He continued:

> In other words, respect for the dead and the martyrs of the Holocaust requires of us a respect for those lives. Those who live have a duty to the departed not to forget. By visiting Poland and by doing so as groups of Jews openly and proudly, we proclaim the victory of the Jewish people over the forces of darkness which tried to destroy us in that unhappy country. We also give hope to small remnants of the Jewish community still left in Poland that the Jews of the world have not forgotten or abandoned them.[44]

He concluded his arguments in support of the visits by noting that Poland was not alone in persecuting its Jewish community – every country in Europe had a bad record when it came to protecting its Jewish community. In addition, Poland had been the centre for Jewish thought and culture for many centuries and if the Jewish community cut itself off from Poland, it was also cutting itself off from its history, which he claimed 'Jews must never do'. Thus, those who visit Poland 'do so within an honourable Jewish tradition of honouring the House of the Living'.[45]

However, most Jewish survivors in Melbourne did not agree with him. When the plans for MOTL were announced, they expressed vehement opposition. The debate began following a Yiddish program on Radio 3EA when Wolf Jablonski, a member of the executive of the Association of Fighters, Partisans and Camp Inmates in Melbourne, spoke in a private capacity in support of participating in the commemoration ceremony. His comments sparked a storm of protest and a spate of articles and letters in both the *Australian Jewish News* and its *Yiddishe Nayes*. Opponents to the proposal also organised a petition to be presented to the Victorian Jewish Board of Deputies (VJBD), which attracted 1,000 signatures. Jacob Rosenberg and Abraham Biderman, both survivors of the Lodz ghetto, were two key leaders of this opposition. Biderman wrote:

> How can we as Jews stand next to the parody of soldiers who beat drums and blow the trumpets, whilst deep in their hearts they despise and hate Jews. How can we commemorate our disaster together with the people

---

44   ibid.
45   ibid.

who facilitated the Holocaust and made it possible for the Germans to destroy six million Jews. Their hands are stained with Jewish blood that is still fresh.[46]

They also expressed their strong opposition to the United Israel Appeal, even warning that participation in the Warsaw ghetto commemoration and MOTL would lead to their withdrawal of support for the United Israel Appeal.[47] Both Biderman and Rosenberg later wrote powerful and award-winning accounts of their Holocaust experiences, Biderman with his *The World of My Past* (1995) and Rosenberg with *East of Time* (2005) and *Sunrise West* (2007).

At the packed March 1988 plenum meeting of the Victorian Jewish Board of Deputies, Rosenberg and Biderman strongly protested against participation and were joined by Abraham Zeleznikow, Bono Wiener and Sam Migdalek. The acting board president, Leon Duval, declared that the executive had discussed the issue and that whilst they did not wish to issue a boycott as it was not appropriate for the board to make recommendations for individuals, it was 'probably wrong for any delegation from the community to attend'.[48] This view was endorsed with the board deciding not to participate in either the Warsaw ghetto commemoration or MOTL because 'it would be inappropriate for the Jewish community as such to be officially represented'.[49] The New South Wales Jewish Board of Deputies supported the board's decision, although Sydney Moriah student Eytan Uliel, who was a finalist in an international competition on Jewish heroism in Israel, joined the Israeli delegation of the first MOTL.

Melbourne Jewish leader Isi Leibler was a pivotal figure in the debate. His private archive, which has not previously been explored, sheds light on his position. In early April, he met with the Polish ambassador Antoni Pierzchala and his assistant W Kaluza in his Melbourne Jetset offices, the headquarters of his travel company. Pierzchala, a fairly senior man, had been Polish ambassador in Lebanon and Egypt and headed the Polish Middle Eastern desk. Whilst Poland still did not fully recognise Israel, Poland did have quasi-diplomatic relations with the Jewish state. During the meeting, Pierzchala stressed what the Polish people were doing to create a better relationship with the Jewish people, including Israel, such as cultural

46   Abraham Biderman, quoted in *AJN*, 19 February 1988, 1.
47   Rutland and Caplan, *With One Voice*, 342–3.
48   'No ghetto delegation', *AJN*, 11 March 1988, 4.
49   ibid.

renovations of museums and restoration of cemeteries. Leibler welcomed these initiatives and explained that whilst the established Australian Jewish leadership welcomed the international gathering being held in conjunction with the anniversary of the Warsaw ghetto uprising, the community had decided not to participate at an official level. Leibler explained:

> As he knew, there were a very substantial number of Jewish survivors in Australia who had terrible memories not only of Nazi bestiality but of the antisemitism they had encountered even after the War by the Polish people.
>
> ... He should understand, however, that the reason that Australian Jewry would not officially participate was because Jewish leaders felt obliged to take account [of] and respect the feelings of those Polish [Jewish] survivors who are adamant in their strong emotional views that it would be an affront to them for Australian Jewry to be officially represented at such an event. I told him I felt obliged to take account of the feelings of these people even if, politically speaking, I did not entirely agree with them. I stressed, however, that whilst there was an effort by some Polish Jewish groups to call for a boycott, this had been resisted. A number of Australian Jews would be participating.[50]

Leibler also stressed that the Polish government needed to face up to its past as a first step in improving Polish-Jewish relations. The ambassador responded diplomatically to this explanation. He tried to emphasise the positive aspects for the Jewish people of participating in commemorations officially sponsored by the Polish government. In particular, he referred to 'the Israel relationship which would lead to a new era'.[51]

Some survivors did participate in the Warsaw commemoration. In a private letter to Isi Leibler, at the time president of the Executive Council of Australian Jewry, Abraham Cykiert described his feelings about receiving an invitation to participate in the Warsaw commemoration and visit his home town: 'My first response was in the negative', but then he received a letter from Lodz, which 'was worded coercively but also touchingly', stating that '... you may be the last member of the remnant of your family who is able to

50 Personal notes about the meeting between Isi Leibler, the Ambassador of the Polish People's Republic Antoni Pierzchala, and his assistant, Mr W Kaluza on Monday 11 April 1988, ECAJ, October 1987–December 1988, Isi Joseph Leibler (IJL) Personal Files, Jan–June 1988, 2421, IJLA-Jer.

51 ibid.

perform the *mitzvah* [commandment] of going on *"Kever Avot"* [visiting the graves of the forefathers] in the still existing Bet Almin in Lodz.'[52] Moved by the emotion that this letter aroused, Cykiert decided to accept the invitation. He stressed this decision was 'stronger than logic' because:

> … after all, of the Yeshiva Beth Yisroel (where your in-law was also a *Talmid* [student]) only two students remained out of close to 3000 of the last pre-war class; I am one of the two. I recall that at the age of 16–17 I was in the group who performed the *Taharot* [purification] for some of our *Haverim* [classmates] who left us in the Ghetto.
>
> I may in fact be the last one to go visiting these *Kvarim* [graves] on a personal basis. As time goes by I am driven more and more by the need to fulfil that duty than by the logic which tells me that my link with Poland has been cut.
>
> As an antidote to the dichotomy between emotion and logic I decided to go, but to sandwich Poland between Yerushalayim [Jerusalem] on both sides.[53]

After the commemoration of the Warsaw ghetto uprising, Lipski wrote in his 'Partisan' column in the *Australian Jewish News* about the simultaneous events in Warsaw. He referred to the activities of a group of Polish dissidents who organised their own commemoration by staging a march to Warsaw's Jewish cemetery, led by Jacek Kuroń, who unveiled a monument to Henryk Erlich and Wiktor Alter, two leaders of the Polish Bund in the 1920s and 1930s, who were executed by the Soviets in 1942.[54] The dissidents were joined by many of the Jews from Israel and the Diaspora. Lipski commented: 'the presence of Jews in the Polish capital on this anniversary turned out to be a positive affirmation which shaped the way events were reported in the international media'.[55]

In 1989, strong opposition was again expressed against participation in MOTL. Neither the VJBD nor the New South Wales Jewish community

---

52 Letter from Abraham Cykiert to Isi Leibler, 8 January 1988, Poland IJL Personal Files, Jan–June 1988, 2421, IJLA-Jer.

53 Letter from Abraham Cykiert to Isi Leibler, 8 January 1988, Poland, IJL Personal Files, Jan–June 1988, 2421, IJLA-Jer.

54 According to some accounts, Erlich committed suicide by hanging himself from the bars of his Kuibyshev (mod. Samara) prison's window. http://www.yivoencyclopedia. org/article.aspx/Erlich_Henryk, accessed 6 July 2013.

55 Sam Lipski, 'Monument to Soviet victims', Partisan, *Australian Jewish News*, 29 April 1988, 14.

endorsed Australian participation. Sydney-based psychiatrist, Dr George Foster, son of a survivor and later president of the Australian Association of Jewish Survivors and Descendants, questioned whether the teenagers had sufficient emotional maturity and raised concerns that they would not take the program seriously. The Sydney leadership reiterated the fear that MOTL was 'in bad taste, insensitive and merely a Hollywood extravaganza'.[56]

In February 1989 the proposed visit of the state-funded Polish Jewish Theatre to Australia reignited the debate. This theatre, located in Warsaw and directed by Szymon Szurmiej, survived the anti-Jewish campaign of 1968. In an editorial in the *Australian Jewish News*, Lipski described the theatre as a 'propaganda tool and a Jewish theatre group without any real Jewish content'.[57] He noted that a Polish historian recently described it as a 'propaganda gimmick'.[58] However, Lipski declared that, despite Poland's past history, Melbourne Jewry should welcome the theatre. The *Jewish News* also published a moving interview of Szurmiej by Michael Gawenda, who introduced his article, entitled 'From the ashes of Poland', as follows:

> Sitting in a Melbourne hotel room talking in Yiddish to Szymon Szurmiej, the director of the State Jewish Theatre in Warsaw, a host of conflicting feelings and thoughts envelop me. The son of Polish Jews, my father's overwhelming love and commitment to Yiddish and Yiddish culture comes back to me. So does his contempt for Poland, the land he lived most of his life, but which he rejected so vehemently after the war that from the time he arrived in Australia, not a single Polish word passed his lips. I inherited both his love of Yiddish and to a lesser extent, his rejection of the country which had been home to generations of my family.[59]

The pain expressed in this article reflected the dilemma that faced Melbourne Jewry. Gawenda's father was no longer alive, but he questioned what his father would have done were he alive. He surmised that he would have attended the show, because of his love of Yiddish culture, but he would

---

56   Rutland and Caplan, *With One Voice*, 342.
57   'The Jewish Theatre of Poland', *AJN*, 3 February 1989, 14.
58   Jerzy Eisler, 'Jews, antisemitism, emigration', in Leszek W Gluchowski and Antony Polonsky, *Polin, Studies in Polish Jewry: 1968 Forty Years After*, vol. 21 (Oxford, Portland, Oregon: Littman Library of Jewish Civilisation, 2009), 59.
59   Michael Gawenda, 'From the ashes of Poland', People, *AJT*, 17 February 1988, 15.

have refused to speak to Szurmiej. In his interview, Szurmiej stated that the Polish Jews in Australia feel 'a mixture of great love combined with great hate and pain'. For most of these survivors, the latter feelings predominated, resulting in their vehement opposition to the return to Poland on any official level, including MOTL. Indeed, Gawenda strongly expressed this opinion a few months later when he describe MOTL as 'a circus', stressing that: 'The idea of thousands of people marching on Auschwitz waving flags is a travesty of what a visit to a cemetery ought to be. A cemetery is not a place for pageants ... this March is a piece of political theatre, a piece of marketing driven by triumphalism'.[60]

Reasons for survivor opposition

In the debate about participating in MOTL and commemorations sponsored by the Polish government, a number of key arguments were presented. Survivors claimed that Jews should not work with the Polish government, because they said many Poles collaborated with the Nazis in the concentration and death camps. Biderman stressed:

> How can we commemorate our disaster together with the people who facilitated the Holocaust and made it possible for the Germans to destroy six million Jews ... Their hands are stained with Jewish blood that is still fresh ...[61]

Many other Polish Jewish survivors in Melbourne shared this sentiment, although the fact that there were many Poles who assisted and rescued Jews and who have been recognised as 'Righteous Amongst the Nations' by Yad Vashem might modify this point of view.

Another powerful reason put forward was that the Poles were only more welcoming for pragmatic reasons, including needing Western support or just wanting Jewish money through the tourist dollar. One Jewish survivor wrote in an article entitled 'Poland tour is a charade':

> Nearly 3.5 million Jews lived in Poland in 1939 and then came the Holocaust. In the years since, the Polish Jews who lived and died there have been quickly forgotten and anti-Semitism is alive and well.

---

60   *AJT*, 22 September 1989, as quoted in Sue Hampel, 'March of the Living', unpublished paper presented at the Australian Association of Jewish Studies Conference, Monash University (February 2008).

61   Abraham Biderman, *AJN*, 19 February 1988.

Suddenly hidden Jewish relics have acquired a dollar value and Polish tourism and cultural authorities have realised they can turn concentration campsites, reconstructed synagogues and other places of Jewish interest into tourist attractions.

Are we going to stand by and watch this charade? Have our memories failed us and have we forgotten the pogroms and Hitler?

No! Polish Jewry vanished without trace. Its shrine is Yad Vashem in Jerusalem. No other place. Only there should we honour our *kedushim* (holy ones).[62]

Others expressed similar sentiments. In his strong opinion piece, Jacob Rosenberg quoted the old saying 'when in trouble turn to a Jew'[63] as the reason why Poles suddenly wanted Jews to return to Poland. Cykiert argued that Poles wanted to mend bridges with the Jews for pragmatic reasons: they needed support from abroad, and expressing anti-Jewish sentiments was counterproductive to achieving this goal.[64] Despite his expressed support for visiting Poland, Lipski pointed out that the Polish government needed the West for both economic and political reasons, and believed it could improve its chances if it could win Jewish support by recognising Israel, inviting Jews to Poland and even admitting responsibility for the anti-Zionist campaign in 1967–8, which led to thousands of Jews being forced out of their jobs and their subsequent emigration.[65] Lipski stressed that Poland still had 'a long way to go, and the Jewish world has every reason to remain extremely sceptical of Warsaw'.[66]

Furthermore, opponents argued that Poles simply wanted to absolve themselves of any guilt associated with the Holocaust. Leon Jedwab returned to Poland in 1979 to visit the mass grave where his family was

---

62   Sam Migdalek, 'Poland tour is a charade', *AJN*, 5 February 1988, 10.

63   Jacob Rosenberg, 'Poland revisited: the same old lies', 19 February 1988, 11.

64   Abraham Cykiert, 'The Polish-Jewish paradox revisited', Outlook, *Australian Jewish News*, 5 August 1988, 21. Cykiert quoted this part of Navon's speech.

65   Dariusz Stola, 'Anti-Zionism as a Multipurpose Policy Instrument: The Anti-Zionist Campaign in Poland, 1967–1968,' *The Journal of Israeli History* Vol. 25, No. 1, March 2006, 175–201. See also Arthur Wolak, *Forced Out: The Fate of Polish Jewry in Communist Poland* (Tucson, Ariz.: Fenestra Books, 2004).

66   Sam Lipski, 'Monument to Soviet victims', Partisan, *Australian Jewish News*, 29 April 1988, 14. Other reasons for improved relations were the impact of Vatican II and above all the actions of the Polish-born Pope John Paul II, who served in the Holy See from 1978 until his death in 2005 and did much to rebuild good relations between the Church and the Jewish world, including being the first pope to visit various Christian sites in Israel in 2000.

buried and to go to Auschwitz. He stressed: 'I can understand going to Poland. But, I am against any formal participation in a commemoration organised by the Polish government to help absolve themselves of their guilt'.[67]

Survivors leading the campaign opposing official Jewish visits also expressed concerns about the contemporary narrative of Polish historians regarding the ongoing Communist obfuscation of Jewish suffering. Rosenberg wrote:

> It is worthwhile examining what is actually happening and at the same time, look at the pages of recent history; history not written by us from afar but by contemporary Polish historians. I hope that such reading will shock our society out of its prevailing indifference, and will at the same time uncover the perfidy and the lies about our tragedy spread by the present day Polish historians who are busy influencing the Jews to visit the old country.

Rosenberg referred to the work of Wacław Paterański, who claimed that Poles saved Jews who had escaped from the Warsaw ghetto and that they had assisted the Jews during the ghetto uprising. He stated that Paterański gave the impression that 'the whole Polish nation was totally involved in saving the lives of Polish Jews', but that there was no truth in these assertions. If the Polish people were so active in assisting Jews, he asked, why did the postwar atrocities, such as the Kielce pogrom in 1946, occur? 'How was it possible to systematically remove Jews from the trains and kill them on the railway lines without a single "fraternal friend" lifting a finger?'[68] He concluded his piece:

> I for one, am not surprised by such historical distortions; one cannot expect any better from the Poles. But I feel disappointed that our present Jewish generation is devoid of even half of the courage of our Spanish ancestors when they were expelled from Spain ... [in Poland] one is a stranger amongst strangers.[69]

Thus, Rosenberg also drew on past Jewish historical traditions, in relation to the expulsion of the Jews from Spain, as a result of a mythical narrative

---

67   Leon Jedwab, 'Poland revisited', *AJN*, 11 March 1988, 13. It is important to note that there was no actual Polish government in Poland itself during the war.
68   Jacob Rosenberg, 'Poland revisited: The same old lies', *AJN*, 19 February 1988, p.11.
69   ibid.

which emerged in Eastern Europe in the 19th century amongst those Jews suffering from persecution in Eastern Europe.[70]

Other writers supported Rosenberg. In his letter to the Jewish press, Leo Cooper declared:

> It is our sacred duty to remember. According to Elie Wiesel, a murderer commits his crime twice; the second time he tries to cover up the traces. It is the responsibility of each Jew not to assist the Polish government in its aim to distort and conceal the truth, lest he become an accessory to this monstrous cover-up.[71]

Thus, survivors argued that formal participation by Australian Jewry at an official level in Polish government initiatives would be a form of historical denial.

Concern about ongoing anti-Semitism in Poland was another important factor in the survivors' opposition. There was some basis for this concern. During his meeting with the Polish ambassador, Isi Leibler experienced this firsthand during a verbal incident with the ambassador's assistant, Kaluza. After Leibler had explained why the Australian Jewish community would not participate on an official level in the 1988 commemoration, Kaluza took umbrage. He accused Leibler of not knowing Polish history, and the Jews of only being concerned with making money. He told Leibler, according to Leibler's account, 'I personally witnessed in my town thousands of Polish Jews who were repatriated from the Soviet Union after the war and settled in my area. These people arrived penniless ... Do you know, within a few years they were all fabulously rich and had huge luxury cars. How do you think the Polish people felt about this?'[72] This sweeping statement elicited a very strong response from Leibler and after their exchange of words he refused

---

70   ibid. Sam Lipski referred to 'the way Jews excommunicated Spain' in his editorial of the same issue, but there is no historical basis for this belief. There is no mention of an official, comprehensive ban (*cherem*) in rabbinic and traditional Sephardi literature, although there were some minor incidents; the idea of a general Jewish ban on Spain was especially popular in Eastern Europe, both among the enlightened thinkers (*maskilim*) and the rabbis who wrote about it extensively. Judah Gordon wrote about the ban in a Hebrew poem; he was one of the first to mention it. Yechiel Goldhaber has assembled some of the sources in a Hebrew pamphlet issued in Jerusalem, 2001. See: http://aleph.nli.org.il/F/11EPNXQVQ5QF1G3VR1CITILSLT8VK L1VQIJB45FRQ9V9J1UQUB-33288?func=direct&local_base=NNL01&doc_ number=003540669&pds_handle=GUEST, information supplied by Professor Shalom Sabar, email correspondence, 21 July 2013.

71   Leo Cooper, Letters to the Editor, *AJN*, 11 March 1988.

72   Personal notes about the meeting between Isi Leibler, the Ambassador of the Polish People's Republic Antoni Pierzchala and his assistant Mr W Kaluza on Monday 11

to speak to Kaluza during the remainder of the meeting, whilst working to maintain good relations with the ambassador. After the meeting, the ECAJ released a bland statement without any reference to this bitter encounter because Leibler felt that 'it would only reinforce the worst feelings many Jews had about some of the people who were still in the Polish government'.[73]

Firsthand experiences also confirmed the problem of ongoing anti-Jewish feelings in Poland. In August 1988, Cykiert published a report of his visit for the 45th anniversary of the Warsaw ghetto uprising entitled 'The Polish-Jewish paradox revisited'. He noted that whilst in the bigger centres Jews were welcomed, anti-Jewish feelings were still very prevalent in the small villages where '[e]very Jew who dares to visit is a threat, a reminder of the past, a ghost in the very houses they took over from their Jewish neighbours who were, they know, murdered.'[74]

Thus, as a result of survivor opposition, Australian Jewry was one of the few communities worldwide which refused to participate officially in March of the Living for 14 years. At international meetings, key Australian Jewish leaders were often reprimanded by other Jewish communities for this decision. When Diane Shteinman served as president of the Executive Council of Australian Jewry in 1995–1998, she was upbraided by Joseph Wilf, a key American Jewish leader and himself a native of Jarosław, Poland, who experienced anti-Semitism in pre-war Poland and was deported to Siberia by the Soviets, but who strongly believed in the importance of March of the Living.[75]

Afterword

During the late 1980s and 1990s, after the collapse of Communism, children and grandchildren of Holocaust survivors visited Poland, often accompanied by their parents. As descendants returned to visit the hometowns and explore the origins of their parents, some began to believe that they should participate in MOTL, provided that there was effective preparation of the students. In 2001 Sue Hampel, a Melbourne-based daughter of Holocaust

---

April 1988, ECAJ, October 1987–December 1988, IJL Personal Files, Jan–June 1988, 2421, IJLA-Jer.

73   Personal notes about the meeting between Isi Leibler, the Ambassador of the Polish People's Republic Antoni Pierzchala and Mr W Kaluza on Monday 11 April 1988, ECAJ, October 1987–December 1988, IJL Personal Files, Jan–June 1988, 2421, IJLA-Jer.

74   Abraham Cykiert, 'The Polish-Jewish paradox revisited', Outlook, *AJN*, 5 Aug 1988, 21.

75   For more background on Joseph Wilf, see http://www1.yadvashem.org/yv/en/museum/donors/wilf_family.asp, accessed 18 September 2011.

survivors, 'reignited the debate, convinced that young Australian Jews deserved this unique opportunity to participate in MOTL'. Hilton Rubin, at the time principal of Mount Scopus College in Melbourne, and Marion Seftel, a history teacher at Masada College in Sydney, supported her. The first group of 28 students participated in the 2001 MOTL and since then the program has gained momentum.

The reasons for this change are complex and understanding them requires further research. They include the ebbing of the pain of the survivors over time, the fact that members of the second generation started to return to Poland and write about their experiences, and the changes on the international scene. After 2001, the Australians stressed the positive values of the program. After focusing on its negative aspects, the Australian Jewish community now strongly endorses the pilgrimage to Poland. Participants stressed that MOTL strengthens Jewish identity and energises the high school participants through their experience of Jewish memorial sites in both Poland and Israel. This view supports Stier's conclusion that '[t]he March of the Living, as an ideological and religious experience is an excellent example of commemorative performance in which the desire for memory has outrun the need for history'.[76]

In 2008 Sam Lipski visited Poland for the first time. After his visit he published a 'Partisan' column in the *Australian Jewish News* titled 'Urging all Australian Jews: go to Poland', in which he stressed:

> Indeed I urge every Jew, especially every Australian Jew, who has any connection with Poland to go there, to confront the complexities of their personal and our national histories, and to experience for themselves the still fledgling, but deeply moving renewal of Jewish life there ... Go to Poland, therefore, not only to commemorate and honour the victims of the Holocaust and to pay respects to our dead. Such remembrance is an obligation, a *mitzvah* for all time. But today's new imperative is to support and sustain those Polish Jews who are emerging tentatively and bravely from the destruction of Jewish life under Nazism and communism. And that means also finding ways to encourage the growing numbers of non-Jewish Poles who are working to restore Jewish culture as part of their lost national heritage.[77]

---

76 Stier, *Committed to Memory*, 184.
77 Sam Lipski, 'Urging all Australian Jews: go to Poland', *AJN*, 13 June 2008, 18.

Thus, Australian Jewry has turned around from strong opposition to strong support of MOTL. With the present enthusiasm for the program, the fact that Australian Jewry refused to participate in the program for 14 years has been forgotten. This generational cycle began with an initial speaking about the horrors of the past in the immediate postwar period, followed by a period often referred to as 'the silence', as most survivors sought to rebuild their shattered lives in the 1950s and so repressed their terrible memories to their subconscious and the regular nightmares recalled by so many of their children. The gradual reawakening and retelling of stories began in the 1960s but gained real momentum in the late 1970s and 1980s. Finally there were the annual pilgrimages and ritual of the return to the death camps and memorial sites in Poland, which for Australian Jews only started on an official level with the community's first participation in MOTL in 2001. This analysis of the changing contours of memory shows how the association with the past has evolved over the generations of Australian Jews since 1945 – a complex and nuanced story. It has also illustrated the largely forgotten story of the emotion and strength of Australian Jewish survivor opposition to any organised return to Poland in the late 1980s. This opposition had largely ebbed away by the turn of the century.

Part IV

Holocaust narratives
on film

Chapter 9

REPRESENTING RAPE IN HOLOCAUST FILM

Exhibiting the eroticised body for the camera's gaze

Adam Brown and Deb Waterhouse-Watson

Rape has been figured and refigured in Holocaust films since the cinema's first engagements with the subject of Nazi Germany. In an early scene of Charlie Chaplin's influential 1940 film, *The Great Dictator*, the Hitler-esque authoritarian ruler, 'Adenoid Hynkel' (played by Chaplin), summons his secretary into his personal office. A tall, 'Aryan'-looking woman obediently enters the room carrying a notepad and pen. Seconds after beginning to dictate a letter to her, Hynkel exudes a mixture of an animalistic snarl and snort, snatching the notepad from the woman's hands and throwing it to the floor. He grabs the back of her head, tilting her body downwards beneath his own and walks her backwards across the room in what almost amounts to an awkward dance to the light musical score in the background. The woman's forlorn cries of 'No, no!' are ignored as Hynkel snarls again with widened eyes and exhales as if snoring. The woman faints as Hynkel lowers her to the couch, the impending rape interrupted only by a ringing telephone. Summoned away, Hynkel seems to immediately forget the woman's presence and leaves the room, while the woman (who had apparently only feigned passing out) sits up to placidly watch her would-be attacker exit. After serving as a vehicle for demonising Hitler, the woman does not even seem to remember the assault when she dictates a letter for her Führer in a later scene.

In the present context of early 21st-century viewing (and perhaps even at the time of the film's release), this scene stands out awkwardly in Chaplin's humorous narrative. The threat of rape portrayed on the screen exhibits a tension between the filmmaker's desire to criticise Adolf Hitler and the more pragmatic technique – common to Hollywood films at the time – of downplaying Hitler's importance and the danger he signified by implying to the audience that he should not be taken too seriously.[1] In any case, with the joke and/or the 'message' being fulfilled, Hynkel's secretary makes no further appearance in the film. Importantly, *The Great Dictator*, already controversial at the time (and to this day) for breaking the taboo of using humour to depict the Nazis' persecution of Jews, was filmed and released prior to the mass exterminations of what is now known as the Holocaust.[2] Nevertheless, many more portrayals of the sexual abuse of women in the context of Nazi Germany and the Second World War – and, more specifically, the Holocaust – have followed Chaplin's satirical work, with examples to be found in every decade since the war's end. As a result, the subject of rape has frequently intersected with eroticised images of female bodies, signalling a highly problematic trend in Holocaust films.

The increasing and important growth of Holocaust narratives – filmic and otherwise – that focus on women's experiences continues to qualify the established male-oriented 'canon' of Holocaust representation. However, the once – or even still – taboo issues of sexuality and sexual violence in this context still linger uncomfortably in the background. The most comprehensive study in this area to date, the collection of essays *Sexual Violence against Jewish Women during the Holocaust* (2010), reveals that many aspects of this subject remain marginalised in popular culture and in academic scholarship.[3] Given the fundamental importance of films to both collective memories of the Holocaust and understandings of gender and violence more broadly, this chapter analyses the ways in which several Holocaust films eroticise the female body through the camera's gaze. Feminist film theorist Laura Mulvey influentially describes this gaze as encouraging male pleasure in objectifying the female form.[4] While a diverse range of Holocaust-related films could be applied to this subject, the works selected for analysis here

---

1   For a detailed exploration of Hollywood's initially guarded treatment of Nazi Germany, see Daniel Anker (dir.), *Imaginary Witness: Hollywood and the Holocaust* (United States: Koch Lorber Films, [2004] 2009).

2   Significantly, Chaplin expressed some regret after the war about *The Great Dictator*, noting in his autobiography that he may not have made the film had he been aware of what would soon take place in the concentration camps. See Charles Chaplin, *My Autobiography* (London: Penguin, 1974), 387–88.

3   Sophia Hedgepeth and Rochelle G Saidel, eds, *Sexual Violence against Jewish Women during the Holocaust* (Hanover, NH, and London: Brandeis University Press, 2010).

4   Laura Mulvey, 'Visual pleasure and narrative cinema', *Screen*, vol. 16, no. 3, 1975.

CHAPTER 9

exemplify the often voyeuristic tendencies of many fiction films depicting events and experiences *during* the Holocaust, particularly those that provide sustained attention to the sexual assault and degradation of women. For this reason, we have excluded films relating to Nazi Germany that portray rape in other settings, such as the notorious anti-Semitic propaganda film *Jud Süß* [Jew Süss] (1940), which portrays a rape committed by the demonised protagonist; and the early Hollywood production *None Shall Escape* (1944), in which a Nazi officer on trial for war crimes is revealed by flashback to have raped (off-screen) one of his school pupils in Poland after the First World War. Likewise, the filmic representation of sexual violence against men in Holocaust films such as *Bent* (1997) and *The Reader* (2008) is an important issue that is beyond the scope of this chapter.

Exploring the competing discourses and trends in how the female body is eroticised or otherwise treated in Holocaust fiction films, we argue that dominant modes of representation continue to reinforce this problematic representation of women in films, such as the recent mainstream production *Zwartboek* [Black Book] (2006). Nevertheless, we demonstrate that some Holocaust films subvert this trend, portraying sexual violence in ways that reject voyeurism, and reveal that film has considerable potential to represent rape in a nuanced and sophisticated manner.

The female body, voyeurism and the camera's gaze

Problematically, mainstream cinema still has a tendency to eroticise the rape victim's body. Indeed, many films depicting rape, such as Jonathan Kaplan's *The Accused* (1988), have been criticised for encouraging voyeuristic attitudes towards rape, despite the filmmaker's apparent attempts to critique such attitudes.[5] In her influential essay 'Visual pleasure and narrative cinema', Laura Mulvey argues that the viewer's perspective is aligned with that of the male protagonist, hence positioning the woman as the object of a voyeuristic male gaze. Mulvey argues that women's 'appearance [is] coded for strong visual and erotic impact so that they can be said to connote *to-be-looked-at-ness*'.[6] She argues that this is the case because 'man is reluctant to gaze on his exhibitionist like',[7] and must therefore control the

5   Tanya Horek, *Public Rape: Representing Violation in Fiction and Film* (London: Routledge, 2004), 91–116; Sarah Projansky, *Watching Rape: Film and Television in Postfeminist Culture* (New York: New York University Press, 2002), 95–96.
6   Mulvey, 'Visual pleasure and narrative cinema', 11.
7   ibid., 12.

'look'. This is particularly problematic when the body is eroticised during a rape, as it therefore positions the viewer to derive pleasure from watching rape. Indeed, Sarah Projansky highlights the 'paradox of discursively *increasing* (and potentially eliciting pleasure in) the very thing a text is working against'.[8] While it might appear counterintuitive to suggest that violent rape might be a source of pleasure, it is important to remember that meaning is subjective, and feminist theorist Susan Faludi relates that many young men who watched *The Accused* 'hooted and cheered' during the rape scene.[9]

These problems also apply to Holocaust films. While intrinsically difficult to depict, we by no means suggest that subjects such as the exploitation of women and sexual violence should not be represented. Such issues are crucial, yet as with the broader contemporary debates over Holocaust representation, and the representation of rape more generally, the question is not *if* they should be represented, but *how*. An ever-expanding literature on Holocaust film has contributed much to legitimising it as an important field of research; however, little substantial attention has been given to the representation of women, sexuality, rape and the voyeuristic tendencies of filmmaking at issue here.[10] While some feminist scholars have discussed Holocaust films using Mulvey's concept of the cinematic gaze, the number and variety of films examined have unfortunately been limited.[11]

---

8   loc. cit., 96.

9   Susan Faludi, *Backlash: The Undeclared War against Women* (London: Vintage, 1991), 170.

10   Works published in the last several years alone include Libby Saxton, *Haunted Images: Film, Ethics, Testimony and the Holocaust* (London: Wallflower, 2008); Giacomo Lichtner, *Film and the Holocaust in France and Italy, 1956–1998* (London: Vallentine Mitchell, 2008); Terri Ginsberg, *Holocaust Film: The Political Aesthetics of Ideology* (Newcastle: Cambridge Scholars, 2007); Millicent Marcus, *Italian Film in the Shadow of Auschwitz* (Toronto: University of Toronto Press, 2007); Caroline Joan Picart and David A Frank, *Frames of Evil: The Holocaust as Horror in American Film* (Carbondale: Southern Illinois University Press, 2006); Toby Haggith and Joanna Newman, eds, *Holocaust and the Moving Image: Representations in Film and Television Since 1933* (London: Wallflower, 2005); Omer Bartov, *The 'Jew' in Cinema: From The Golem to Don't Touch My Holocaust* (Bloomington, Ind.: Indiana University Press, 2005); Janet Walker, *Trauma Cinema: Documenting Incest and the Holocaust* (Berkeley: University of California Press, 2005); Joshua Hirsch, *Afterimage: Film, Trauma, and the Holocaust* (Philadelphia: Temple University Press, 2004).

11   See, for example, Marguerite Waller, 'Signifying the Holocaust: Liliana Cavani's *Portiere di Notte*', in Laura Pietropaolo and Ada Testaferri, eds, *Feminisms in the Cinema* (Bloomington, Ind.: Indiana University Press, 1995), 206–19. Other examples by Cottino-Jones and Scherr are cited below.

Many films have contributed to what Holocaust historian Saul Friedländer has characterised as 'a vast pornographic output centred on Nazism'.[12] The infamous (semi- or fully) pornographic films *Ilsa, She-Wolf of the SS Special Section* (1975), *Salon Kitty* (1976), *Deported Women of the SS* (1976) and *SS Hell Camp* (1977), among many other Nazi (s)exploitation films of the 1960s and 1970s, have been criticised as encouraging a perverse voyeurism. Lynn Rapaport argues in her analysis of *Ilsa, She-Wolf of the SS* that 'the Holocaust is not just being sexualized, but it is also being gendered – a woman in power is evil, a Nazi, a feminazi'.[13] In these and other films, any attempt – if there is even an attempt – to critique the fetishistic aspects of Nazi ideology and practice can potentially, and problematically, reinforce these ideas. Of course, we are not attempting to draw parallels between these kinds of films and more authentic attempts to engage with World War II history on film, but the common intertwining of themes of sex, death and 'moral compromise' in films about the Nazis makes for a problematic cultural context for any filmmaker who attempts to represent women's experiences.

Liliana Cavani's controversial film, *Il portiere di notte* [The Night Porter] (1974), still prompts vigorous debate over the intersection of sex, the Holocaust and film. Exemplifying the trend of eroticising the female body in order to symbolise the apparently amoral environment of wartime Europe, *The Night Porter* portrays the tormented sexual relationship between a former Nazi officer and the camp inmate he repeatedly raped and sexually abused, who renew their destructive and fatal relationship after the war. Marga Cottino-Jones strongly criticises *The Night Porter*, arguing that the camera's 'voyeuristic effect and its subtle manipulation of the spectators' gaze and reactions' reveals the power of the image 'to overwhelm and ravish, to enlist a voyeuristic pleasure of almost any subject, no matter how monstrous'.[14]

In his essay on the 'grey zone', prominent Auschwitz survivor Primo Levi strongly condemned the filmmaker's (intentional) blurring of the fundamental distinction between victim and perpetrator. Levi wrote that Cavani's film was 'false', a sign of 'a moral disease or an aesthetic affectation or a sinister sign of complicity; above all, it is precious service rendered ... to the

---

12   Saul Friedländer, *Reflections of Nazism: An Essay on Kitsch and Death*, trans. Thomas Weyr (New York: Harper and Row, 1982), 74.

13   Lyn Rapaport, 'Holocaust pornography: Profaning the sacred in *Ilsa, She-Wolf of the SS*', *Shofar: An Interdisciplinary Journal of Jewish Studies*, vol. 22, no. 1, Fall 2003, 63.

14   Marga Cottino-Jones, '"What kind of memory?": Liliana Cavani's *Night Porter*', *Contention*, vol. 5, no. 1, 1995, 107.

negators of truth'.[15] Scholar Rebecca Scherr sums up many of the issues at hand, arguing that in Cavani's film,

> eroticism emerges as the central trope for examining the difficult subject of Holocaust experience and memory ... replac[ing] the absence of sexuality characteristic of memoirs of camp experience with an overabundance of erotic imagery, a sign that indicates a general discomfort with the historical facts or with the methods one can employ to represent the Holocaust. Moreover, it is the female body that becomes the site for displaying this erotic impulse. The authors project a kind of sexual paranoia, and as readers/viewers watch these sexualized bodies they share the experience of navigating between sex and violence, and sex and death, in a fictional Holocaust universe.[16]

The problematic appropriation of the female body is part of a much broader phenomenon in Holocaust representation, with themes of perversion, sadomasochism, rape and nymphomania figuring in several films.

Reiterations of a familiar theme: Problematic portrayals of sexuality and rape

Most depictions of rape in Holocaust films are fleeting. To take one example, the implied rape of a young girl in NBC's highly influential television miniseries, *Holocaust: The Story of the Family Weiss* (1978), is briefly used as a metaphor for the ferocity of the Nazis' persecution of Jews on *Kristallnacht* ['Night of Broken Glass'] in 1938. The traumatised girl, who can no longer speak, is then murdered as part of the Nazis' 'euthanasia' program; thus the rape is ultimately subsumed within the seven-and-a-half hour narrative that seeks to touch on 'all' aspects of Nazi persecution. On the other hand, some representations of the (actual, planned or potential) degradation and assault of women form major points around which a film's plot pivots. The variety of representations is aligned with the diversity of 'uses' to which the device or trope of rape is put in filmic terms.

---

15   Primo Levi, *The Drowned and the Saved*, trans. Raymond Rosenthal (London: Michael Joseph, [1986] 1988), 32–33.

16   Rebecca Scherr, 'The uses of memory and abuses of fiction: Sexuality in Holocaust film, fiction, and memoir', in Elizabeth R Baer and Myrna Goldenberg, eds, *Experience and Expression: Women, the Nazis, and the Holocaust* (Detroit: Wayne State University Press, 2003), 279.

Emphasising the 'silence' that has formed in historical writing and testimonial narratives around the subject of rape during the Holocaust, Zoë Waxman writes that 'when writing rape into the Holocaust, historians and other custodians of memory also need to ensure that they are not imposing on survivors their own concerns and preoccupations'.[17] This point can readily be applied to the appropriation of rape by filmmakers to generate meanings of various kinds and for various agendas. A brief survey of Holocaust cinema reveals that films represent acts of rape and eroticised images of the female body in a number of ways: as a means of signifying a male survivor's trauma; a way to construct binaries between a narrative's (male) 'hero' and 'villain'; a tool for engaging in sheer comic absurdity; or a vehicle for exploring the apparently amoral environment viewed as a byproduct of Nazism and its atrocities.

Sidney Lumet's film *The Pawnbroker* (1965) is as much concerned with contemporary 'race relations' in the United States as it is with the Holocaust, intertwining the traumatised back story of Holocaust survivor Sol Nazerman with the social tensions of 1960s America. In one of the film's most pivotal scenes, an African-American prostitute attempts to use her body to entice the pawnbroker to give her a better price for her locket. While the woman strips off all her clothes in front of Nazerman, she repeatedly tells him to 'Look', arguably reinforcing the racialised and sexualised stereotype of the 'Othered' Black woman.[18] At the same time, the camera cuts to images of Nazerman's experience in Auschwitz, including a panning shot of several women forced to be camp 'prostitutes'.[19] Juxtaposing the African-American woman's exposed breasts in the present day with the naked body of Nazerman's wife just prior to his witnessing a Nazi officer raping her, the female body serves as a conduit to Nazerman's repressed memories, which are ignited by the woman's physical provocation. Nazerman orders the woman out of his store, and his enraged groan and clenched fist serve as a prelude to the well-known 'silent scream' at the end of the film, which signals the release of his repressed trauma.

---

17   Zoë Waxman, 'Testimony and silence: Sexual violence and the Holocaust', in Sorcha Gunne and Zoë Brigley Thompson, eds, *Feminism, Literature and Rape Narratives* (New York and London: Routledge, 2010), 126.

18   For a detailed exploration of this stereotype in a cinematic context, see Frank B Wilderson III, *Red, White & Black: Cinema and the Structure of U.S. Antagonisms* (Durham, NH, and London: Duke University Press, 2010).

19   It should be noted that the forced prostitution of women in the camps is better characterised as 'rape slavery', though the former term is more prevalent in Holocaust literature.

Several decades later, the depiction of eroticised female bodies and sexual abuse in the context of the Holocaust would take an entirely different form in Steven Spielberg's Hollywood blockbuster *Schindler's List* (1993), a film that has inspired a critical industry of its own.[20] One scene in particular that has attracted considerable attention is the (in)famous 'shower scene', which takes place after a group of Jewish women are temporarily diverted from the promised safety of Schindler's factory to Auschwitz. With subtle intertextual leanings to Alfred Hitchcock's *Psycho* (1960), the building tension and emotional catharsis (when water bursts from the ceiling rather than the anticipated gas) rely heavily on a voyeuristic gaze on the female body, which is arguably eroticised, if only briefly, in the undressing room sequence shortly beforehand. Reflecting a widely held view, Barry Langford writes that the scene parallels the redemptive trajectory of the film's overall narrative, and has the effect of '"pornographising" genocide; that is, it issues an explicit "come-on" to the spectator, its exploitative address underlined by the naked female flesh on ample display'.[21] Scholars have also commented at length on the scene in the cellar where the threat of rape looms large over Helen's eroticised body as Amon Goeth stalks and then beats her.[22] Crucially, Helen's character functions to make clear the distinction between 'good' and 'evil' men through the different ways that Oskar Schindler and Goeth treat her, rather than being a person in her own right.

An even more dubious representation of (attempted) rape can be found in a more unconventional 'rescue story', the Czech film *Divided We Fall* (2000), which focuses on a married couple who are generally indifferent to the plight of Jews being deported from their town, although they do secretly (and reluctantly) care for an escaped victim. In one scene, what could be portrayed as a chilling and callous attempt at rape is trivialised and mocked. A collaborator, Horst, attempts to rape the main female character, Marie; however, the event occurs in a brightly lit picnic setting and uses elements of slapstick. When the scene begins, Horst tells Marie that he is 'preparing an offensive', which seems to tally with early feminist arguments that rape

---

20   For a detailed account of the popular and scholarly reception of *Schindler's List*, see Alan Mintz, *Popular Culture and the Shaping of Holocaust Memory in America* (Seattle: University of Washington Press, 2001), 125–58.

21   Barry Langford, '"You cannot look at this": Thresholds of unrepresentability in Holocaust film', *The Journal of Holocaust Education*, vol. 8, no. 3, Winter 1999, 36.

22   For a detailed discussion of the 'shower scene' and the representation of Helen, see Sara R Horowitz, 'But is it good for the Jews? Spielberg's Schindler and the aesthetics of atrocity', in Yosefa Loshitzky, ed., *Spielberg's Holocaust: Critical Perspectives on Schindler's List* (Bloomington: Indiana University Press, 1997), 126–32.

is an act of violence rather than of sex,[23] yet this sentiment is portrayed as ridiculous through Horst's failure to complete the 'offensive'. When Marie cries that Horst is attempting to rape her, Horst asks, 'What rape? Nobody's here. We're here alone', as if he could not possibly be a rapist. The comic absurdity of the scenario renders the attack titillating and a potential source of pleasure. Marie kicks her attacker in the groin before expressing genuine concern that she hurt him, showing how easily the rapist could be overcome and making light of the threat. In the film's climactic happy ending, Horst, who is not even a doctor, helps deliver Marie's baby, further marginalising and dismissing the threat of rape.

Images of rape and the voyeuristic gaze on the woman's body serve a different purpose again in Lina Wertmüller's 1975 film *Pasqualino Settebellezze* [Seven Beauties], which follows the comedic exploits of Pasqualino, whose journey encompasses his days as a roguish scoundrel and murderer in Italy, an inmate in an insane asylum, and a prisoner in Auschwitz. The adventures of the egotistical (and mostly unsympathetic) protagonist, who is determined to survive the war at any and all costs, are propelled by his various encounters with female bodies, which are portrayed by turns as erotic and grotesque. Invariably, the film's camerawork invites the viewer to adopt the male's gaze on women – from the obese Nazi officer who exchanges food for sex, to the woman tied to an insane asylum bed whom he rapes. While representations of sexual assault in any medium should legitimise the suffering of the victim and indict the perpetrator, the film's portrayal of rape immediately shifts to the physical torture of the perpetrator (along with Pasqualino's other suffering), thus effectively writing the victim of rape out of the narrative.

Eli Pfefferkorn writes that *Seven Beauties* presents 'the painful ambiguities that derive from survival in extremities that shame man into hiding',[24] yet he does not take into account the eroticised (or grotesque) bodies of *women*, nor the exploitation of these bodies (by both protagonist and camera). Upon deserting the Italian army on the way to Stalingrad, Pasqualino stumbles across an isolated villa in the forest, peering inside to see the naked back of a woman playing the piano and singing. Signalling a tension between two (apparently insatiable) appetites, Pasqualino ceases to encircle the room like

---

23 Susan Brownmiller was an early proponent of this argument in her book *Against Our Will: Men, Women and Rape* (London: Secker & Warburg, 1975), 194–197.

24 Eli Pfefferkorn, 'The case of Bruno Bettelheim and Lina Wertmüller's *Seven Beauties*', in Yisrael Gutman and Avital Saf, eds, *The Nazi Concentration Camps: Structure and Aims, The Image of the Prisoner, The Jews in the Camps: Proceedings of the Fourth Yad Vashem International Historical Conference, Jerusalem, January 1980* (Jerusalem: Yad Vashem, 1984), 676.

a predator staring at the woman's body, and ventures into the kitchen to fill his mouth and pockets with food while engaging in comic banter with an old woman who cannot understand or stop him. The film's frequently voyeuristic gaze constructed around the semi-naked bodies of women, along with the comedic portrayal of rape, perhaps signals less 'a scathing comment on the breakdown of human compassion and moral responsibility by the civilized world', as Pfefferkorn contends,[25] and more an ambivalent representation of an amoral wartime Europe left ravaged in the wake of Nazi Germany's destructive agenda. A similar representational agenda seems to be at work in the 2006 film *Black Book*, one of the most recent re-articulations of this voyeuristic trend in Holocaust film.

The erotic and the abject in Paul Verhoeven's *Black Book* (2006)

Black Book follows a similar thematic line to Wertmüller's much earlier production, focusing on the 'compromises' necessary to survive in an apparently amoral world. Unlike *Seven Beauties*, however, the flawed protagonist of *Black Book* is a Jewish woman, Rachel Stein, who takes the name Ellis de Vries when masquerading as an 'Aryan' to assist the local Dutch Resistance. The film's director, Paul Verhoeven, who also made *Robocop* (1987), *Basic Instinct* (1992), *Showgirls* (1995) and *Starship Troopers* (1997), is well known for his excess-driven plots, and *Black Book* is no exception. After her entire family is killed in a bloody massacre, Ellis joins the Resistance and is assigned to seduce a high-ranking Nazi officer, Müntze, with whom she soon falls in love. The film is clearly intended to work against the exploitation of women by Nazism and, more broadly, by men; however, the aesthetics employed throughout the narrative undermine this surface ideology, positioning the viewer to view the female body simultaneously as an erotic object and an embodiment of the abject.

While the female figure serves to varying degrees as a sexualised prop in the films already mentioned, Ellis functions as an agent in *Black Book*. Nevertheless, she *only* has her 'feminine wiles' to draw from – violence is left to the men. The film does consciously play on (and with) the idea of using one's body to subvert the perpetrators' goals; however, significant contradictions lie at the heart of the narrative. Her constant central positioning within the frame, and the way she stands out from any background and all other

---

25   ibid., 674.

people, encourages viewers to see her body as an erotic spectacle. Adopting an appearance not unlike Marlene Dietrich, Ellis sings for the Nazis and frequently wears transparent clothing (even on impractical occasions when spending time with the Resistance and not trying to seduce any Nazis). A close-up shot early in the film draws the viewer's gaze to her pubic hair while she dyes it blonde for extra 'Aryan' effect. Even more problematically, when Müntze realises that Ellis is Jewish as she tries to seduce him, she succeeds in winning him over by drawing his hands to her breasts and her hips, repeatedly asking him, 'Are these Jewish?' Although this may be intended to imply that she is – like all women – human, the question actually attaches very degrading connotations to the physique of Jewish women.

Torn between the Nazi perpetrator-occupiers and the Resistance (which are portrayed as equally brutal as the war ends), the figure of Ellis is emblematic of the film's depiction of wartime Europe: she acts as a metaphor to portray the aesthetic sheen of power and the powerful – the beauty that disguises a rotten foundation. In this sense, Ellis becomes the embodiment of not only the erotic, but also the grotesque and abject. At one point, she is shown as completely mired in the abject when she attempts to avoid detection as a spy by using a toilet to clean grease off her foot (ignoring the sink that stands alongside it). Although the audience is clearly positioned to identify and sympathise with Ellis throughout the film, the devices used to this end rely on a voyeuristic gaze that takes in a compilation of degrading images of women which the film, on the surface, seeks to critique.

Women's experiences are again brought to the fore after the liberation, with one disturbing shot portraying several women publicly humiliated by Resistance members who cut off their hair and label them 'Nazi whores' with a sign. However, the effectiveness of this image is undermined shortly afterwards by perhaps the film's most confronting scene, when the Resistance forces a group of imprisoned collaborators, including Ellis, to strip naked in a factory surrounded by concentration camp-like fencing. Ellis, whose naked body is foregrounded by the camera's gaze while the bodies of those around her are hidden, is singled out and, when she refuses to sing for the drunken crowd, she is bombarded with a barrel of human excrement from above. While a Nazi officer tells a resister early in the film that 'You are a pile of shit on the road to German victory', Ellis becomes a pile of shit in the wake of German defeat. To further the 'shock value' of the scene, one of the resister-now-perpetrators hoses her down as if he is urinating on her. As one scholar of Holocaust film has recently noted, 'filming for shock effect can transform a scene from a war crime to a kind of commercial pornography that … [injures] the image of survivor women'.[26] In short, even though Ellis is clearly the victim in *Black Book*, the voyeuristic depiction of her body – by turns erotic and grotesque – is exploited by both characters and filmmaker, transforming it into a site of voyeurism to explore the dark natures of Nazism and humanity.

Performing history in/through film: Deconstructing the gaze

In an essay published in 2010, Yvonne Kozlovsky-Golan provides the most recent discussion of sexual abuse of women and girls in Holocaust cinematic memory, identifying the female body as 'public property' and contending that women are used 'as a vehicle for conveying the Nazi/Fascist message, for carrying out their sex crimes, sexual exploitation, and pimping, and as a means through which pure evil works itself out in all its ugliness'.[27] While this might indeed apply to many of the films noted previously, this is not always the case. Several recent Holocaust films engage seriously and sensitively with the traumatic experiences of women, and some arguably succeed in avoiding patriarchal objectification. Although Kozlovsky-Golan suggests that fictional dramatisations of rape 'can often transmit the reality better than words can', she laments that 'the bounds of cinematic representation of sex and sexual abuse of women during the Holocaust' have not been broken.[28] However, through a self-reflexive emphasis on performativity and intertextuality, Michael Verhoeven's *Mutters Courage* [My Mother's Courage] (1995) and Audrius Juzenas' *Ghetto* (2006) deconstruct the male gaze and, as a result, subvert the voyeuristic sexualisation of women common to other Holocaust films.

My Mother's Courage offers a heavily ironic representation of the deportation of Hungarian Jews to Auschwitz in 1944. While the above examples of 'Holocaust comedies', *The Great Dictator, Seven Beauties* and *Divided We Fall*, demonstrate problematic tendencies in their combination of comedy and rape, which tend to belittle, marginalise or degrade the victim, Verhoeven's film reveals that this is not an inevitable outcome of the

---

26 Yvonne Kozlovsky-Golan, '"Public property": Sexual abuse of women and girls in cinematic memory', in Sophia M Hedgepeth and Rochelle G Saidel, eds, *Sexual Violence Against Jewish Women During the Holocaust* (Hanover, NH, and London: Brandeis University Press, 2010), 247.

27 ibid., 241.

28 ibid., 249.

genre.[29] Verhoeven's sensitive engagement with the fraught issue of sexual assault is partly achieved through the employment of humour at various points throughout the film. Having claimed that '[w]e have no right to assert that this is reality precisely because it is a true story', Verhoeven privileges self-reflexivity over a conventional linear narrative. The narrator – played by George Tabori, whose real mother's story of survival is dramatised in the film – physically intrudes on the 'set', interacting with, and often making fun of, the characters or the actors who are playing them. This mode of representation repeatedly highlights the constructed nature of the film, but also subverts the potential eroticisation of the female body. The film is part comedy, part tragedy, and includes three instances of rape within its narrative, with the effectiveness of these more serious moments enhanced as they are preceded by scenes of comic banter.

While waiting to board the train, protagonist Elsa Tabori makes friends with another Jewish deportee, Maria, who tells Elsa how she was raped by several Hungarian collaborators. Flashbacks show the young girl being chased by several men, who hold her head down in a flushing toilet before forcing her onto a table as she struggles and cries out. One then starts to remove his belt. While the dramatisation ends there, opening up the possibility of the rape being elided, the portrayal of Maria's experience continues through her statement that she does not think she screamed (although the dramatised re-enactment suggests she did). The filmmaker uses shot-reverse-shot, moving back and forth between the characters' faces, which presents lingering views of the girl's traumatised visage and Elsa's sympathetic expression and comforting embrace. This technique encourages an empathetic understanding of the victim's trauma.

A similar validation and lack of eroticisation are employed when Elsa is raped in the cattle car by another deportee, shattering her previous flashbacks of pleasant family life and representing an experience that is seldom mentioned in discussions of deportation. The rapist's aggressive face is relegated to the edge of the frame, while the camera's gaze focuses primarily on Elsa's shocked, then horrified facial expression rather than on her body, as she attempts to fight the man off. This actively negates the potential for eroticisation. Afterwards, Elsa brushes herself down with the seemingly compulsive need to 'wash away the rapist' that many victims experience. This

---

29   For a discussion of the value of humour in Holocaust representation, see Lynn Rapaport, 'Laughter and heartache: The functions of humor in Holocaust tragedy', in Jonathan Petropoulos and John K Roth, eds, *Gray Zones: Ambiguity and Compromise in the Holocaust and Its Aftermath* (New York: Berghahn, 2005), 252.

takes the place of the 'showering' scene, which Projansky argues is important in signalling to the viewer that rape did actually take place.[30] Mulvey argues that denying the camera's presence prevents the audience from being aware of it and is therefore crucial for naturalising the objectifying gaze.[31] The self-conscious camerawork in *My Mother's Courage* actively disrupts this problematic effect. After the rape scene, the film immediately shifts to an explicitly intertextual connection with Claude Lanzmann's paradigmatic film *Shoah* (1985), recreating the well-known figure of the train conductor looking out from the locomotive. Once again exposing the artifice of the fictional narrative, *My Mother's Courage* implies that the 'reality' of this trauma can never be represented fully.

Another self-reflexive film that engages with the complexities of rape during the Holocaust is the German production of *Ghetto*, adapted from Israeli playwright Joshua Sobol's stageplay. Portraying the vexed issue of Jewish behaviour in the Vilna ghetto prior to its liquidation, the film's narrative focuses on the order to establish a theatre in the ghetto to 'keep up morale' by SS officer Kittel, who, in one of the film's many subplots, has become infatuated with the theatre's lead singer, Haya. Released in 2006, the film in many ways implicitly rejects the redemptory aesthetic of *Schindler's List*. Unlike the tension between Goeth and Helen in Spielberg's film, the relationship (if it can be called that) between Kittel and Haya is not eroticised, even though her body is used at times to influence the Nazi perpetrator.[32]

One instance of rape is depicted in *Ghetto*, during a scene in which Kittel and other Nazi soldiers stage a kind of 'celebration' with the members of the theatre troupe. Throughout the scene, the artificiality of the situation is emphasised through the visibly uncomfortable expressions of the Jewish victims present (who have been ordered to 'keep the Germans happy'), the frequent onscreen presence of a Nazi camera operator, and the black-and-white footage of the scene (apparently being filmed by the Nazi) that is

---

30 Projansky, *Watching Rape*, 109. The third (implied) rape in the film occurs in flashback, immediately following this scene, as Elsa remembers seeing her doctor-father with a woman in his surgery.

31 Mulvey, 'Visual pleasure and narrative cinema', 17.

32 For an analysis of the contrasting representations of 'privileged' Jews in *Schindler's List* and *Ghetto*, see Adam Brown, 'Marginalising the marginal in Holocaust films: Fictional representations of Jewish policemen', *Limina: A Journal of Historical and Cultural Studies*, vol. 15, 2009 http://www.limina.arts.uwa.edu.au/previous/vol11to15/vol15/ibpcommended. Further discussion of the depiction of 'privileged' Jews in film can be found in Adam Brown, *Judging 'Privileged' Jews: Holocaust Ethics, Representation, and the 'Grey Zone'* (Berghahn, New York, 2013).

intermingled with colour film. The fast editing and lively rendition of 'I am the Naughty Lola' nevertheless implicate the audience as spectators of the onscreen entertainment, until a sudden change in the soundtrack combines haunting sounds, an absurd speech about Jewish productivity by the film's Schindler figure, and the screams of a Jewish woman who is violently raped by two German soldiers. The bloodied woman falls to the floor in front of the stunned and guilt-ridden group, confronting the Jews with their extreme situation. The blood arguably signifies that the rape was an act of violence, rather than sex, negating its eroticisation.

Connoting determination in the face of tragedy, another woman sings a song of survival and lament – 'We will fight and we will strive to carry on and stay alive!' – until she is cut off when Kittel forces a phallic cigar into her mouth and changes the song. This actually heightens the effect of the Jewish lament, because it disrupts the audience's emotional response. Further, when an intoxicated Kittel informs the head of the Jewish Police, Jacob Gens, that he is to organise 2,000 Jews to be 'selected' and delivered to Lithuanian militia (evidently to be shot), the ambiguous figure of Gens exposes Haya's breasts to the obsessed Kittel in order to 'bargain' him down to 600 victims. The image of Haya trapped between the two men who barter over her body is thus linked to the abuse of the woman who has just been raped. The use of the onscreen camera in this scene, like the self-reflexive elements of *My Mother's Courage*, again disrupts rather than normalises the eroticising gaze.

Conclusion: Towards a new aesthetic?

Mulvey's concept of the 'gaze' emphasises 'the silent image of woman still tied to her place as bearer of meaning, not maker of meaning'.[33] In the area of Holocaust film, representations of female victims of Nazi persecution have frequently given history heavily gendered meanings, (re)inscribing patriarchal understandings of the event. Ever since the secretary of Chaplin's 'Hynkel' was marginalised in *The Great Dictator*, the eroticisation of the female body and trivialisation of rape have permeated collective memories through the screen. Indeed, there are many more films that could be discussed in relation to this subject than could be covered here and further research on rape and the Holocaust is needed. It is clear that filmmakers have begun to confront social and cultural anxieties around rape in the unprecedented context of the Holocaust, although there remain considerable obstacles to this. The

---

33 Mulvey, 'Visual pleasure and narrative cinema', 7.

eroticisation of the female body is still a commonplace trope in mainstream films in particular, and this has informed much of Holocaust cinematic history. Nevertheless, films such as *My Mother's Courage* and *Ghetto* show that film can and does have a crucial role to play in mediating sexual violence, revealing the potential to disrupt the voyeuristic gaze and represent women's experiences during the Holocaust in a complex and nuanced manner.

Chapter 10

FROM 'EICHMANN-AS-VICTIM' TO 'NAZI-AS-JEW'[1]

Deconstructing justice in American Holocaust trial films

Danielle Christmas

As early as 1946, when Orson Welles's *The Stranger* depicted the postwar pursuit of a hiding Nazi war criminal, Hollywood investments and box office returns have demonstrated the popular appeal of performances about Holocaust justice. Although the narrative diversity of Holocaust performances – from the long-familiar incarnations of *The Diary of Anne Frank*[2] through more recent films like Robert Young's *Triumph of the Spirit* (1989) – demonstrate the cultural appeal of any and all Holocaust narratives, Holocaust accounts constructed around the trial trope have been exceptionally successful at leveraging a formulaic courtroom structure into critical acclaim and mainstream consumption. Films ranging from *Judgment at Nuremberg* (1961) and *The Man in the Glass Booth* (1975), all the way to *Music Box* (1989) and *The Reader* (2009), have helped produce a uniquely Holocaust version of the classical theatrical trial trope, a transformation that I will show has deconstructed and reconstructed the new notion of Holocaust justice that followed Israel's trial of Adolf Eichmann.

---

1   Robert Skloot, 'Holocaust theatre and the problem of justice', ed. Claude Schumacher, *Staging the Holocaust: The Shoah in Drama and Performance* (Cambridge: Cambridge University Press, 1998), 18.

2   These include, among other films about Anne Frank, George Stevens's 1959 play-to-film adaptation and the British Broadcasting Corporation's 2009 diary-to-miniseries adaptation of the same name.

In this essay, I will first outline what I am calling the pre- and post-Eichmann versions of the Holocaust trial, as described and contested by Hannah Arendt and Shoshana Felman. Next, I will discuss two American Holocaust trial films, *Judgment at Nuremberg* and *The Man in the Glass Booth*, which illustrate what I claim is the evolving account of Holocaust justice. These films, as I will show, gesture towards resolution just as they suggest that perpetrator testimony – and by extension, perpetrator victimhood – is the factual and emotional mirror of survivor testimony and victimhood. Finally, I will argue that Holocaust trial narratives after Eichmann – and by consequence, the very notion of Holocaust justice produced and reproduced by these performances – ultimately reify the idea that Holocaust justice hinges on a centring of the perpetrator, a centring that reveals the aesthetic possibilities and ethical consequences associated with blurring any and all distinctions between Nazi and Jewish subjectivities.

The Eichmann trial: 'Two opposing positions, each partially right'?[3]

In 1960, Israeli Prime Minister David Ben-Gurion announced Mossad's capture of Holocaust architect Adolf Eichmann to the Knesset and the world: Israel would finally hold accountable one of the so-called architects of the Final Solution, who had eluded the tribunals at Nuremberg. Justice would finally prevail. But Israel's breach of Argentina's sovereignty by kidnapping Eichmann gave pause, as did their assumption of jurisdiction for a crime that had been committed over a decade earlier on a different continent. Because of its controversial genesis, the Eichmann trial did not win Jews in the Diaspora or in the young Israeli state many friends, especially in the American media,[4] though it succeeded in doing one thing that Jews had failed to do following the Second World War: it brought the Holocaust into the public imagination and conversation and, according to Peter Novick,

---

3   Stefan Machura and Stefan Ulbrich, 'Law in film: Globalizing the Hollywood courtroom drama', trans. Francis M Nevins and Nils Behling, *Journal of Law and Society* 28.1 (March 2001): 125.

4   In remarkably Christological – and barely restrained anti-Semitic – language, the *Washington Post* called Israel's trial of Eichmann a 'passion play in the guise of a trial' and 'a prostitution of the forms of law', whereas the *Wall Street Journal* suggested that his prosecution had 'an atmosphere of Old Testament retribution'. Aside from what amounts to veiled Jew-baiting, the trial was also framed as an instrument of 'Communist aims' in the shadow of an escalating Cold War and the attending need for US-Germany solidarity. Quoted in Peter Novick, *The Holocaust in American Life* (New York: Mariner Books, 1999), 129–30.

branded the genocide as 'a distinct – and distinctively Jewish – entity'.[5] As one of the earliest televised trials in the history of television, Israel's prosecution of Adolf Eichmann was accessible and theatrical in a way that the Nuremberg trials never were.

While the diplomatic conflicts arising from Israel's capture of Eichmann brought the Holocaust into the media, the testimony of Jewish survivors themselves brought the Holocaust into people's homes. This centring of victim testimony literally and figuratively boxed Eichmann into the periphery and created a new and controversial strategy that challenged the primacy of the perpetrator, as well as the very notion of defendants' rights as memorialised by due process: the right to a fair trial before an independent and impartial tribunal, in which the accused is presumed innocent until proven guilty. It was this primacy of testimony and the extraordinary death and concentration camp narratives shared by the featured Holocaust victims that made the Eichmann trial so compelling and made the Holocaust suddenly so urgent for the average and uninformed viewer. This testimony changed forever the prevailing historical account of the Second World War and cemented an identity shared by Jews in Israel and the diaspora – for my purposes, especially American Jews – as survivors, one-and-all, of the Holocaust. More than just raising American interest in the juridical proceedings around a single criminal, the discussions begun by Israel's capture of Eichmann in 1960, the televised trial in 1961, and his execution in 1962 inspired a dialogue around the meanings and mechanisms of post-Holocaust justice that continues, politically and aesthetically, into the present.

Although several popular American media outlets memorialised the tenor of debates around Israel's trial of Eichmann, Hannah Arendt's series of essays for *The New Yorker*, later published as *Eichmann in Jerusalem* (1963), had a dramatic influence on this public discourse. Although the televised trial made the home of every viewer a private theatre-cum-courtroom, Arendt's credentials differentiated her gaze, privileging her account over others. Already the distinguished author of *The Origins of Totalitarianism* (1951) and, perhaps more importantly, a Jewish refugee from Nazi Germany for whom the trial was necessarily both professional and personal, Arendt undertook the task of describing the Jerusalem courtroom, the judges, the prosecutor and the defendant. Arendt's Eichmann is a mediocre man in just another government job, and this unexceptional character embodies her provocative thesis regarding the 'banality of evil'. Arendt describes the trial as profound for what it reveals

---

5   ibid., 134.

about the nature of the Nazi perpetrator: he is a 'terribly, terrifyingly normal' careerist who represents one of many orderly totalitarian cogs.[6] While she incisively questions the legitimacy of 'the court of the victors'[7] and the legal statutes defining the newly conceptualised 'crimes against humanity', Arendt is principally interested in the failure of the Israeli prosecutors to grapple with this 'new criminal'. Instead, they invoke what she defines as showmanship and theatrics that undermine the formal goals of the trial and diminish the possibility for anything like justice to come out of the Eichmann episode.

Arendt's critiques of the Eichmann trial betray her absolute commitment to a conservative theory of justice, by which I mean the long-standing and often uncritical commitment to the inherent fairness of due process. Her measures of Israel's failure in the Eichmann case – the (in)appropriateness of the 'victors' court' as the site of judgement, the legal definitions deployed in the trial, the inaccurate psychosocial evaluation of the perpetrator-subject, the theatrical primacy of victim testimony – implies that *if only* these problems had been resolved, the Eichmann trial would have been a success. In other words, Arendt implicitly concludes that *if only* Eichmann had been extradited by the right means, tried by the right state, judged by the right statutes, assessed by the right psychological theories and adjudicated by the right and formal modes of justice, his prosecution would have been both fair and successful. But Israel naturally failed to meet Arendt's standards of success because it never attempted to satisfy these standards. Instead of subscribing to her preferred conservative approach, Israel sacrificed the guise of impartiality for a cathartic ritual in which survivors were given a hearing and the Holocaust was given its due prominence.[8] Even without an explication of this victim-centred, testimony-driven approach to Holocaust justice, it is clear that Arendt is unsympathetic to the ideological goals of the trial given her seemingly uncritical commitment to due process, even and especially in exceptional circumstances like the Eichmann trial.

---

6   Hannah Arendt, *Eichmann in Jerusalem: A Report on the Banality of Evil* (New York: Penguin, 1963), 276.

7   While Arendt distrusts the impartiality of a 'court of the victors', this critique is more relevant when evaluating the justice of the Nuremberg tribunals, at which the victorious Allied powers put the Nazis, their former opponents, on trial. Despite her choice of words, using 'victors' where 'victims' would have been more truthful, the Israel-Eichmann opposition does not fit that analysis so neatly.

8   Israel almost certainly used the Eichmann trial as a stage on which to rehabilitate their international image from aggressor against Palestinians to victimised survivor – a strategy that inclined Arendt and other journalists to scepticism of the whole venture, from kidnapping to execution.

Holocaust trauma theorist Shoshana Felman has written extensively of Arendt's limited evaluation of the Eichmann trial in her book, *The Juridical Unconscious* (2002), and takes *Eichmann in Jerusalem* as her point of departure for claims regarding the role of trauma in the courtroom. For Felman, because Arendt evaluates the Eichmann trial on solely legal terms, she misses the transformative power of trauma in expanding the trial's goals and possibilities. Felman argues that an account that narrowly focuses on the knowable – e.g., rational legal categories like perpetrator and victim, innocent and guilty, or sentenced and acquitted – disregards the necessary role of the unknowable in the construction of the trial: the hidden traumas that are at the core of small- and large-scale crimes of violation, like rape or genocide. In this analysis, since trials have to cope with trauma, the law's attempt to realise a finite justice is doomed to failure because it cannot realise the nature of a trauma-based case. This means that the trauma-based trial, be it the trial of a war criminal like Eichmann or of an alleged murderer like OJ Simpson – both of which are key examples for Felman – will never succeed on solely legal terms because narrative excess[9] is implicit in its per-formance; thus, an honest evaluation of an event like the Eichmann trial requires the observer to pair the legal lens with extra-legal psychoanalytic, or 'therapising', discourses. According to this version of trauma theory, the same Eichmann trial that fails Arendt's legal test succeeds when judged on the basis of its transformative power for the victims of trauma. More than advancing an expanded account of the trial function, trauma theory suggests – somewhat problematically – that aesthetic representations of trials, in-cluding film representations, overwhelmingly provide the same account of justice by privileging these therapising discourses and de-privileging the juridical paradigm.

Felman's analysis overlooks the formal elements implicit in the classical trial trope, those very elements characteristic of due process. Trial narratives, rather than reverting to Felman's therapising discourses in order to explore and perform trauma, use 'classical structure elements such as one finds in Sophocles's *Antigone,* which is about the conflict between two opposing

---

9   I am using 'narrative excess' to mean all of those elements of survivor testimony that are not relevant to the juridically assessed narrative, whether it be emotional reactions (crying, fainting) or tangents (remarks with no factual bearing on the case). Felman might concur with the *Yad Vashem Bulletin* writer when he affirms 'the right of [Eichmann trial] witnesses to be irrelevant'. The dramatic testimony of Eichmann trial witness Yehiel De-Nur/K-Zetnik, who follows a long metaphysical tangent by becoming speechless and ultimately fainting, is a perfect example of a moment of narrative excess. Quoted in Arendt, *Eichmann in Jerusalem*, 225.

positions, *each partially right*.'[10] This feature of the trial drama, in which both sides present competing versions of the event and the most convincing account wins, complicates any firm assignment of guilt and thus any fixed notion of perpetrator identity. As Susan Sontag wrote, 'The trial is a dramatic form which imparts to events a certain provisional neutrality; the outcome remains to be decided; the very word 'defendant' implies that a defense is possible.'[11] The trial film that demands two 'partially right' stories, even as it implies disillusionment with the judicial process, aligns itself with a conservative centring of the perpetrator in the name of fairness and due process. It is no surprise, then, that films that subsume these structural elements are inconsistent with Felman's conclusions, even if their commitment to exploring the performative potentials of the courtroom might suggest otherwise.

Narrating justice and eliding difference in *Judgment at Nuremberg* (1961) and *The Man in the Glass Booth* (1975)

Since Israel's prosecution of Eichmann opened the possibility of a victim-centred narrative, popular filmmakers have developed narrative strategies to subvert this innovation and maintain Arendt's conservative interest in a trial process that follows a script and permits closure. Popular films especially have maintained the conservative account of the trial in the face of ever-emerging traumatic Holocaust narratives as a means of constraining their emotionally chaotic and often chronologically dislocated plot structures, while conversely deconstructing this very same account. The Eichmann trial, the principal point of departure for this discourse, offers the format of a trial as a mechanism for understanding what happened at Auschwitz, Mauthausen and Dachau. The trial, then, becomes a hegemonic metaphor for adjudicating the Holocaust as it further infiltrates cultural discourse.

Two Holocaust trial films illustrate the transformation of 'Holocaust justice' as a concept, both the pre-Eichmann conservatism favoured by Arendt and the victim-centred innovations celebrated by Felman. Following an evaluation of the pre-Eichmann theory of the Holocaust trial posited in the 1961 film *Judgment at Nuremberg*, I will discuss how *The Man in the Glass Booth* of 1975 manifests Arendt's 'new [bureaucracy-minded] criminal' through the overlapping of victim and perpetrator subjectivities – the

---

10 My emphasis. Machura and Ulbrich, 'Law in film', 125.
11 Susan Sontag, 'Reflections on *The Deputy*', *Against Interpretation and Other Essays* (New York: Delta, 1966), 127.

effective elimination of any distinction – and reifies the trial trope even as it undermines the trial's ability to capture the depth of Holocaust trauma. While exploring this conservative notion of the trial, the filmmakers exhibit a preoccupation with Holocaust justice narratives, a preoccupation that reflects larger cultural trends. Peter Novick distils the Jewish interest in reproducing a Holocaust narrative, citing Israel's interest in benefiting from international sympathy, an American discourse increasingly rooted in identity politics,[12] and the assimilationist threats of intermarriage and secularism. Given the stakes of this newly Holocaust-centred identity, leaders in the American Jewish community expressed anxiety at what they perceived as the increasing social acceptability of Holocaust denial, which risked opening the possibility of historical doubt and nuancing Nazi guilt, both threats to what Novick calls an increasingly sacralised Holocaust narrative. Though the interest in preserving this narrative has led to the reproduction of Holocaust trial representations, it has also led to an equally frequent reproduction of nuanced perpetrator guilt and scepticism of the post-genocide justice enterprise. Aside from these Jewish leaders and their organisations, Alan Mintz describes the relationship between this new Holocaust narrative and American cultural reproduction, arguing that a number of films, including *Judgment at Nuremberg,* have given us the kind of Holocaust America needs, a Holocaust that enables a culture of remembrance and supports national identity politics, most obviously by fortifying the increasing centrality of Holocaust memorialisation to American Jewish identity.

Jewish screenwriter and producer Abby Mann created *Judgment at Nuremberg* as a teleplay in 1959 and, following its broadcast success, collaborated with director Stanley Kramer to produce it as a film in 1961. The story is a fictionalised account of the third Nuremberg trial, often called the Judges' or Justice Trial. This particular trial reframed the 'camp commandant' image of the Nazi perpetrator by trying several high-level Nazi judges who enforced Germany's Nuremberg Codes; because the codes, upheld by them, imprisoned innocent Jews and sanctioned Nazi war crimes, the judges are charged with having effectively legalised Nazism and, by doing so, legitimising a breach of international law. In the film, Chief

---

12   Alan Mintz describes this as a transformation from what, in his essay on *Judgment at Nuremberg,* he calls the move from 'silence to salience' of the Holocaust narrative based on the need for American Jews – eager to become relevant to 1960s identity politics – to develop a collective memory of suffering. Alan Mintz, 'From silence to salience', *Popular Culture and the Shaping of Holocaust Memory in America* (Seattle: University of Washington, 2001), 3–35.

Justice Dan Haywood, an American judge, presides over the prosecution of several German judges, including Ernst Janning, a formerly upstanding jurist accused of ordering the execution of a Jewish man for having an illicit relationship with a German woman named Irene Wallner – a 'race defilement' crime of which Janning knew the man to be innocent. With this as the context for the trial, Haywood develops a friendship with Mrs Bertholt, the widow of a Nazi officer, who attempts to convince him of collective German innocence. The viewer grasps the stakes at hand: at this trial, as in the entire Nuremberg Military Tribunals, the German people are collectively on trial.

With these German stakes in mind, *Judgment at Nuremberg* also asks: What are the stakes of this particular Holocaust trial narrative for 1960s America? For example, how can a film like *Judgment at Nuremberg* give a racially divided country the Holocaust trial that it needs, a Holocaust trial that, as Mintz argues, reconciles identity-based persecution with a culture of collective remembrance? In his analysis of the film, Henry Gonshak points to the salience of Jewish racial persecution for the American context, especially the resemblance between the segregationist Jim Crow laws of the American South and the Nuremberg Codes of Nazi Germany. Gonshak draws specific attention to a courtroom scene in which the prosecutor 'show[s] ghastly footage of the liberation of the camps, [and] the camera cuts for a second to the face of a black American GI ... Does this slaughter of innocents remind the GI of the lynchings of equally innocent blacks in the American South?'[13] Gonshak goes on to note the American parallels to 'the Feldenstein Case, where a German Jew was executed for allegedly romancing an Aryan girl, which may have reminded viewers of the way Southern blacks (such as Emmett Till) ... were beaten or killed or arrested for supposedly dallying with white women'.[14] The America that screened Stanley Kramer's film – a film about the culpability of a judge who 'violate[s] legal or moral principles accepted by civilized nations' – was the America of Martin Luther King and Jim Crow.[15] So did the movie attempt to balance these American interests with the questions of Nazi guilt and innocence at the centre of the real-life Nuremberg trials? Not according to Kramer: 'Do you think [the movie studio] wanted to make ... [a Holocaust] trial [film]? They weren't interested

---

13   Henry Gonshak, 'Does *Judgment at Nuremberg* accurately depict the Nazi war crimes trial?' *The Journal of American Culture* 31.2 (June 2008): 159.
14   ibid.
15   Paul Bergman and Michael Asinow, *Reel Justice: The Courtroom Goes to the Movies* (Kansas City, Miss.: McMeel, 2006), 126.

at all in war guilt and those people in the ovens and the crooked judges.'[16] If filmmakers start from a premise that 'war guilt and those people in the ovens' will never matter on their own terms, then the commitment to ticket sales will always trump a sincere inquiry into contested notions of justice. And while box office returns may confirm the popularity and social urgency of allusions to the civil rights movement and identity politics more broadly, this leveraging of a specifically Jewish trauma for (distinctly American) social purposes reinforces a cultural discourse in which the Holocaust trial in representations is a metaphorical means to an end.

At one point during the film version of the Justice Trial, former-Judge Janning's defence attorney, Hans Rolfe, aggressively questions Irene Wallner to establish the fairness of Janning's decision to sentence the trial's victim, a Jewish man, to death. However, when Wallner becomes emotional, Janning, in an act of conscience, interrupts his lawyer to prevent Irene's further traumatisation, admitting that in this case as in many others, he knowingly found an innocent Jew guilty. During deliberations, the American government pressures Haywood and his fellow judges to acquit the judges in order to curry German favour for America's emerging conflict with Soviet Russia. Haywood rejects political expediency for ethics when he sentences the four accused judges, including Janning, to life imprisonment. Haywood's ruling is resolute, although he prefaces the sentencing by explaining how,

> Janning ... is a tragic figure [who I] ... believe loathed the evil he did. But compassion for [his] present torture ... must not beget forgetfulness of the torture and death of millions by [his] government ... This trial has shown that under the stress of a national crisis, ordinary men – even able and extraordinary men – can delude themselves into the commission of ... atrocities so vast and heinous as to stagger the imagination.[17]

At the end, when Haywood visits Janning in prison at the latter's request, the German judge begs for the empathy of his American counterpart: 'The real reason I asked you to come [is that] ... I want to hear from a man like you ... not that he forgives, but that he understands.'[18] In response to

---

16   In order to mitigate the studio's lack of interest, Kramer 'studded it with people to get it made', casting Hollywood stars like Spencer Tracy, Marlene Dietrich, Montgomery Cliff and Judy Garland for minor as well as major roles. Judith E Doneson, *The Holocaust in American Film* (Philadelphia: The Jewish Publications Society, 1987), 97 quoted in Gonshak, 'Does *Judgment at Nuremberg* accurately depict the Nazi war crimes trial?' 154.

17   Stanley Kramer, Director, *Judgment at Nuremberg*, 1961.

18   ibid.

Haywood's incredulous response – 'How can you expect me to understand sending millions of people to gas ovens?'[19] – Janning offers his final protest, one that is familiar from the testimony of so many admitted Nazi criminals, by insisting that he 'did not know it would come to that! You must believe it! You must believe it!'[20] And Haywood, quite expectedly, provides the equally familiar answer of a juridically dispassionate – if personally compassionate – instrument of the justice system: 'Herr Janning, it came to that the first time you sentenced to death a man you knew to be innocent.'[21] At the film's close, a final note descends from outside the narrative arc of the movie and reads: 'By 1959, of the ninety-nine [perpetrators that the Nuremberg Military Tribunals] sentenced to prison terms, only three were still serving their sentences.'[22]

Despite the sobering implications of the film's postscript – the ultimate sense that the difficult effort of calling war criminals to account is, in fact, a futile one – Haywood's pronouncement persists in our minds and centralises his heroism. He chose the moral and juridical right over political expediency, doing the right thing despite his balanced evaluation of, and growing affection for, the German people. Janning wins some of our sympathy because he was bound to enforce the law for better or worse, his pre-Nazi record was honourable, and he had initially resisted Nazi ideology – but even he is found guilty and sentenced to life imprisonment. He himself believes his sentence to be a just one. Due process and the resolution that it confers prevail, even if some other sentences imposed at Nuremberg may have been light.

Aside from being the earliest Hollywood account of Nuremberg, *Judgment at Nuremberg* was one of the first to use real concentration camp footage and expose the general public to images of the death camps. When the prosecutor, Colonel Tad Lawson, plays the footage in an attempt to win back the favour of the tribunal judges who express sympathy for the defendants, he also curries favour with an audience increasingly persuaded by the compelling case for German victimhood as told by Mrs Bertholt. In the trial performed onscreen (and the trial for which the audience sits in judgement throughout the performance), Mann, the author, has ensured fairness. Janning's and Germany's guilt is by no means assured as the story unfolds, and Mann's extraordinary efforts to make Janning a valiant figure

19   ibid.
20   ibid.
21   ibid.
22   ibid.

who, in the end, holds himself accountable, gives the narrative its tidy, ethical ending. One of the greatest critiques of Nuremberg, which Arendt echoes, is that the tribunals risked being victors' justice, but Mann discredits this with Haywood's sympathy for Janning; this is not victors' justice, but judgement *in spite of* a desire to be lenient.

What does it mean that the perpetrator is the sympathetic foil of Haywood, our American hero? And that we gaze at the concentration camps without encountering any survivors? What should we make of the fact that a middle-aged German woman's trauma while testifying stands in for the trauma of all Nazi victims, especially the absent Jewish victim that Janning sent to death? What does it say that the Jewish figure nearest the centre, the man accused of having a relationship with a German woman, is absent, sent to his death years before by the same perpetrator-judge who commits a dramatic act of conscience? For Mann, Janning renders these questions irrelevant; his plea for the empathy of Haywood, a man of legal conscience, and his noble use of the trial-stage to protect the victim that he formerly violated, occupy centre stage.

Despite the contemporary inclination to read the film's closing note about the failure to enforce Nuremberg's sentences as an ironic statement about the tribunal's seeming lack of utility and value, the story resists this reading, finally and fully memorialising the fairly administered trial as the ultimate means of reconciliation and adjudication. When Haywood meets privately to say goodbye to the opposing attorney, Rolfe says, 'In five years, the men you sentenced to life imprisonment will be free', a point to which the morally pragmatic Haywood responds, 'I have no doubt that what you suggest may well happen. It is logical in view of the times in which we live. But to be logical is not to be right. And nothing on God's earth could ever make it right.'[23] In this scene, as throughout the film, Haywood's unwavering moral sensibilities seem to be as optimistic as they are naïve.

The Man in the Glass Booth, on the other hand, assumes an entirely different aesthetic strategy and – informed and inspired as it was by the Eichmann trial – refuses the optimism of its predecessor. Arthur Hiller's film adapts actor and writer Robert Shaw's 1967 novel and 1968 play of the same name.

---

23 ibid. Lawrence Langer is unimpressed by Janning's shift from public assumption of guilt at the trial to this private plea for exoneration, concluding, 'Janning's declaration of guilt is not enough, psychologically or artistically: not enough for himself, because he still has not penetrated his motives, and not enough for us, because we still do not know how such a decent man came to lend his judicial prestige to the Nazi cause.' Lawrence Langer, 'The Americanization of the Holocaust on Stage and screen,' *Admitting the Holocaust: Collected Essays* (Oxford: Oxford University Press, 1995), 173.

Explicitly reminiscent of the Eichmann case, the film tells the story of Arthur Goldman, a wealthy Jewish businessman living in a Manhattan penthouse who is kidnapped by Mossad, taken to Israel and tried as a Nazi SS officer. The first half of the film shows Goldman's bizarre behaviour in New York, where he abuses his employees, expresses constant anxiety about being under surveillance and holds private Jewish rituals in a room that contains religious, concentration camp and Nazi paraphernalia. He's on the edge of sanity, wielding a gun and hoarding cash in fits of paranoia.

After Mossad captures him and formally identifies him through dental records, he flies to Israel, where the second half of the film takes place. Here, Goldman transforms himself into Nazi Colonel Adolf Karl Dorff and incites his captors by refusing to disguise or repent for his actions. Mrs Rosen, the Israeli prosecutor, deposes him, asking why 'in the reports of the Einsatzgruppen I notice plain words do not occur: we have "final solution", "evacuation", and "special treatment", [while] on the other hand, in *your* reports, you always stated "extermination" or "killing". Why is that?' The smug Dorff offers his maxim – 'always call a spade a spade' – before going on to explain how 'those euphemisms you speak of were best for keeping orders – they didn't want the typists to get the message … But in my case, I'm not here to tell you I didn't enjoy it – I'm here to tell you I did. No clerk, Rosen! Issued my own orders, plotted my own plots, had a ball.'[24] Dorff wears his Nazi uniform and seems eager to use the trial as a larger stage from which to repeat this message, unremorseful and cruel, as he makes his opening statement and questions witnesses in a courtroom full of Holocaust survivors. Like Eichmann, Dorff endures his trial in a bulletproof glass booth for his own protection; unlike Eichmann's booth, Dorff's is soundproofed, and the judges operate an 'off-switch' when Dorff has one of his many long-winded outbursts.[25]

Following the climactic revelation that the medical doctors, two key witnesses, have been paid to provide false testimony, the film quickly evolves from farce into tragedy, a shift that is well-captured in a short passage from the same point in Shaw's play. Just as we learn that Dorff is, in fact, Arthur Goldman – not a ranking Nazi officer, but a Holocaust victim who inexplicably falsified a Nazi identity by faking medical records and grafting

---

24 Arthur Hiller, Director, *The Man in the Glass Booth*, 1975.
25 This is reminiscent of Shoshana Felman's commitment to prioritising testimony – privileging speech as the signifier of (for her, victim) enfranchisement in the courtroom – and the suggestion that its repression is a form of violence; in this case, Dorff's silencing is tantamount to suffering violence at the hands of his Israeli judges.

over his camp tattoo – the suddenly frail and silent Goldman can only listen as the prosecutor and judge try to work out the truth:

JUDGE: What was the point of all this, Goldman?

MRS. ROSEN: He likes bad jokes.

JUDGE: I understand his need to put a case. I understand a concern for justice, a concern for law. I understand his need to put a German in the dock, a German who would say what no German has said in the dock. I understand that, I understand his guilt. Even so, I would not have done this, would never have done this.[26]

In the final scene of both the play and its film adaptation, Goldman stands paralysed in his booth and the viewer recalls Goldman/Dorff's post-abduction references to himself as a Christ-like martyr. The viewer can only wonder at Goldman's ultimate motivation for this deception: Is he a repentant collaborator, as one witness seems to suggest? Is he using this ruse to work through survivor's guilt? Or is it Goldman's answer to the simple need for, as the judge puts it, 'a German who would say what no German has said in the dock'? As the guards attempt to get into the booth, sealed from within, the lights fade on Goldman who, dying from this final trauma, is exhibiting the ultimate 'narrative excess' before being silenced forever.

This film raises several issues, the most obvious of which has to do with the real political consequences of the Goldman/Dorff figure. What does it mean that so many survivor-witnesses misidentified Goldman as Dorff, including the most sincere and deeply disturbed victims of the real Adolf Karl Dorff, presumably still in hiding? Critics of the post-Eichmann prosecution of Nazi war criminals raise the risk of 'getting the wrong guy' and, since most perpetrators will not own their crimes as eagerly as the play-acting Dorff does, Nazi-hunters like Simon Wiesenthal have been forced to meet rigorous evidentiary tests when accusing a perpetrator with an assumed identity. Shaw's suggestion that a number of Holocaust survivors are gullible enough to confirm Goldman/Dorff's assumed identity – and that some are even willing to accept Goldman's bribes in order to go along with his scheme – undermines the very foundations of Israel's prosecution of Eichmann. If several witnesses, dental records and the word of the perpetrator himself cannot accurately validate a presumed perpetrator's identity, the ethical prosecution of Nazi war criminals is impossible. By abandoning due process in

---

26   Robert Shaw, *The Man in the Glass Booth* (New York: Grove, 1968), 71.

the Goldman/Dorff case – and, implicitly, the Eichmann case – Israel runs the risk of destroying the ritual of collective memory.

Following the Eichmann kidnapping, several media figures accused Israel of acting like a rogue Nazi state, advancing a trope that is central to Hiller's film: namely, the eliding of difference between Jews and Nazis. According to playwright and Holocaust literary scholar Robert Skloot, 'There are a variety of problems associated with the emerging trope of 'Nazi as victim', the principal of which is this precise problem of subjectivity-collapse: this trope finally 'leads from "Nazi as victim" to "Nazi as Jew"'.[27] *The Man in the Glass Booth* provides us with a despicable Nazi who celebrates his crimes, earning the viewer's disdain and desire for a swift and just retribution. However, Shaw and Hiller turn this disdain on its head by blurring Jewish and Nazi identities in a way that reflects the very shift in aesthetic attitudes towards Holocaust justice that Skloot fears. Annette Insdorf writes that the film's focus 'on individual responsibility ... depict[s] the breakdown or transfer of identity among bystander, survivor, and victim, and [this focus] locate[s] the drama within the self, where a Jewish or Nazi identity is gradually assumed'.[28] This narrative construction of a localised drama of guilt takes our inquiry into Dorff's crimes out of the courtroom. Instead, we are disillusioned with the trial's incapacity to sort out the complicated issues of identity that the film posits as integral to questions of guilt. This is all the more concerning given the firm link between the film's title, *The Man in the Glass Booth*, and Eichmann's trial. It is extremely meaningful, then, that a narrative which ostensibly retells Eichmann's story actually turns into the story of a trauma-ridden Jew. Quite literally, this story turns a Jew (Goldman in New York) into a Nazi (after Dorff's capture by Mossad) and back into a Jew (during the courtroom climax in which Goldman and Dorff are revealed to be one and the same).

When history becomes fiction and Nazis become Jews

The shift in popular performances of Holocaust justice, highlighted by the specific films discussed in this essay, illustrate the complementary shift in American notions of Holocaust justice following the Eichmann trial. Before the Eichmann precedent, *Judgment at Nuremberg* provides a Jewish-produced, narrative resolution in which the central figures – an American

---

27   Skloot, 'Holocaust theatre and the problem of justice,' 18.
28   My emphasis. Annette Insdorf, *Indelible Shadows: Film and the Holocaust* (Cambridge: Cambridge University Press, 2003), 159.

gentile and German Nazi, both arbiters of the law – show how the juridical space is capable of allowing good to prevail and the guilty to be punished. After the Eichmann trial, *The Man in the Glass Booth* uses a figure who resembles Eichmann to respond to Israel's victim-centred account of justice by collapsing distinctions between Nazi personhood and Jewish personhood and refocusing audience attention to identity (*i.e., Is he a Nazi or is he a Jew?*) These issues, rather than the Holocaust event itself, take up all the narrative space. The story halts once he is a confirmed Jew, and forestalls our knowledge of his survivor experience.

Although not all post-Eichmann films necessarily or explicitly suggest that the viewer is finished with the work of remembering once the credits are running, they maintain a commitment to the perpetrator-centred narrative and share the notion that some dysfunction of the trial mechanism itself, rather than any structural problem with the guarantee of due process, is the reason why the trial might be incapable of adjudicating genocide. Instead of ethical frames of judgement, administrative questions drive the narrative inquiry into Holocaust justice at work in these films. The implication that proper functioning of the trial makes closure possible reproduces the ideal of a foreclosed narrative in which the trial has adjudicated the latest Holocaust story and cleanly assigns subject positions: victim, perpetrator, penitent, survivor, resister, bystander. These circumscribed signifiers, reached through due process, are wholly compatible with Arendt's ethos in *Eichmann in Jerusalem*, an ethos that seems to frame so many Holocaust trial film productions.

Finally, *Judgment at Nuremberg* and *The Man in the Glass Booth* are representative of, rather than exceptions to, the representation of Holocaust trials in aesthetic culture in general and cinema culture in particular. These films are the foundations of a Holocaust film sub-canon, a body of trial narratives that has inspired hundreds of social and scholarly responses, most recently and resoundingly to Stephen Daldry's much-discussed adaptation of Bernhard Schlink's novel, *The Reader*. Taken as parts of a whole, these movies theorise a version of Holocaust justice in which the trial will always fail. Essentially, the narrative trend has changed the purpose of the trial from a just remedy (which it cannot provide) to a means of engaging non-juridical remedies. These filmmakers remain committed to the trope of the trial as the ideal means of exploring Holocaust justice, while positing it as the only juridical option which can, at best, open the door to extra-juridical, ad hoc remedies. In the end, these films support Arendt's theory of justice, even as they reflect filmmakers' discomfort with this theory and their sympathy for the very victims that they neglect. Regardless of the motives behind these films, they advance a narrative of Holocaust justice in which, as Robert Skloot warns, 'the idea of history as fixed, of goodness as pure, and of victims as worthy – or even as victims at all – is deconstructed and re-envisioned'.[29]

---

29   Skloot, 'Holocaust theatre and the problem of justice', 26.

CONTRIBUTOR BIOGRAPHIES

Kimberly Allar earned her BA in history from Amherst College and is currently a PhD candidate in history at Clark University, Massachusetts, USA. Allar has been awarded fellowships from the European Holocaust Research Institute, the Deutscher Akademischer Austausch Dienst, the Ben and Zelda Fellowship at the United States Holocaust Memorial Museum in Washington DC, and the Saul Kagan Fellowship in Advanced Holocaust Studies, Claims Conference on Jewish Material Claims Against Germany. She is currently working on her dissertation, 'Training Nazi camp guards. Dachau, Ravensbrück, and Trawniki in comparison' which examines the recruitment and training of concentration camp guards in Nazi Germany.

Dr Fay Anderson is a senior lecturer in the School of Media, Film and Journalism at Monash University, Australia. She has published widely on war journalism, media history, photography and violence. Fay Anderson and Richard Trembath's co-authored book, *Witnesses to War: The History of Australian Conflict Reporting*, was published by Melbourne University Publishing in 2011 and was a finalist for a Walkley Book Award in the same year. In 2012 Fay was awarded an Australian Research Council Grant with Michael Gawenda, Kate Darian-Smith and Sally Young to investigate the history and significance of Australian press photography.

Karen Auerbach is an assistant professor of history and Stuart E Eizenstat Fellow at the University of North Carolina at Chapel Hill, USA. Previously she was a lecturer in the Australian Centre for Jewish Civilisation. She is the author of *The House at Ujazdowskie 16: Jewish Families in Warsaw after the Holocaust* (Indiana University Press, 2013) and numerous articles in English and Polish.

Dr Adam Brown is a lecturer in media studies at Deakin University, Australia, and works as a volunteer at the Jewish Holocaust Centre in Melbourne. He is the author of *Judging 'Privileged' Jews: Holocaust Ethics, Representation and the 'Grey Zone'* (Berghahn, 2013), co-author of *Communication, New Media and Everyday Life* (Oxford UP, 2012), and is currently writing a monograph on women in Holocaust film. Intensely interested in animal and human rights issues, Adam's interdisciplinary research has spanned Holocaust representation across various genres, surveillance and film, mediations of rape, digital children's television and multiplatforming, and board game culture.

Dr Danielle Christmas is a Postdoctoral Research Fellow in the Department of English and Comparative Literature at the University of North Carolina at Chapel Hill, USA. She has taught and published on topics ranging from American narratives of Nazi fugitives to the so-called African Hottentot Venus Saartje Baartman. Her current manuscript, 'Auschwitz and the Plantation: Labor and Social Death in American Holocaust and Slavery Fiction', concerns how representations of Holocaust and slavery perpetrators contribute to American socioeconomic discourses. In 2014, she was awarded a Cummings Foundation Fellowship at the United States Holocaust Memorial Museum to support this research. Most recently, her article on William Styron's *Sophie's Choice* and *The Confessions of Nat Turner* will appear in the journal *Twentieth-Century Literature* (2015). You can find out more about her work at her website, www.daniellechristmas.com.

Dr Esther Jilovsky is Research Fellow in the School of Languages and Linguistics and part of the Affiliated Faculty of the Program for Jewish Culture and Society at the University of Melbourne in Australia. A graduate of the University of Melbourne and the University of Oxford, she was awarded her PhD by Royal Holloway, University of London, in 2011. Her book *Remembering the Holocaust: Generations, Witnessing and Place* (Bloomsbury 2015) traces how survivors and subsequent generations write about visits to Holocaust sites. She is co-editor, with Jordana Silverstein and David Slucki, of *In the Shadows of Memory: The Holocaust and the Third Generation* (Valentine Mitchell 2014), a volume dedicated to the experiences of the grandchildren of Holocaust survivors. Dr Jilovsky has published articles and book chapters about Holocaust memory in the second and third generations, the role of place in Holocaust memory, and German-Jewish identity.

Tom Lawson is Professor of History and Associate Dean (Academic) in the Faculty of Arts, Design and Social Sciences at Northumbria University, UK. He is the author and editor of several books including *Debates on the Holocaust* (2010) and (with James Jordan) *The Memory of the Holocaust in Australia* (2008). He is the co-editor of *Holocaust Studies: A Journal of Culture and History* published by Vallentine Mitchell. His latest book, *The Last Man: A British Genocide in Tasmania*, was published by IB Tauris in 2014.

Laura S Levitt, professor of Religion, Jewish studies and gender at Temple University, USA, has chaired the Department of Religion and directed the women's studies and the Jewish studies programs. She is the author of *American Jewish Loss after the Holocaust* (2007) and *Jews and Feminism: The Ambivalent Search for Home* (1997) an editor of *Judaism Since Gender* (1997) and *Impossible Images: Contemporary Art after the Holocaust* (2003). Her current project 'Evidence as archive' builds on her prior work in Holocaust studies to consider the relationship between material objects held in police storage and artefacts housed in Holocaust collections.

Dr Rebekah Moore is a graduate of the University of Tasmania and holds a PhD in history from the University of Western Australia. Her dissertation examined the interaction between morality and historical practice, and the ways in which ethical concerns have shaped and driven debate within the historiographies of the Holocaust and Stalinism. After eighteen months assisting the Commission on Delivery of Health Services in Tasmania, Dr Moore is now working in a strategic policy role with the Australian Government Department of Health.

Salvador Orti-Camallonga has a PhD. in history from the University of Cambridge (Downing College), UK. He has previously studied at the London School of Economics and Political Science. Salvador's research focuses on the Spanish perception of the Jewish extermination after the Second World War, and concentrates on the reasons why the remembrance of this event triggers so much controversy in Spain. In parallel to his investigation, he has completed an internship at the Department of Political Affairs in United Nations Headquarters, New York.

Suzanne D Rutland MA (Hons) PhD, Dip Ed, OAM is professor in the Department of Hebrew, Biblical & Jewish Studies, University of Sydney, Australia She has published widely on Australian Jewish history, including Jewish migration and Jewish women in Australia, as well as writing on the Holocaust, Israel, Soviet Jewry and Jewish education. Her latest books are *The Jews in Australia* (Cambridge University Press, 2005); co-authored with Sarah Rood, *Nationality Stateless, Destination Australia* (Melbourne, 2008); and, co-authored with Sam Lipski, *Let My People Go: Australia and the Soviet Jews – the Untold Story*, to be published by Hybrid Publishers, Melbourne. In 2008 she received the Medal of the Order of Australia for services to Higher Jewish Education and interfaith dialogue.

Dr Deb Waterhouse-Watson is a Lecturer in the School of Communication and Creative Arts at Deakin University, Australia. Her book *Athletes,
Sexual Assault and 'Trials by Media': Narrative Immunity* was published by
Routledge in 2013. Deb's current research project analyses representations
of sexual violence and football in the courtroom and news media, focusing
on discourse and narrative. Other research interests include board game
culture, gender in Holocaust film and popular fiction.